The Prodigal Father

Other Hay House Titles
of Related Interest

*FACING LIFE'S CHALLENGES: Daily Meditations for
Overcoming Depression, Grief, and "The Blues,"* by Amy E. Dean

FROM ONIONS TO PEARLS: A Journey of Awakening and Deliverance,
by Satyam Nadeen

*INSTEAD OF THERAPY: Help Yourself Change, and
Change the Help You're Getting,* by Tom Rusk, M.D.

THE POWER IS WITHIN YOU, by Louise L. Hay

*RE-CREATING YOUR SELF: How You Can Become the Person You
Want to Be, Living the Life You Desire,* by Christopher Stone

(All of the above titles are available at your local bookstore, or may be
ordered by calling Hay House at 760-431-7695 or 800-654-5126.)

Please visit the Hay House Website at:
hayhouse.com

The Prodigal Father

*A True Story of Tragedy,
Survival, and Reconciliation in
an American Family*

Jon Du Pre

Hay House, Inc.
Carlsbad, California • Sydney, Australia

Published and distributed in the United States by:
Hay House, Inc., P.O. Box 5100, Carlsbad, CA 92018-5100 • (800) 654-5126
(800) 650-5115 (fax)

Editorial: Jill Kramer • *Design:* Summer McStravick
Interior photos courtesy of the author

Library of Congress Cataloging-in-Publication Data

Du Pre, Jon.
    The prodigal father : a true story of tragedy, survival, and reconciliation in an American family / Jon Du Pre.
        p. cm.
    ISBN 1-56170-674-4 (trade paper)
        1. Du Pre, Jon. 2. Television journalists—United States—Biography. I. Title.

PN4874.D87 A3 2000
070'.92—dc21
[B]

                                                                      99-059123

ISBN 1-56170-674-4

03 02 01 00   4 3 2
1st printing, May 2000
2nd printing, May 2000

Printed in the United States of America

To
Kasey,
Jessie,
and Jonny.

Thanks for asking, Kasey.

CONTENTS

"Which of us has looked into his father's heart?
Which of us has not remained forever prison-pent?
Which of us is not forever a stranger and alone?"

— from *Look Homeward, Angel,* by Thomas Wolfe

✤✤✤

"We love with horror and hate with
an inexplicable love whatever
caused our greatest pain."

— Erika Burkart

❧ PREFACE ❧

I hadn't meant for this story to end up as a book. Neither had I intended that anyone other than the members of my immediate family would read it. My sole objective was to jot down, in journal form, some thoughts about my upbringing and to preserve them for a time when my children would be old enough to understand—hoping, of course, that by the time they reached their teenage years they'd still care about anything their dad had to say. To my astonishment, I've discovered that there are others who, as they heard about my story through casual conversation, emotionally connected with it at one level or another.

In the years it has taken me to write this book and see it published, it has become abundantly clear that my efforts have not just been for my family and me, but for fellow survivors—people I don't know and will never meet. They are the children, the stepchildren, the foster children, the orphaned children, the pupils, the protégés, or the admirers of preoccupied people. Whether their hero spent too much time at work, in bars, or on the couch in front of the television set; or whether their father suddenly disappeared into homelessness, they are acquainted with abandonment. They understand the abiding ache of disappointment, the recurring sting of resentment, and the sometimes crippling lack of confidence in their ability to sustain a relationship with a friend, a lover, a spouse, or perhaps, most frightening, a child.

I could have suppressed the bad memories of my early years. I could have languished in therapy. I could have emulated my predecessor and drowned my demons with drink. Any of those options might have seemed socially acceptable, psychologically diagnosable, medically reimbursable—hell, maybe even fashionable! But I chose a different way. Mine was a rough road to what was, at best, an unsure cure, but it was a direct route. I'll leave it to the reader to decide whether you think my way was good sense or foolishness.

Some people have used words such as *courageous* and *selfless* to describe what I've done. However, although I appreciate these kind and generous sentiments, I have to say I don't see it that way at all. What I did was motivated by fear and driven by an entirely selfish sense of survival. I don't want to be anybody's champion. I just want my kids to know I'm doing the best I can with what I've got.

My simple hope is that this story offers a little encouragement at a time when so many of us are so quick to deflect the responsibility for how we live our lives, to victimize ourselves by blaming someone else for our problems, and to allow our families to disintegrate at a terrifying rate. This story is my testament to the fact that no matter how we contrive to screw up our lives, the spirit of family never quits.

❦ ❦ ❦

⚜ ACKNOWLEDGMENTS ⚜

There are a few people who, whether they know it or not, played critical roles in making this book possible. I wish to thank them with all my heart:

Marquis Anthony Du Pre, my elder brother. The bow of the ship takes a beating when it sails through rough waters. Marq cut a wake for his younger siblings. Now, by allowing me to write about him in this book, Marq endures a terrible intrusion into his privacy. I hope he understands why I'm doing it. His disappointments are mine as well, and so they are part of my story. Witnessing my older brother's suffering has enabled me to navigate many perils, such as the way he held my hand and led me through danger when we were children. Marq will always be my hero.

Daryl James Du Pre, my younger brother. His attitude has enlightened me and changed for the better the way I see the world. His enormously generous spirit and prodigious recollections of harrowing experiences have added a wealth of compelling material to this book—not to mention his talent with paint, rags, brushes, and masking tape, which has turned my home into a palace!

Ted Jensen, my surrogate dad. As if he hadn't had enough children already (six), he reached out to three lost boys, and, enduring the loss of countless gallons of milk, took it upon himself to shepherd us through the final crucial years of our adolescence.

Lynn Packer, my college professor. He noticed me sitting in the back of his class and took it upon himself to make a reporter out of me. Beyond his class lectures, it was his brilliant and courageous example that taught me what it means to be a journalist.

Ann Gaunt, my wonderful aunt. After years of silence from our side of the family, she responded to my out-of-the-blue inquiries with compassion and enthusiasm and showed me that my brothers and I had loving relatives who'd been rooting for us all along.

Jimmy Du Pre, my favorite uncle. Without asking why I was suddenly turning to him for help, he rallied in support of my search for my father.

Alan Webber and Bill Taylor, magazine publishers. An almost accidental conversation with them caused me to consider the fact that something as simple and abstract as an idea could have great power. Their inspiration turned my ideas into action. Their recommendation that I contact a friend of theirs turned action into success.

Richard Pine, my literary agent. From the moment he read my unsolicited, hastily written two-page letter of introduction in 1994, he believed in the power of this story. Through unforeseen, sometimes bizarre twists of bad fortune that threatened to banish our book to the publishing industry's trash heap of good intentions gone bad, Richard never flinched. He simply started over and found a new home for my orphaned book.

Jill Kramer, my editor. She was the sensitive, sensible, smart, self-confident editor I needed. After years of beating my head against brick walls trying to get this book published, and just when I had given up, Hay House rescued it, and Jill made the experience amazingly positive and pleasant.

Most important:

Tom Congdon, my collaborator, and, dare I say it, my mentor. Tom had once helped a guy named Peter Benchley turn *Jaws* into a phenomenal bestseller. He had once helped a successful newspaper columnist named Russell Baker turn *Growing Up* into a Pulitzer Prize–winning work of American literature. Then he decided to help me, for no other reason than that he loved the story. With inexhaustible patience and a master teacher's touch, Tom taught me how to write a book. Whatever my reader finds worthwhile about this work I owe to Mr. Congdon's generosity, wisdom, and guidance.

Gina, my wife. She married "down," thinking she could salvage me. She has forgiven me for my boorish and abusive behavior more times than I care to count. Her spiritual strength and emotional endurance have saved our marriage many times. Okay, honey, I'm done writing. Let's dance!

❧❧❧

CHAPTER ONE
The Journey Begins

I make my living looking into the lens of a television camera and telling people what's happening. It's an odd sort of job, being a news broadcaster. I never see the people I talk to, except at restaurants or supermarkets when they ask for my autograph. I smile and banter as I scribble, but ask myself what my name on a napkin could possibly mean to them. I'm just a face, a voice, a bearer of tidings, good and mostly bad. Sometimes when the attention makes me uncomfortable, I realize I'm still the quiet teenager with a constant look of worry on his face who lived in fear that people could just glance at him and know the whole sorry truth about his life.

In the TV news business, young anchormen and women tend to move from job to job, scrambling for better deals at glitzier stations in bigger places. My scramble started in the Rocky Mountains and took me through the Upper Midwest. Then in 1993, when I was 34 years old, I landed the main anchor spot at a station in Boston. I was 15 years younger than the city's other anchormen, all of them well seasoned and well respected. I should have been intimidated, grabbing a plum position in the nation's sixth-largest television market. Instead, after the childhood I'd been through, I felt I'd left my past behind and arrived at my great reward. At least that's how I felt for a while, anyway.

Like riding a new bicycle or pleasing a new lover, it takes time before you feel comfortable at a new anchor desk. Five months into my Boston gig, I had the feeling I was settling in. It was about that time that the first big snow hit. New England was in for the snowiest winter in 50 years, and a sizable part of my duties that season would be heralding blizzards, telling people how hard the storm would hit and what it would do to their lives.

My producer had decided to play the storm late in the show, after we came back from a commercial break, as an introduction to the weather segment. When the floor director yelled, "Stand by!" I set myself in the posture I used for serious stories. Gently leaning on my left elbow, as I'd been trained, I turned my head slightly to the right, just far enough to focus on the center of the big studio camera lens with what I'd been taught was my dominant eye. The tally light on the camera lit red, and I drew a deep breath.

"Brace for a squall, Boston!" I began. "A major storm's coming our way, and it's carrying a big load of snow." The director in the booth cued the videotape operators, and onto the screen came footage of a blizzard from the year before. Without looking at the studio monitor, I knew what sort of scenes there would be: sheets of white sweeping past the Prudential Building, probably, and snow-buried cars on Beacon Hill.

"And wouldn't you know," I said, "that it's going to hit early tomorrow morning, just as hundreds of thousands of commuters are trying to enter the city."

Then I adjusted my tone, moderating my professional detachment with just the right touch of manufactured sympathy. "The police," I said, "will find frozen bodies in the usual places, under the viaducts and in the alleys." The file footage, I knew, was keeping up with me, showing bent, bundled figures plodding along, dark shadows against the white. "Officers are patrolling the downtown streets," I said as the videotape continued to roll—images, no doubt, of men and women hunkering in corners and crannies. "Police say it's an impossible job . . ."

At this point, as I neared the end, I glanced up from my script at the studio monitor and saw the last of the file video. I saw a ragged old man curled on a manhole cover, trying to stay warm in the steam rising from the sub-street sewer system. My breath left my lungs. I thought I heard myself gasp. The fear that my audience might have heard the same sound instantly shredded my composure. Suddenly, I realized that the expression on my face had changed and I couldn't control it. I needed to finish the rest of the sentence: " . . . finding all the indigent street people and bringing them to the shelters." Camera three took me on a close-up. My director hadn't noticed my distress. I choked and altogether missed my last line, a nimble lead-in to the weatherman's segment.

It only lasted a few seconds for the viewers at home. The way most people watch television, with little of their conscious attention, my gaffe probably went unnoticed. From my side, it was like being in a car wreck—your mind speeds up and you watch everything happen in slow motion. The silent pause that was supposed to be my last sentence seemed like several minutes. When I failed to speak, the director switched over to the weatherman, who launched into his standard blizzard quips. "That's right, Jon," he chirped, responding to the line I never uttered. "We'll need backhoes to dig ourselves out of our driveways tomorrow!"

The station had recently brought in some broadcast consultants to critique our on-air delivery and help us communicate emotion without seeming emotional. They were fond of saying that an anchor had to not only convince the audience that he knew what he was talking about, but that he *cared*. I had just revealed that, for a journalist covering a blizzard, I cared too much.

In the postbroadcast meeting, Mike, our constantly anxious producer, didn't mention my flub. He was concerned instead about where in the program the blizzard segment had been slotted. "We should have run the frozen man story up higher," he said, pushing his fingers through his hair. "I didn't like tossing into the weather segment on a downbeat." What he meant was that he didn't like leading into our happy-talking weather guy's routine on a note of misery and death.

None of my colleagues seemed to have given the tragedy of people dying in the frigid New England night a second thought. They'd all read, written, and reported the story many times before. It was the sort of news fodder our producers regularly plugged into the newscast for a little jolt of pathos. As the anchor read the same old story, the videotape editors loaded the same old cassettes into the playback machines and showed the same old file footage, and the folks at home saw the pathetic ragged man lying on the manhole cover. The image had become one of the staples of the news consumers' diet, part of the mix. The shock value had worn thin.

When we returned to the newsroom, Karen, my incurably self-conscious colleague, continued the anchorwoman act as she took calls from viewers commenting on her hairstyle and wardrobe. I got a call from a man who was phoning yet again to insist that there was a Martian mind-machine in his satellite dish and that our station was part of a conspiracy to cover it up. No one was calling to ask where the people stranded in the storm might be huddled and how the public might help. But we'd done our job. We'd attracted an audience and had gotten them to watch a few high-priced commercial spots, and we'd reminded them to stay tuned for the *Arsenio Hall* show.

I could hardly blame the audience or my co-workers. Like them, I too had built up a professional veneer over the years, one that shielded me from the horror of some of the news I reported every day. But when it came to this particular story on this particular night, the veneer was thin. The old man in the file footage that night had broken through. I knew that when I went to bed and closed my eyes, I'd see him again, coiled on the sidewalk. For me he was more than a fuzzy image on the television screen. He had a face. He had an identity. He was my father.

I had no reason to think that my dad was anywhere near Boston, but for a moment the man looked so like him—the same crouched shoulders and strong-looking legs, the bulk of the body, the distinctively French nose and jawline. And the setting was the same. I knew my father was on the street somewhere that night. Why not here?

It had been years since I'd learned that the old man was down and out. For all my supposed knowledge as a newsman, I'd come no closer to understanding what had happened to him. In some part of my mind, my father was still the exuberant, hilarious, larger-than-life hero of my boyhood, still my champion and motivator, still full of hope and ambition. He was still the handsome young FBI agent, the legal counsel to a prominent U.S. senator, the successful prosecutor turned civil rights attorney who defended the poor and defenseless, often pro-bono and at risk to his own safety. He still had his pretty wife, his $700 suits, his collection of automobiles, his speedboat, his ultramodern dream house built on the perched clearing of his 35-acre lakefront property, all of which had made me the envy, if only briefly, of my childhood buddies and some of his business associates. It was so hard for me to accept that this man, my father, was out there somewhere, not unlike many of the pathetic, detestable people whose charity cases he had once championed. So, to protect myself from the thought, I simply tried to put it out of my mind entirely. I tried, but it had never worked.

Driving home after the show on the empty midnight highways, the first flakes of the incoming snowstorm brushing my windshield, I was once again hit by the questions, the same ones that haunted me whenever I had time to think: *Where was he sleeping that night? What did he eat? What about shoes? Did he wear shoes? What if somebody tried to take his shoes? Could he defend himself? And what, in the end, does a person who lives on the street do when he gets sick? Cold? Lonely? Why didn't he call?* Nineteen years, except for that once, and he'd never called. When had he slipped away into this kind of existence? And why?

And then the most painful of all the questions: *Was it my fault? Could I have saved him? Can I save him still?* And then, *Can I save myself from* becoming *him?*

"I'm too old for this shit," I heard myself mumble.

I wondered what normal people, the ones whose parents didn't sleep on the street, thought about as they drove home from work. Yet here I was again, speeding along in my red Volvo 850, one of the anchorman's conspicuous indulgences, feeling guilty that my father, now 66, was on the street somewhere this very night trying to cadge a place to bed down.

As I had so often, I thought back to the days when my dad seemed to be the most indefatigable man in the world. I recalled his command of everything and everyone around him, his irrepressible humor, his dogged devotion to his cause, and mostly his knack for convincing me that I could achieve anything I wanted enough to work for. For all his miserable failures, he'd done plenty of good. I'd grown up determined to be counted as one of his successes. I owed a good deal of my achievements in life to him.

❦❦❦

My father enters my first memories at his best, as a showman—the ringmaster of fun and excitement. I was playing in the kitchen of our little brick rambler in Mauldin, South Carolina, one day when our babysitter looked out the window and spotted him. "Your daddy's home early."

My father's daily homecoming was always an event, a moment my brothers and I awaited eagerly. To have him home early was unbearably wonderful. I ran to the window, and there he was, getting out of the car, pulling out a big white cardboard box, and coming up the walk. We boys, bouncing on our toes like pogo sticks and squealing with glee, met our hero on the porch. Marq was seven, I was five, and Daryl was two.

"Hey, hey, boys! Daddy's home and he's got a party!" he yelled, holding the box over our heads. "Follow me inside."

Like a waiter in a fancy restaurant, he set the box down on the living room coffee table. "How do you think she'll like this!" he said in his game-show host's voice, carefully removing the top.

Inside was a white cake with pink rose petals in frosting all around its rim. In the middle, in a flowing frosting script, the baker had written *Happy Birthday, Mommy!* This was the first time I'd ever seen a cake with someone's name written on it, and I was fascinated.

"You know what today is, boys?" he asked, lowering his voice as if telling a secret, making the occasion as suspenseful as a little boy could stand. "Today is Mommy's birthday."

He closed the box and set it down. "Okay, boys, huddle up."

Dad often got us together in a make-believe football huddle when he wanted to tell us something like "Let's go swimming" or "Let's drive down for ice cream sodas," or "Let's rake the leaves." We gathered around him, heads together, eyes wide and mouths open.

"First thing," he said. "That closet over there . . ." (we gaped at the closet door) ". . . is full of presents for your mother. There's one from each of you and two from me. Okay, here's the play. We hide the cake in the closet with the presents. When she comes in, we're sitting on the couch watching TV. As soon as she comes into the living room, I give the signal and everybody jumps up and yells, 'Surprise!' Then we bring out the presents and the cake, and we

light the candles and let her blow them out, and we sing 'Happy Birthday.'"
The three of us looked at each other with delight.

"But," my father said, "you've got to promise to keep still until I give you
the cue." We crossed our hearts and hoped to die.

Mommy's shopping trip must have been to China. It seemed to take all
evening. For three little boys, the wait was thrilling and agonizing. Finally, the
kitchen door opened and in walked our mother, both arms loaded with grocery bags. Daryl started to make a noise. Marq and I grabbed him and held
him down on the couch and covered every opening that might let out air and
blow the lid off our secret plan.

"Couldn't someone help me with the groceries?" she started to scold. Daryl
wiggled free. "Mommy!" he piped. "Don't look in the closet! Your cake's in
there, and all your presents!"

Marq and I were furious. The secret was out, and we couldn't put it back
in his mouth, although we tried. Our mother didn't seem to mind a bit. "Oh,
my goodness!" she said as Dad swung the closet door wide. "All for me? What
a wonderful surprise!"

Dad brought the presents over and stacked them around her on the couch.
We boys were dying to see what "our" presents to Mom would turn out to be.
Mine was some fancy bath soap, and I couldn't have been prouder if I'd picked
it out myself. Marq gave her pretty handkerchiefs, and Daryl gave her some
nail polish. She hugged and kissed and thanked us.

Dad's main present to her was a full-length, lime-green nightie. "Bob!"
she said, gasping. "Where in the world did you get this? It's beautiful!" She
stood and held the nightie to her body. "Come here, you," she said to Dad, reaching up to give him a kiss more fervent than any I'd ever seen before.

"Hey," Dad said, flushed with pleasure, "we'll have to give that thing a
road test tonight," and my mother answered with a saucy laugh. I thought that
was pretty strange, Mom wearing her pajamas in the car out on the highway,
but I accepted it as just one of those baffling, thrilling things grown-ups did.

"Time to cut the cake," our game show host announced. We scampered
to the seldom-visited dining room where Dad ceremonially lifted the cake from
the box and placed it on a platter that looked like it had been cut from a giant
crystal. We boys clustered around and watched raptly as he lit the candles. "Make
a wish, honey," he said. My mother looked at each of us, shut her eyes, and
made a wish, and we all understood what that wish was: that this happiness
would last forever.

"Blow out the candles," we boys began chanting.

"I'll need your help," she said. "Everybody blow!"

We all took deep breaths and blew and blew until all the candles were out. My father handed my mother a silver knife, and she began cutting.

"Chocolate!" we boys howled in unison when the first slice came out.

"My favorite," Mom said. We all knew it was.

As we boys sat in a circle on the living room floor, Dad put a Ray Charles record on the phonograph and set the needle on a song that made everybody loosen and sway with its seductive melody and suggestive lyrics, something about holding and squeezing and stop teasing. "Get up off that couch, Birthday Girl," Dad said in a soft, low voice, his hand extended. Mom glided into his arms, as only a trained dancer could do. The two of them moved in unison around the center of the room. We boys beamed as we watched them in each other's arms, moving to the music, hugging and kissing each other. As I looked back on the scene, it had a mythic glow. It seemed to bypass my comprehensive ignorance of sex to give me a glimmer of how I was created and to assure me that I was the result of an act of love.

The Mom's-birthday memory always led to another memory far less assuring. It was six years later, and I was 11 years old. We were living in Anderson, 30 miles from Mauldin. I was sitting on the curb outside the YMCA, alone in the dark, waiting for Dad to come and pick me up and take me home. He was nearly two hours late, and I was cold. Finally, I saw his tan Mercedes coming down the street, and I ran out to meet it. "Hop in, Jonny!" he said.

He turned the car around in the parking lot and headed in the wrong direction, away from home. "Where are we going?" I asked.

He responded in that voice he always used when he wanted something to sound a lot better than it was. "Guess what, Jonny," he announced. "We're going to a friend's house on our way home. You'll like her." He said it as though I was in for a treat. I was so tired that I barely took in what he'd said. I didn't mind the detour; at least I was off the curb and in his car.

He drove to the far east side of town, where almost no white people lived. After ten minutes, he pulled up at a modest brick home, and we got out of the car.

"This woman's name is Miss Tilly," he said. "She's a client of mine. I need to take care of a little business with her." I still thought nothing of it. My father often took me with him on business calls, to see his clients in their homes— the county jail and the state prison. He knocked, and an attractive and gracious woman answered the door and invited us in.

She shook my hand and said, "You must be Jon." I was surprised she knew my name. She ushered us into the living room where her children were sitting, watching television. They looked startled. I was sure they hadn't had many white people in their house. She introduced me to them, and my father acted as though he expected us to become instant playmates. The girl was nine, and the little boy was seven. We were told to make ourselves comfortable in the living room and watch as much TV as we wanted.

"There are plenty of snacks," Miss Tilly said.

"You kids won't need to bother us for anything while we get our work done," my father quickly added. They disappeared down the hall, leaving us kids to stare at each other and wonder what to say.

We pretended to watch television, but we couldn't help glancing back and forth. No one said a word. For an hour-and-a-half we sat there, looking at each other, passing potato chips and pretzels. Although we didn't know exactly what was going on, we sensed the nature of what our parents were doing down the hall. Those two kids looked at me with resentment, but I didn't blame them a bit. I'd accompanied the white man who'd come to soil their mother somehow.

I stood up as soon as I heard a door open down the hall. "Okay, Jonny," my father said, "let's go." Miss Tilly didn't come all the way out of the dark hallway, but I could see that her hair was mussed and she was wearing a bathrobe. There were no good-byes. My father opened the door, and the two of us walked out.

He had more instructions for me as we drove home: "Now, when Mom asks where we've been, I just want you to say, 'Dad had to work late on a special case.' Okay? We don't want Mommy to get mad at us, right?"

I wanted to scream. I knew I hadn't done anything wrong, but still I felt dirty. My father was doing something wrong, something hurtful to Mom, and I was his little alibi. He was counting on me to keep his secret for him, and I would, because I didn't dare do anything that would spark another of those fights my parents had been having. I felt so guilty I couldn't stand myself. And I felt rage because I hadn't done anything to feel guilty for.

Luckily my mother was in bed when we got home that night, so I didn't have to face her questioning. I kicked off my shoes and went straight to bed with my clothes on. I lay there for hours, staring into the dark, just trying to breathe slowly as my feelings tore at my heart.

✤✤✤

Boston's blizzard had struck in earnest by the time I turned off the Southeastern Expressway at Hingham, a little harbor town 18 miles south of the city. My neighborhood was already tufted with white. I pulled up into the snow-covered driveway, and inside my house, I knew that my wife, Gina, and our children lay sleeping, peaceful and safe.

When I thought of Gina, my first impulse was to feel sorry for her. Early in her marriage she'd discovered there was something wrong with her new husband, an anger just under the skin that broke through like an erupted boil whenever I was corrected or criticized, or even made to feel inferior through some act of generosity on her part. In our seven years together, she'd had to tread cautiously. She'd learned which of my buttons never to press. Money was a dangerous topic; if a bill went unpaid for even a day after the due date, I'd explode. "I shouldn't expect a trust fund baby like you to appreciate the importance of handling money properly! You think I work my ass off just so you can live like a princess? What if I throw you out in the snow and make you fend for yourself? You'd max out your credit cards and starve to death!" If she offered even the mildest critique of my on-air performance, I'd lash back with sarcasm. "If you were anything more than a talking hairdo, you'd still be on the air!" She never knew when some minor complaint might trigger a rebuke—like the time she asked whether I'd forgotten Valentine's Day.

She'd just handed me an envelope and a small box wrapped in shiny red paper. The envelope contained a love note. In the box was a new watch. The beautiful gift made me feel inadequate; in my ruined family we hadn't celebrated Valentine's Day. When she wondered aloud if perhaps I might have a gift for her, it was as though she were putting me down for growing up in a family that never showed love for each other, that was plagued by so many problems that we barely made it to school in the morning, let alone recognized Valentine's Day. I blew up in her face. "Does the whole world have to make it a fucking holiday every time greeting cards go on sale?" She shrank from me and moved quickly from the room, leaving me with my amazement and horror. What could have made me punish my generous wife for my own thoughtlessness? Where had that weird, mistargeted rage come from?

Gina grew accustomed to being crushed in arguments, to being embarrassed in front of our friends, to taking the blame for little things that went wrong—the baby's stinking diaper, the burnt toast, the bounced check. She had the resilience to handle it all, while I teetered on the verge of a breakdown. I knew that demons from my past were threatening to destroy this new life that meant so much to me. But I couldn't even name them.

I'd begun concocting a life for myself the day my childhood ended, the day my father left our home. I'd stumbled through adolescence and become an adult only to find that I didn't have the first clue how to be a man. The world expected me to know what I was doing, but I was a patch job, a man cobbled from wreckage, and one of the parts I hadn't been able to fabricate for myself was intimacy. Instead, there was resentment. I could convert my resentment into a kind of high-octane fuel powerful enough to propel me through most obstacles, but it was burning up my marriage.

I wondered how deep Gina's well was, how much longer she could keep on greeting abuse with compassion. I wondered if there might come a time when she'd decide that the benefits of this one-sided relationship simply weren't worth the pain. It sickened me to think she might be worrying that I was passing my defects along to our children.

I promised myself that when I got home that night I wouldn't, for once, wake her up and talk to her about my torments. I'd keep them to myself.

I tried. I got into bed carefully so as not to wake her, and kissed her and tried to sleep, but I couldn't. My mind kept replaying the blizzard video, as I knew it would, and then once again I began obsessing over my childhood and its destruction.

"Jon?" Gina whispered. "You're awake, aren't you." It was more an accusation than a question.

"No," I whispered in the other direction.

"Yes, you are. I can feel you jerking."

"Sorry. I guess I'm just a jerk," I said.

She rolled over and faced me in the dark and put her warm hand on my cheek. "Honey," she said, as she'd said so often, "you've got to concentrate on this thought: You *survived*. Your brothers went to jail, you got yourself an education and a career and a family. You should be grateful for your success."

I started to dispute what she said about my brothers. "Went to jail" made it sound like they'd committed armed robbery when it was really minor—no weapons, no violence, no stolen money. But I knew what she meant; my brothers' lives had been badly hurt by what happened. They hadn't really survived.

"You're right," I said, and she was. My life had become everything that, as a castoff child, I'd yearned for it to be. "I'll think about you and my beautiful kids and this beautiful house."

"And remember," she said, "when you're not terrible, you're wonderful. The kids adore you." She kissed me. "And so do I." She snuggled against me. "Let's go to sleep."

I waited until her breathing became slow and even. I thought the lovely thought she'd given me, and still I was edgy, anxious. I couldn't believe it—this feeling that something was missing, that although I had everything I wanted, it amounted to nothing. However irrational, the fear that I could lose everything I'd achieved was real, and it terrified me. All during my troubled youth I'd taken as a God-given certainty the fact that once I'd created my own sweet family and won a measure of prosperity, I'd possess a deep and lasting contentment. It hadn't happened.

Out of sheer exhaustion, I finally fell asleep. The next day I was tired—too tired, really, for the ritual roughhouse with my four-year-old son, Kasey. Every morning we'd turn the family room floor into our own wrestling mat or karate ring or football field. We wrestled and chopped and tackled each other. The first to knock down his opponent five times was the winner, so long as it was Kasey.

"Okay, Daddy!" he said when he'd swallowed the last spoonful of breakfast cereal. "Time for the karate championship!"

I was dragging when we began, but I got myself into it, and we were having fun. Then, right in the middle of our pretend fight, he stopped and looked at me with a curious, almost perplexed expression on his face.

"Dad," he panted, his karate guard down, "where's Grandpa Bob?"

The question had come out of nowhere. It took me a few seconds to figure out what he was talking about. He'd heard his parents speak of a visit from a strange old man who had appeared on our doorstep a few years before. The man had played with Kasey on the floor for half an hour, then he'd gone away. Kasey remembered that we'd introduced this man to him as "Grandpa Bob" and that we'd spoken of him as if he was somehow important—important to Kasey.

I was stunned, not only by the timing of his inquiry, but by its laserlike accuracy. His curiosity had led him to the one subject that this all-knowing, all-powerful father was afraid to examine. Kasey wanted to know where his grandfather had gone. He wanted to know why his father's father was missing from the family photo, the picture that defined this little boy's identity. And there I knelt, unable to utter a word. My mind ran through all the pat answers that parents use to brush off children's difficult questions. Long seconds passed. Finally, I forced out something like, "Grandpa Bob is traveling. Grandpa Bob is on the road."

"Is he dead?" Kasey asked.

"No, I think he's still alive."

"You don't know?"

"No."

"Why don't you know?" he pressed.

"I'm pretty sure he's still alive, Kasey." I tried to sound authoritative, hoping that would satisfy the boy and end the conversation.

"Then why doesn't he come to visit?" he went on.

"You ask too many questions!" I shouted at my curious little boy. He flinched at the boom of my terrible voice and cowered at the sight of my facial expression transforming instantly from pleasant to menacing. I reached for him, to pull him to my chest and give him a hug, but the nimble four-year-old stepped back and dashed out of the room and up the stairs. I heard him whimper as he fled.

"I'm sorry, Kasey," I mumbled as I stared after him. "I just don't know."

Then I noticed Gina, standing at the kitchen sink, glaring at me with a look of disapproval.

"You wanna ration of your own?" I threatened. "Just give me that pissy look and you can have your own ration of shit!" She turned away quickly and continued washing dishes.

"That was mean. Kasey didn't deserve to be—"

"Shut up!" I roared. "Mind your own business." And as I was leaving the room to go upstairs to apologize to my shell-shocked little boy, I muttered, "You should know by now you can't lecture me. I already know it's mean as soon as it happens. I don't know why I do it." Gina didn't bother to look up.

This wasn't supposed to have happened. Kasey had torn away part of the pretty picture I had painted over my old life. I thought I'd done a good job of making things seem just right—the new family, the house, the job. Now I wasn't so sure. Suddenly it all felt like a sham.

I realized in that moment that we both needed an answer to Kasey's question. Thirty years had passed since my father left my brothers and me alone in a dingy two-bedroom apartment with our broken-spirited mother. He'd stolen a piece of my identity when he disappeared. Now I needed to pass it along to my son, and I couldn't. I'd spent the first part of my life worshiping my father and the rest of it trying to forget him. Kasey's question now made me realize why the image of the old man on the manhole cover had disturbed me so deeply. It had reminded me that the most important man I had ever known had deserted me. And not only that, he'd vanished into a world shrouded from my sight.

As terrifying a prospect as it was to me, I knew what I had to do. It was time for me to go down into his gray world and find him. I had to get as close to him as I could and stay there as long as he'd let me. I'd go back through his life with him, tracing his path from loving father to deserter, his slide into desolation, until I understood. I'd thank him for what he did right, and make him answer for what he did wrong.

How strange to go searching for the father I'd spent most of the last 15 years trying to forget. But I had no choice. As I'd just learned, I couldn't cancel him out. I felt an overpowering practical need to come to terms with his ruin. I needed to make sure that, through ignorance of some dark emotional inheritance, I didn't do to my own life and my children's lives what he had done to himself and his family. If it could happen to my father, it could happen to me. It could happen to anyone.

In the many years leading up to this decision, I thought that my troubles were unique. Long afterward, however, when I'd made it through to the other side, I learned I'd had a recognized disorder afflicting people who once had been put through hell and had gotten stuck there. I fit right into the pattern of what psychologists referred to as Post-traumatic Stress Disorder. It was first recognized when Vietnam vets came back from southeast Asia in such emotional turmoil. My anger and resentment were standard symptoms, along with my guilt and my shame and my fear that it was all my fault. Many victims of the disorder are blind-sided one day, years after the devastating experience, by a vivid image that brings it all back and precipitates an emotional crisis, and this was precisely what happened with me. In my case, it was the videotaped glimpse of the old man freezing on the sidewalk.

Therapists urge sufferers to confront their demons. I didn't know that. I did so out of desperation.

❧❧❧

CHAPTER TWO
The Amazing PB&J Sandwich

In 1955, Robert Owen Du Pre was a newly appointed, 26-year-old FBI agent stationed in Los Angeles. The Cold War was in full swing, and the FBI was intent on rooting out subversives. My father's job was to spy on members of the motion picture industry suspected of Communist sympathies.

A secretary in the Bureau's Los Angeles office, Darlene Hammond, was engaged to one of the other agents, and she asked the dashing southerner, Bob Du Pre, if he'd like a blind date with her friend from grade school, a UCLA student named Marquise Peek. The four went to the Los Angeles Coliseum, where they watched the July 4th fireworks show.

Marquise was impressed by the G-man's looks. He had curly brown hair and a slender, 6'1" frame that hung a suit without a wrinkle. His eyelids slanted sensuously like the young Paul Newman's. But it was his sense of humor that won her over. "He was relentless," she used to tell her children. "He just kept wisecracking until you laughed because you were punch drunk."

In appearance and in fact, she was the classic Southern California drum majorette—pretty and petite, with an arresting figure and perfect bright white teeth. Her hair and eyes were dark brown, and (to continue the Hollywood imagery) she had the distinctive black eyebrows of the young Elizabeth Taylor.

Her parents, Marquis and Marie Peek, were German Lutherans from Indiana who, licked by the Depression, had limped out to Southern California. Marquis, an infantryman in World War I, got a job as a guard at Joliet State Prison, then as a cop in Montebello, a Los Angeles suburb.

A short man who bunched up his lips and thrust his jaw forward, he was a very straight arrow, very concerned about morals and standards of behavior. When he was a boy, he'd been so distressed by his sister's promiscuity, as he saw it, that he'd run away from home to go live with relatives. He was quick to anger. "Mom was the disciplinarian," my mother once told me, "but my father had the temper. You never wanted to be around when he lost his temper." She told of a time at dinner when suddenly, for no apparent reason, Marquis jerked back and pushed himself away from the table, jarring everyone's plate as he sprang to his feet. He took the sandwich he'd been eating, threw it on the white-tile floor, and stomped out of the room. "Mom just kept eating," my mother said. "She never raised her head." No one wanted Officer Peek's attention when he was angry, so no one asked what caused the outburst.

I felt the long, strong arm of the law on that side of the family when I was five years old. My brothers and I were staying with Grandpa and Grandma Peek for a month in the summer of 1963. I had my own room. On our first night there, as he tucked me in, Grandpa laid down the law. "Whatever you do," he said, "don't pull down on the curtain rod above that window. I'm sick of putting it back up again." He turned out the light and left the room.

From my bed, I saw a huge white moon hanging in the sky, bigger than any I'd ever seen. It looked as if it might land in the backyard. I parted the curtains, and down came the rod, but I was transfixed by the moon and hardly noticed.

Suddenly my head snapped to one side; Grandpa's hard, flat hand had struck my cheek. "You need to listen to instructions," he growled in the dark. I never saw him. He went out, and my ears rang like sirens until, after a long while, I fell asleep.

These two instances of my grandfather's violence would soon repeat themselves in my life, by proxy and with remarkable similarity.

Grandma Marie was a stout woman with a weathered face, and, incongruously, a head of fluffy brown curls. Her deep wrinkles made her look stern, but when she smiled, they all seemed to fit. Whatever girlhood dreams of her own she might have privately mourned, she was determined that her pretty little daughter would have it better. She wanted Marquise to take dancing and singing lessons, but there was no money for it on the salary a cop made in the 1940s, so she took a job in a restaurant baking pies. For years, her pie money not only paid for the lessons, but also for material to make dresses and costumes for Marquise that were fancier and frillier than those of any other girl in the class.

The greatest expense was straightening Marquise's teeth; orthodonture was rare among working-class people in those days. My mother remembers how her mother, during the war years, scrounged for coupons for the rationed gasoline that would enable her to drive Marquise to and from the orthodontist's office in Los Angeles, 15 miles away. When Marquise decided she wanted to go to college, her mother shook the family purse and came up with the tuition.

Grandma's aim wasn't to make a professional performer out of her daughter or to give her a career in Hollywood. She didn't approve of the lives led by actresses and dancers. She wanted her daughter to possess the graces that would attract a fine man to marry her.

After the fireworks show, Marquise asked Bob Du Pre to dinner the next Sunday. It turned out to be a cookout served at the backyard picnic table.

"Want some more corn?" her father asked Bob.

"Don't mind if I do," Bob replied and held out his glass, grinning. The joke was lost on the Peeks. He had to explain that where he came from, Walhalla, South Carolina, "corn" was the term for moonshine. The Peeks, both teetotalers, smiled tautly. But Marquise could tell that her parents liked Bob. He had charmed them. The small-town cop was impressed by the tall, confident FBI agent and was flattered by his attentions to his daughter.

That afternoon, Bob took Marquise to the beach at Santa Monica. While they were wading in the surf, he slipped his hand down into her bathing suit and cupped her buttock. She was embarrassed. "Stop that. I don't go that far," she protested, reflexively blurting the defense her mother had practiced on her countless times.

Marquise's prudish posturing caught Bob's attention. The girls he'd dated back in South Carolina, the girls he'd enjoyed when he'd served in the Navy, never said no. This was something new.

Marquise soon realized that Bob didn't want to hear about her college life; unfortunately, it was all she had to talk about. He didn't like her friends either; they were too young for him, and he found them boring. He wanted to talk about himself and what he wanted to do in life, which was to be an attorney in private practice. She was afraid she was too unsophisticated to interest him.

But Bob *was* interested. One evening, a month after they'd met, they went out to dinner. "We kept looking into each other's eyes," my mother recalled, "and then he asked me to marry him. He didn't say he loved *me*, so I never got to say that I loved *him*. I *assumed* he loved me."

What seemed to be on Bob's mind was not love, but speed. They'd have to be married right away, he said, because the Bureau was about to transfer him to New York. If he was married at the time of the move, the Bureau would pay to move his wife, but not if the marriage came afterward.

Marquise was only 20 and hadn't finished college. They'd known each other scarcely six weeks. But her parents did not object. No need to ask this dynamic fellow questions; he'd been checked out by the FBI, after all, so he must be a model citizen. The Peeks considered ambitious young Agent Du Pre a good catch.

On September 2, just two months after their blind date, the drum majorette and the government spy stood under the 50-foot-tall stained-glass window of the Westwood Baptist Church on Wilshire Boulevard and presented themselves to be married. Bob's older brother, Frank, was his best man, and two buddies from the Bureau were ushers. Bob's parents had written and said they were sorry, but they couldn't afford to make the trip.

There was no time for a honeymoon. The day after the wedding, the new couple was on the train for New York. By the end of the week, the beautiful coed from paradise, the indulged daughter barely out of her teens, was just another lonely housewife in a nondescript apartment house in suburban Long Island, far from the forbidding city where her husband worked endless hours.

The day before the wedding, Marquise's mother had taken her aside and tried to give her some maternal advice. She said nothing about the happiness to be found in the sharing of one's life. She said nothing about marriage being hard work, requiring effort from both parties. Marie Peek wanted to tell her virgin daughter what a nasty business sex was. She went on and on until Marquise stopped her. "Mom," she said, "I don't want to hear about it."

But she soon discovered that Mom wasn't entirely wrong. One evening she was watching television, and Bob came into the room and said, "Let's go to bed."

"This movie is really good," she said. "Come over here and watch it with me."

"I'm going to bed," he said huffily and made for the bedroom. Ten minutes later, he came back. Now he was angry. "If you won't have sex with me," he said, "I'll rape you."

At first she thought he was joking: If he'd wanted to have sex, why hadn't he said so? "You can't," she said, laughing. But he was serious. He got down on the sofa and began tearing at her clothes and working himself over on top of her. She was athletic and had strong legs and managed to squirm free.

In bed, he was exasperated by her inexperience. Much later, looking back over years of marital grief and responding to his accusations, she wrote him a long letter, and in it, she said, "If you wanted to marry a virgin, then once we were married, why didn't you teach me what you wanted so that you would be more satisfied and happy at home?"

"Foreplay," she told me in a remarkable conversation I had with her many years later, "was never Bob's specialty. He always did it for himself. He'd never wait for me. In all our time together, I never once had a climax with him. That's the way it was. I think it might have had something to do with his early adventures, making out in the back seats of cars and so forth, always in a hurry to finish before the girl's father came along or a cop shined his light in the window. The hurrying got to be part of it."

The New York period was misery for the immature, mistreated bride, but it was also bad for Bob. The FBI routine had become a grind, unsuited to his restless, impulsive temperament. When my brothers and I were little, he told us exciting tales of tracking "Commies." He had a scar on his arm, and he said he'd gotten it in a shootout with Communist undercover agents. Years later, he confessed that he'd made that up, and he described what the day-to-day work was really like. "I got to drive up on the sidewalk a few times," he said, "but other than that, it was just long, long hours sitting in cars, listening to tapped phones with nobody interesting on the line, watching people who didn't do anything suspicious, and drinking enough coffee to kill a water buffalo. Most days I was bored out of my skull."

He began playing hooky, spending his afternoons working out in a Manhattan boxing gym, or otherwise just wandering around the midtown area. He also fell into the habit of going to bars after work with other agents, and with secretaries from the office. He was getting home later and later. My mother, all alone in the apartment and now pregnant with her first child, expected him to hurry home after work. When she asked him where he'd been, he'd say, "We stopped for a drink," and leave it at that. My mother began to resent this office-based social life he'd created for himself.

It became clear to her that he was deliberately excluding her from that life. The occasion that brought this home to her was the FBI Christmas party their second year in New York. Marquise was eager to go. She wanted to meet Bob's friends. She'd had a baby two months before—a squaller named Marquis Anthony, named after her father and her twin brother who had died as an infant—and this was her first chance since the birth to get out of the apartment and have some fun. Neighbors had agreed to sit the baby, and she'd bought a dress and had her hair fixed.

Bob had told her he couldn't come out to Long Island and pick her up, so she said she'd drive herself. She didn't know the highways or the city, but she was determined to go. When she tried to start the car, however, the battery was dead. She phoned Bob and asked him to come get her, but he refused. He went to the party by himself, and she got the feeling that that was the way he preferred it. She wondered if he was ashamed of her. She sat up and waited for him, but he didn't get home until five the next morning.

From the very beginning, my father had talked and talked about his old flames. The stories seemed designed to make my mother feel inadequate, but she put up with them, not knowing how to make him stop. A frequent figure in these reminiscences was a girl named Ginger. She was a knockout, he said, a real pistol. He would have married her, but he hadn't been ready to settle down. One day Ginger called my father at the FBI in New York. She was in town, she said, and wanted to meet his wife. The three of them had dinner at an expensive restaurant.

Ginger was indeed a knockout. She was a water dancer with a water park in Florida and had come to New York to perform on the *Dave Garroway Show*. The chemistry between Bob and Ginger seemed strong, and Marquise felt shut out. The next two nights in a row, Bob came home very late. She knew what was happening but tried not to let herself think about it.

At the same time that he was building a separate life for himself, Bob was closely restricting Marquise's contacts with outsiders. He got twitchy and cross whenever she talked to a stranger. He did what he could to prevent her from keeping up her Los Angeles friendships. He learned she'd been corresponding with two girls she'd known and an old boyfriend, and he became enraged. "You can't write letters to a man," he shouted. "That's highly improper!" The contradiction between his restrictions on her and his fast and loose ways with his own women friends in the city was not lost on my mother. But she didn't complain. She didn't dare. She let layers of resentment fold over each other inside her.

Marquise became pregnant again, and soon afterward, for reasons undisclosed, my father quit the Bureau, beginning a behavior my mother would later call "the pattern"—the practice of walking away from good jobs, fed up and embittered. "He hated every boss he ever had," she said, "including himself."

He got a job in Washington as a legislative assistant to one of South Carolina's senators, Strom Thurmond. My father's politics in no way matched those of the segregationist Dixiecrat Thurmond. Taking a position in the senator's office was more about career positioning than political ideology. By the end of his four years in Washington, Bob Du Pre's pattern had repeated itself again—he was angry and disheartened.

Nearly 40 years later, Thurmond, the senior member of the U.S. Congress, remembered my father with clarity and fondness. "Your daddy was an ambitious, talented young man," he told me. "He had such a keen intellect and such an impressive conversational style. He was a real up-and-comer. Bobby could have done almost anything he wanted in this town if he'd stayed with it."

Thurmond's fervent appraisal of my father so many years later might have seemed feigned except that the senator also remembered "courting" Dad's sister, Ann. My aunt remembered, too. "Well, now," she said when I asked her, "it's not something I would brag about. You don't have to announce it to the world." I asked Aunt Ann if Dad owed his job to the senator's romantic interest in her. Nonsense, she said. He owed it to the senator's indebtedness to their father, a county chairman of the Democratic Party in South Carolina, who routinely delivered the vote for Thurmond.

I was born in Washington in 1958, providing "the biggest news in the Thurmond office that day," according to a Washington wire service article picked up by several South Carolina papers. With a birth weight of nine pounds, six ounces, I irreparably stretched and rumpled my mother's belly, she told me years later.

When I was three, my father, sick of running errands for Thurmond—including repeated fetchings of glasses of fresh-squeezed orange juice—got himself appointed assistant U.S. attorney for South Carolina, posted in Greenville, the federal seat for the western end of the state. Soon he became chief assistant prosecutor, the lead man on the team of assistant district attorneys who argued the cases.

He and my mother bought a small, red brick rambler in Mauldin, a coagulation of strip malls and gas stations just down the road from Greenville.

It was a hot noon in the spring of my fifth year. My best friend and I were squatting by a tiny creek near the Mauldin house. We'd caught a dozen polliwogs in the creek and were holding them in pools we'd made with the red mud of the bank. The polliwogs were our prisoners, and we were standing guard over them from our fort, a large cardboard box we'd opened up and propped against a tree. We were ready to capture as many more of the slippery little polliwog spies as the enemy sent our way. We were deep into our fantasy. No other world existed for us, no care beyond maintaining vigilance against our imaginary foe.

"Jon!" My mother was calling me from our back porch. I knew just how long it would be before she called again, at a higher pitch.

"Jon!" she called, right on time. "Come and eat!" I also knew that I'd be in trouble if I dawdled until the third summons, "Jon Mason Du Pre, where *are* you!" So I broke open the mud dike around our polliwog pond and freed our prisoners, and then, not even pausing to say good-bye to my playmate, I ran for the house.

There was my mother, standing on the porch in her hot-weather clothing— green polyester shorts, unbuttoned white blouse with the shirttails tied in a knot above her navel, and a green band around her head, holding her dark brown hair up and back.

"Take off your shoes," she said. "Come in and wash your hands." I passed my hands quickly under the faucet and smeared the mud onto the towel. My mother sat down at the kitchen table and went back to the article she'd been reading in the *Ladies' Home Journal*. I climbed onto my chair and felt the cool blue rim of the white enamel tabletop pressing against my naked chest. Before me on the table was the usual glass of milk, and, on a plate, something entirely outside my experience. I stared at it. It was a peanut-butter-and-jelly sandwich, its red sweetness runny in the Carolina heat and oozing from between the thick, spongy slices of white bread. But this was no ordinary peanut-butter-and-jelly sandwich. My mother had cut it diagonally, from corner to corner.

I had never seen a sandwich sliced that way before. My mother had probably done it out of boredom, to vary her routine, hardly thinking about it, but to me it seemed like a brilliant new idea, an inspiration, a work of art on a paper plate.

She mistook my awe for distaste. "Eat your sandwich," she commanded.

To eat this perfect object seemed a sacrilege, but after a moment, I picked it up and carefully bit off one of the amazing corners. Then, horrified that I was destroying the shape, I nibbled at the other corners and at the edges to restore the original triangle. As I ate, I maintained the triangles as long as I could, savoring every tiny bite. When I was done, I looked up at my mother reverently. She sat across the table reading her magazine, unaware that she had just created a moment that would last a lifetime. I'm certain that it was in that moment I came into consciousness. The sublime experience of eating that sandwich brought me to an awareness that I was someone's child, part of something larger than myself, and that I lived under the care of a mother and father who nurtured and protected me. My world would never be the same again.

✤✤✤

Our house looked like every other house on the block—three bedrooms, with a small living room that opened onto a dining area adjacent to a cramped kitchen. It was my home, where my family lived, and I loved it. I considered myself the luckiest little boy in the world, with the most wonderful parents, having the best childhood a kid could have.

Mixed in among these memories from that first summer is the standard one in which a young boy learns the hard lessons of life. It begins with me tagging along with my mother as she shopped. We were headed for the bland, gray, aluminum-fronted row of stores down the street from our house. First, we passed the cobbler's shop with no name; in the window was a small dusty heap of repaired shoes no one had ever picked up. Then we passed the Barbecue Hut, where almost nobody ate. And then we arrived at Gilbert's Rexall Drugs.

As we entered, the screen door brushed a hanging bell, which announced our entrance with a tinkle. Immediately in front of us was a big green oxygen tank on wheels. The display always made me nervous. It looked like an atomic bomb that might explode at any moment. All around me, rising from the white linoleum floor to a place higher than I could see, were shelves laden with at least one of everything anybody could ever think to ask for. There were stacks of perm kits for women who wanted big southern bouffants. There were trusses and plasters and liniments waiting to be bought by aching textile mill workers.

Down at the back of the store, next to the cash register, was a display that always made my eyes widen and my mouth water. Perched on the counter, between the spinning postcard rack and the key-ring stand, right where customers could see it as they opened their purses and wallets and made impulse purchases, was a three-gallon, clear-glass jug filled with jawbreakers—big candy balls—red, yellow, and green. While Mr. Gilbert was helping my mother find the hand lotion she liked, I reached in, took one, and slipped it into the pocket of my shorts.

When we got back on the sidewalk, I fished it out and put it in my mouth. My mother, seeing me sucking on something, grabbed me by the collar and made me open my mouth. Then she dragged me back into the store and marched me up to the counter.

"I want you to tell Mr. Gilbert what you just did, young man," she said sternly. "Go on, tell him." Looking at the floor, feeling my mother's hand tightening on my arm, and with the candy cramming my mouth like a bowling ball, I mumbled out my offense. "Tell him you're sorry," she said, and I did.

As Mr. Gilbert considered, I waited anxiously. "Young man," he said finally, "how much money do you have in your pocket?" I shook my head: none. "Then you should work for your candy, don't you think?" I nodded. He handed me a broom twice as long as I was. "Start sweeping, son," he said. "When I think you've done a jawbreaker's worth of work, I'll tell you."

I saw him wink at my mother but failed to realize that they were sharing amusement at the little corrective charade they were playing out for my benefit. For half an hour while my mother was off doing her other shopping, I struggled with the broom, toggling it clumsily across the linoleum. The jawbreaker took forever to dissolve in my mouth and came to taste sickeningly sweet. I felt embarrassed and alone. When my mother returned, Mr. Gilbert told me I'd served my time.

Marq, my older brother, was an energetic and adventuresome seven-year-old. He was something of a Huckleberry Finn, brash and eager to try everything. It was all I could do to keep up with him, but I tried, every waking hour, up and down trees, through the woods and across the creek and back again. One day he told me he'd found a collection of glass jars in Mr. Albrecht's garage. Mr. Albrecht was the next-door neighbor, a grouchy old man. Marq took me back through the hedge and into Mr. Albrecht's garage. He showed me how to smash a jar full of paint on the cement floor and pointed out the crazy patterns the bright colors made as they splattered and mixed. I grabbed a jar and joined in. We'd broken 10 or 12 bottles, when the door swung open. There was Mr. Albrecht, in shock.

He told our mother. She sent us to our bedroom and made us stay there for the rest of the afternoon, until Dad got home and could discipline us. We were scared. When we heard Dad's car in the driveway, Marq and I dove under the bed. We both believed that when our executioner came through the door and failed to see us, he'd leave and we'd get a reprieve.

The bedroom door opened. I could see my father's shiny black wing-tipped shoes step toward the side of the bed. "Come on out here, boys," he barked, "and take your licks."

When I crawled out, I was astounded to see that he wasn't angry. Our pathetic effort to hide had tickled him, and in any case, having just gotten home from work, he was in no mood to whip his boys. "Tell you what," he said. "You stand beside me, and when I slap my belt on my leg, you scream like I'm whipping you. That way, Mommy will think you got your licks, and I won't have to spank you. Is that a deal?"

"It's a deal!" we shouted.

My father swatted his leg with the belt, trying to produce a genuine lashing sound. Our make-believe screams, mixed with giggles, weren't very convincing. When we emerged from the room, we saw that my mother was smiling, and I realized she'd been in on the ruse. Mr. Albrecht, for some reason, wasn't popular with my parents. They'd had to tell him they'd whip us but they'd never meant to, certainly not to please Mr. Albrecht. Our real punishment had been the long afternoon of dread.

I was considered too young for first grade, but all summer long I pestered my parents to let me start school in the fall. One late summer evening, Mom and Dad sat down in the living room and talked. I was in the kitchen, not far away, and could hear them, and I realized that they were talking about me.

"Well, what do you think?" my mother asked. "Should we send him to school? He'd be smaller than the other kids."

"Yes," my father said, "I guess he would. But Jonny's a pretty bright kid. I think he's smart enough to do it."

Did they intend for me to overhear that conversation? Had they already decided to send me, but were now just trying to build up my confidence? If so, it worked. All these years later, I still can hear my dad saying, "He's smart enough; he's a little bit smarter than most five-year-olds," and my mother agreeing. And I remember my reaction: If Mom and Dad thought I was smart, maybe I was.

Five or six days before school opened, I was playing by the creek, dropping sticks into the water and running along with them as they followed the current. I stepped on a board with a nail in it, and the nail lanced up through my sneaker and into the arch of my foot. The nail held the board to the bottom of the sneaker, and I was afraid to pull it out, so I hopped into the back yard on the other foot screaming, "Mama! Help!"

The doctor gave me a tetanus shot, but it was my mother who made it all better. On the way home, she stopped at the shoe store. "Pick out any pair you want," she told me, smiling affectionately, her hand gently touching my head. I went straight for the brown leather construction boots. "Those have nail-proof soles," the salesman said. Everywhere I went in them, I fearlessly crushed sticks and bugs and nails in boards. For a year, I took them off only to bathe, and even then they stood right by the tub. If my mother didn't pull them off my feet, I slept in them. At the end of that year, when they were two sizes too small for me, my mother had to talk me out of them. I was glad I'd stepped on that nail. I got a new pair of boots, and my mother had shown me tenderness.

I also saw her other side. Marq and I came home from school one afternoon to find that she had wallpapered the bedroom we shared. She'd used old travel posters she'd been collecting, making a sort of montage of them. It was beautiful. "Now, boys," she said, "I want to say something to you, and I don't want you to forget it. Never, never peel back the corners of those posters. If you see a corner curling, never pull at it or peel it off. Tell me so I can glue it down. Don't you ever peel back the corners."

One day I was sent to my room for something I'd done. I went over and sat on my bed, with nothing to do. I looked at the posters and saw that a corner of one of them had curled. I couldn't resist the temptation to peel it back. I decide that if I took off just the little turned-up part, my mother would never notice. I pulled, and a big section of the bottom of the poster tore loose.

It was as if my mother had been standing at the door listening for the sound of the ripping paper. She burst through the door the moment I did it. She was furious, out of control. "What did I tell you!" she screamed. And then even louder, "What did I tell you!" She came at me with fists clenched and started beating me, hitting me wherever she could land a punch. I scrambled all over the room, ducking and dodging, trying to dodge her blows. Finally, she pinned me down on a corner of my bed. I saw her fist coming straight at my nose. It was a sight I would always remember.

She got up, stormed out of the room, and slammed the door shut behind her. I lay there sobbing, shaking, confused. There was something terribly wrong with what had just happened. I couldn't comprehend what it might be. I could only wonder, in a whimpering voice, why I had caused it. "Why did you peel the wallpaper, Stupid? Why did you peel the wallpaper? What did she tell you? What did she tell you?"

More and more often, my mother flashed into fury over minor incidents. Once she asked Marq and me to clean up our bedroom. She was having guests that evening, she said, and she wanted everything tidy. An hour before the guests were to arrive, I heard her yell. We ran to the bedroom door and looked in, and there she was, yanking out our dresser drawers and throwing the clothes all over the room, shouting at the top of her voice.

"I asked you boys to clean this room! Can't I get you to do anything? All right. If you want to live in a mess, live in a mess!" She wrenched a mattress from one of the beds and threw it on the floor. For four or five more minutes, she ransacked the room.

To outsiders, we looked like a happy family. My parents got along with their neighbors. People passing our house saw well-kept lawns and gardens. No one could know that we were in the twilight of our time together.

To me, we seemed to be in fine shape. If there was an inconsistency between a mother who delicately cut my sandwich and one who pounded me with her fists in rage, it didn't dawn on me.

I've asked myself why in later years I regarded my mother so differently from my father, why I blamed him but let her off the hook. It may have had something to do with her aloofness. She hardly ever hugged or kissed us, and our relationship with her was cool. My mother never disappointed me because I never expected much from her. She was never my hero.

I had no idea what was going on in her life or in my father's, no suspicion that torments were tearing apart their marriage. All in good time.

❧ ❧ ❧

CHAPTER THREE ❧
Twelve Black Horses and Three Green Elves

My parents had always talked about the dream house they would some-day build. "There won't be a house like it anywhere in the South," my father would say with a sweep of his arm, full of excitement. "I hope it looks like those places I saw in Bel Air when I was a kid and my father took us driving," my mother would reply, her eyes gleaming.

The dream house was the only important thing that I can remember both my parents being enthusiastic about, the only thing I can remember them ever working on together. It got under way in 1965, when they bought 35 acres of lakefront property near Anderson, a small city almost 40 miles west of Mauldin. I was seven by then and spent hours in the waiting room of the architect's office while my parents argued with him over the house plans. It would sit on top of a hill looking down on Lake Hartwell. It would have a redwood-paneled exterior, curving slate connecting walls, and a split-cedar shingled roof—a vision from the portfolio of Frank Lloyd Wright.

My parents subdivided 25 of the 35 acres into building lots, which they hoped to sell off, and kept 10 acres for the dream house. While it was being built, they moved us into temporary quarters, a rental house in a pleasant development called Stonewall Woods. My brothers and I loved it there. It was a real neighborhood, full of children our ages. We had woods to explore, football and kickball and softball games in the big yard across the street, great Halloweens, lots of birthday parties—everything that makes living in a neighborhood nourishing. It was a healthy, happy time. It lasted about a year.

We went to Centerville Elementary School. I remember my third-grade teacher, a red-haired woman who took us beyond the subjects third-graders were supposed to study. Every Friday, just before lunchtime, she would start talking in a way none of us understood but which was tremendously pleasing to our ear. Her strange talk signaled that it was time to listen to the French records. The people on the records said things from deep inside their throats, and we kids tried to repeat the sounds. I found out the first time we had French class that I was good at rolling the *r*. My teacher's compliments inspired me to try extraordinarily hard to speak fluent French. My red-haired beauty also taught us how to operate a cash register, how to read a thermometer, and how to move our foot from the gas pedal to the brake. "Look how fast you move your foot!" she used to cheer. It wasn't the extracurricular lessons that interested me. Rather, it was my teacher's approval I craved.

I was happy at Centerville Elementary, except for the times when I passed the big kids' hallway after lunch break and saw everyone kicking Tyrone. I'd never met him. He was a fifth-grader. I knew his name because I'd heard it shouted. "Tyrone! Hey, Tyrone! Look over here, Tyrone!" Tyrone walked precisely down the middle of the long hall that stretched the distance of the big kids' half of the school. He folded his arms and lowered his head as he walked. Along the way, kids would walk up beside him and shove him or punch him on the arm or kick him on his butt. There were even a few girls who sneaked up behind him and slapped him on his head. Tyrone never tried to defend himself. He just looked straight ahead and kept walking. I remember being angry at Tyrone for not striking back.

I only saw one person come to his rescue—my big brother, Marq. When Marq walked beside Tyrone, the other children shouted at Tyrone, but they didn't punch him or kick him. The mysterious thing was that I never saw a teacher when the big kids tried to hurt Tyrone, except for my brother's teacher, who grabbed Marq by the arm and pulled him back into her room. When Marq told Dad and Mom he'd gotten in trouble for walking with Tyrone, our parents erupted. They wanted to know all about Tyrone's troubles, every detail. I was flattered by their sudden interest in what I had to say, and was deeply impressed by the way they acted together.

The entire family rode together in Dad's Mercedes the next morning. Marq and I took it as a reward for having done a good deed, although we still weren't sure exactly what the deed might have been. Dad and Mom spoke vaguely and softly when they explained why they were going to school with us. They turned in to the principal's office as I went down the hall toward my classroom. They never told me what it was all about except that it wasn't about me or Marq or Daryl. They only said, "The kids won't pick on that boy anymore." And they were right. That weekend they announced that at the end of the school year the family was moving out of that school district. Unaware of the reasons for our move, I was quietly heartbroken. We were going to live in an apartment they'd hurriedly constructed in the basement of the dream house.

The basement was the only part that had been completed. It was small, the floors raw cement, the walls unfinished. "We won't be down here long," my father said buoyantly. "This is just temporary. A couple of months at most. They're going great guns on the upper story." But there were arguments between the workmen and my father, about unpaid bills, as best as I could tell, and the work became sporadic. At first it was fun for us boys, living in a semi-abandoned construction site. We built forts out of scrap lumber and rigged swings and trapezes from the joists. Then it got to be dreary and uncomfortable and something we were ashamed of when friends came to play. My father's hearty reassurances began to ring false, a burden to listen to. I would spend more years in that basement than in any other place I've ever lived.

One day that summer, the summer of 1965, my father called my brothers and me into the living room to watch something on television. He was sitting on the edge of the big coffee table, leaning into the screen to get a close look at what the Huntley/Brinkley report was showing. We saw film footage of blacks marching along an Alabama street carrying signs. Whites were shooting water at them from fire hoses, knocking them down.

"What do you think of that, boys?" he asked, not expecting an answer. I was struck by how some of the dark people in the pictures folded their arms and lowered their heads when the policemen hit them with sticks. The pictures reminded me of Tyrone at Centerville Elementary, and I wondered if he was getting a beating again as he walked down the hall, now that my parents and my big brother weren't there to protect him.

Late one afternoon, Marq, Daryl and I went to see Dad at his office. As always, we pestered him until he agreed to take us home. Usually he drove north on Main Street to Clemson Highway, across the lake and home. On this day, he got onto Murray Avenue one block west of Main and proceeded north. Traffic slowed, and when we got to the Rec Center at Murray and Roberts, it stopped. I was amazed; that was the first time I'd ever seen traffic in Anderson. We sat up in our seats and strained our necks to see what had stopped us. My father sat grasping the steering wheel, saying nothing, focusing on the activity ahead.

"Take a good look at this, boys," he said solemnly. "This is what hate looks like." We stood on our seats to see the terrible thing Dad had identified, dead ahead of our car.

The sight of them made me shudder—a dozen men wearing white robes and pointed white hoods riding the biggest, blackest horses I'd ever seen. They rode in a circle, carrying signs, right in front of the Rec Center where I played football and basketball. None of them spoke, and neither did the people watching from the sidewalk and the stopped cars. No chants, no cheers, no jeers. The only sound to be heard was the clacking of hooves on pavement.

I was about to be frightened by the scene when I noticed the reflection of my father's face in the rearview mirror. I'd never seen that look before. His eyes narrowed into a squint, not the way he looked when he strained to read toy assembly instructions, but the kind of look that made me think he could see right through the sheets to the men hiding beneath them. It was as if he were memorizing them, pondering something, maybe planning something. I found myself watching my father as he watched the procession before us. Somehow I knew that as long as I stayed close to him, I didn't have to be afraid of the men in the sheets or the 12 black horses.

"This is what happens when ignorance gets the best of decent men," he said as he drove us home. Years afterward he told me that he knew plenty of Klan members from all parts of the community. After that day, if we were with him, my father would always take that alternate route out of town. Every time, if they were there, he would sit and stare at the men on the horses.

"These are cowardly people," he said once, never moving his gaze from them. "They're ashamed to show their faces. That's why they wear those hoods. They're ashamed of their own bigotry." I didn't know what that word meant, *bigotry,* but the way he sneered when he spoke it, the way he popped the *b* and made it sound almost like a *p,* told me that it was a detestable thing. "They stand for everything I'm fighting against."

I'm sure he deliberately drove to the Klan rallies so that we could see them and hear his speeches on bigotry.

❧❧❧

When my father felt that he'd established himself well enough in the legal scene in that part of South Carolina, he quit his job as prosecutor and set up his own law practice in Anderson. He rented a storefront office in an 80-year-old brownstone at 128 East Benson Street. I stood on the sidewalk with him that Saturday afternoon as, gleaming with pride, he watched the sign painter stencil his name on the window, then slowly apply the gold paint.

Robert O. Du Pre
Attorney at Law

"How's that, Mr. Du Pre?" the man asked as he finished.

Dad stood back and studied the lettering. This was what he had dreamed of when he sat in those law classes at the university.

"Put an accent mark over the *e*," he said. With a few careful strokes of his thin brush, the man added the accent.

Robert O. Du Pré
Attorney at Law

"There. That adds a touch of class to the name," he said, pleased, talking to no one in particular.

My father's new practice specialized in criminal defense and civil rights litigation. Some of his civil rights cases went up to the Federal Court of Appeals. Why this South Carolina homeboy who'd hunted Commies for the FBI and worked for a Dixiecrat like Strom Thurmond made the switch to civil rights lawyer . . . why he quit a prestigious government job to strike out on his own and bring in clients from the streets . . . these are questions I have never been able to find answers for. Did it involve some sort of conversion experience, or was it necessity or opportunism? Was it personal conviction or rebellion against his parents' segregationist background? Or was it what my mother called his "pattern"? I was too young to be informed. But already I was beginning to sense that he was a man of contradictions, a man who often took actions inconsistent with past behavior and who had raised unpredictability to a lifestyle.

My father took on as many civil liability, malpractice, divorce, and ordinary criminal cases as he needed to make his business pay, but most of his clients were blacks charged with crimes. He might as well have asked that sign painter to add the famous lines on the plaque at the Statue of Liberty: "Give me your tired, your poor . . . the wretched refuse of your teeming shore." The couches in his waiting room soon filled with the down-and-out from every county in the northwestern part of the state. There were burglars and bandits and drunks and drug pushers and wife beaters and gas station robbers. My father would take just about anybody's case, anyone who had dark skin. It wasn't long before my father's law practice became known as the last refuge for anyone who was in trouble with the law, oppressed by the system and down on their luck.

He gave priority to his black clients. "The Civil War's over. It's about time somebody brought these rednecks into the 20th century," he liked to say, meaning that the boy from Walhalla was declaring his own private war. If he had ever wanted to see what he was up against, all he had to do was walk a half block to Anderson's town square, its geographic, judicial, and cultural center. There stood a 40-foot granite memorial to "Our Confederate Dead." One of its inscriptions began: "The spirit of chivalry was not dead in 1861 when the soldiers of the Confederacy went forth to battle for the love of home and country and for the preservation of constitutional liberty." Another legend, on a stone shield, stubbornly predicted: "The world shall yet decide in truth's clear far-off light that the men who wore the gray and died with Lee were in the right." Although the inscriptions were weatherworn and barely legible, many of the citizens of Anderson still believed them.

My mother echoed Dad's counterrevolutionary cry. "These southerners!" she would say. "They're still fighting that damned war."

At the age of eight, Daryl was too young to think much about it, but Marq and I believed in our parents and were proud of what we saw as our father's brave stand, even if it brought us occasional difficulty. Once in a while we were jeered at in school because our daddy was a "nigger lawyer." We were big boys, however, especially Marq, and our size tended to discourage the taunts. Once, though, we became more directly involved.

It was another hot summer day. The three of us had been playing in a patch of poison ivy, and now our hands and legs were swollen and unbearably itchy. We looked so bad that my mother was afraid we'd scare the other children at the doctor's office, so she decided to take us in through the back door.

We arrived at the door and were about to go in when my mother stopped, looked up, and saw the inscription on the sign hanging over the entrance. "Coloreds Only," she read aloud, and then exclaimed, "Coloreds only!" She was furious to discover that the man who had been our family doctor for five years still had a segregated office in 1969.

She jerked us inside by the arm and sat us down in the waiting room. Black children and their parents stared at us, probably because our faces were swollen with the poison ivy rash, but also because we were undoubtedly the only whites they'd ever seen in the waiting room reserved for our doctor's second-class patients. We sat there for about an hour. My mother fidgeted in her seat and huffed with impatience as she sat. There were no magazines piled on the coffee tables. There was no mood music playing over the intercom. There were no countryscape paintings decorating the walls. The cramped room was pale green and stark. Finally, she'd had enough.

"Let's go," she said, abruptly rising to her feet and taking us by the arms. Everyone looked at us as we stumbled toward the back door, where my mother paused and turned. "You people don't have to put up with this kind of treatment," she said to the room. I noticed her hand, clutching Daryl's and mine, begin to quiver. "You can walk right in that front door," she said, her voice beginning to crack, "and there's not a damn thing Dr. McCallum can do to stop you." They answered with blank stares and silence.

Mom tugged us back around to the front of the building and into the whites' waiting room. She walked directly up to the check-in desk. "I want to speak to Dr. McCallum," she declared to the receptionist.

"He's seeing a patient right now, ma'am," the woman said softly.

"Fine," my mother shot back. "Then you tell him I want all our files sent over to Dr. Wardlaw's office immediately. Dr. McCallum will no longer be our family physician." And with that, she turned and marched out of the office, chin up, her children trotting along behind her. It was one of the moments that defined my mother for me, and her outrage over our town's stubborn refusal to abandon its racist traditions seemed to be one of the precious few points on which she and my father agreed.

Mom hadn't liked Mauldin, and she didn't like Anderson. She once defined it as "40,000 people who think they're better than the hicks who live in the boondocks but resent people who live in real cities." Anderson wasn't crazy about her, either. The other women in town shunned this assertive Californian. They'd all known each other since they were children and talked a lot about which family you came from and how much money you had. She wasn't part of their world. She dressed in bright-colored pants, and they wore long, floral-print dresses. She let her hair fall, and they puffed theirs into stiff soufflés. Mom made fun of their slow southern drawl. "My God," she said to my father, "all those biddies talk about is who comes from old-South plantation money and who doesn't. I mean, this is the '60s, and these women are still living the Civil War!"

Mom decided to start a business, the Marquise Du Pre School of Dance. She said she wanted to put her training as a drum majorette and theater arts major to use, but there was more to it than that. She enjoyed defying the set-tled wisdom of Anderson, which held that a woman belonged in the home. She built a studio in one of the dilapidated three-story buildings on East Benson Street, not far from my father's office. At first, students were scarce, so to make the school look more popular, she made my two brothers and me attend the tap and ballet classes.

Little Daryl didn't mind. He was a plump, merry, free-spirited fellow who enjoyed all things artistic. Marq and I hated the very thought of dance. I was 10, and he was 12. We were the only boys in the studio, and ruffians through and through.

Worst of all, Mom said we had to wear leotards. Boys dressing up like Tinkerbell and prancing around the room—we knew how that would go over in a place like Anderson. We could never escape our shame; a mirror cover-ing the wall on one side of the room constantly reminded us of it. We dealt with embarrassment by disrupting things. I'd guffaw at Marq and point at his legs, and he'd slam into me and send me sprawling. Sometimes our shoving matches turned into fistfights.

"Boys!" Mom would bark at us. "Stop the body contact!" Then she'd turn back to the girls, smile, and calmly lead them through their pliés and tendus and battements. Luckily, none of the girls in the class went to our school, so at first we were able to keep our shame a secret.

Within a year, though, my mother's hard work and enterprise began to pay off, and she had enough students to move into better quarters. She decided to present her class to the entire town in Anderson's Christmas parade.

"Every entry needs to have a theme," she told us, "and the theme of the Marquise Du Pre School of Dance is that we are Santa's helpers."

To the girls' delight—and to our horror—she went on to describe what our elf costumes would look like. She had all the patterns, and she would work with everyone's mothers to make sure the costumes turned out just right.

"Marq and Jon and Daryl," she said, "you will wear green tights with green turtleneck shirts, and red slippers with bells on the toes. And I will make red Santa hats for you."

I felt sick to my stomach. Marq went pale. So far we'd been able to keep this whole thing a secret, but everyone in Anderson would be at the parade, lined up along North Main Street on December 20th, and we were going to frolic along in front of them all, dressed like pixies.

The day of the parade, the class took up its position around the corner from the Osteen Theater at Greenville Street and Main. My mother darted about, shouting names and inspecting costumes to make sure everyone was in place and in uniform. Daryl was right in the middle of the group, tugging at his costume, making sure he looked just right. Marq and I were edging off to the side, desperately trying to figure out how we could make a break for it.

"Marq and Jon," my mother called out, "come over here." We dragged ourselves to her. "I want you two to march at the front of the class. You will carry the school banner." She handed us two eight-foot wooden poles around which was wrapped a green wool sheet. We unfurled it. *Marquise Du Pre School of Dance*, it read in big red sequined letters. Marq and I gaped at each other in disbelief. Any chance of sneaking through this parade was gone. We were going to lead the procession.

As soon as we made the turn onto Main Street, jeers began to rise from the crowd. Marq and I hung our heads and stiffened.

"Do the elf walk!" Mom called from the rear. "Do the elf walk!" The elf walk was a dainty little shuffle step Mom had invented—a right, left-right, left, right-left, with every other step crossing behind the heel. I grudgingly shifted into it, painfully aware that it made me sway merrily back and forth, jingling the bells on my toes.

I looked over at Marq and was shocked to see he wasn't elf-walking. I was doing it alone. "Marq!" I whispered urgently.

"I'm not gonna do it," he said, looking straight ahead like a prisoner on his way to the gallows. I instantly stopped elf-walking.

"Boys!" Mom cried. "Boys! The elf walk! The elf walk!" Marq and I pretended not to hear her, clomping along grimly and trying to look as masculine as the circumstances permitted.

The catcalls from the crowd grew louder. I thought I recognized some of the hecklers' voices but didn't dare turn my head to see.

"Dew Pree! Wut the hail yew doin' out ther?!"

"Wut yew sposta be, boa, a daincin' fay-ree?"

"Mawk and Jon is shu-ga plum fay-rees!"

At the end of the parade, the minute our group turned off Main Street, Marq and I threw down our poles and raced toward our car, tearing off pieces of our costumes as we went. We got in the car and locked it and crunched down in the back seat, lying low so no one would see us, both of us on the verge of breakdowns.

The parade gave Mom's school great exposure, and enrollment boomed, but for a long time I faulted her for insensitivity, for making her two virile sons endure that humiliation. I think she simply hadn't realized we weren't little kids anymore, hadn't noted how manly we'd become. I also believe she did not associate dancing with being effeminate. I eventually forgave her, but I still don't like parades.

Despite her success with the school, my mother remained unpopular in Anderson and frustrated in her attempts to blend into a culture that would always regard her as a stranger. She and Dad threw parties at the still-unfinished lake house for Dad's business associates and their wives, but they developed no real friendships. Their life was becoming like their dream house—impressive outside, spiritless within.

❦❦❦

I realized as I grew that my parents fought a lot. For a while, they did it when they didn't think we were around. As time went on, they lost the ability to be judicious about it and launched into heated debate whenever the mood hit. The arguments provided my brothers and me with a great deal of insight into the sordid details of our parents' bad marriage. My mother complained about my father's drinking and about money, and there were caustic references to some other behavior of his that was evidently too dreadful to be articulated—women, I now realize. More and more often, my mother's lightning-quick temper would break through. One night we were sitting around in our basement quarters eating watermelon. My parents were bickering back and forth, a low-level bicker, not a screaming argument. Dad said something that set her off; I don't remember what, because we weren't listening, we were just watching TV and eating watermelon.

"Screw you, you bastard!" she screamed.

She took her half-eaten section of watermelon and hurled it straight up in the air with all her might. It splattered on the ceiling and fell to the floor. We boys looked at her in amazement. She just sat there, motionless. We turned to my father for reassurance. His head was down, his spoon poised above his plate. "Marquise," he said quietly. "Don't."

The spot on the ceiling, pale red at first, later brown, would never be removed. Every time I passed under that stain, I'd look up and shudder.

The tension spread throughout the family. It seemed to affect Marq in particular. As Mom's manner became more defiant, her temper hotter, her self-control more brittle, so did his. One morning as we were getting ready for school, Marq was moving slowly. Mom began to browbeat him.

"Get moving, Marquis Anthony Du Pre!" she barked. "If you'd get your lazy butt out of bed in the morning, we wouldn't always be rushing to school!"

I saw Marq tighten. He was 14, tall and muscular, and he'd inherited Mom's short fuse. Instead of cowering that day, he turned and grabbed Mom by the lapels of her bathrobe and shoved her up against the wall. I saw her expression change from anger to fear. She'd had no idea how volatile he was, or how strong. Dad reacted instantly. He dove across the room, wrapped Marq in a bear hug, and held him until he stopped shaking and let Mom go.

Several years ago, Grandma Marie, my mother's mother, paid me a visit. She spoke of Marq, and I asked a question that had been on my mind for a long time. She'd always been a wonderful grandmother to me, I said, but I'd noticed she'd always gone out of her way to be kind and helpful to Marq, and I wondered why. I told her I knew it wasn't favoritism; there seemed to be another kind of reason behind it.

Grandma burst into tears, as if she'd just been waiting for someone to ask. "You just don't know what your mother did to Marq when he was a child," she said. "You were too young to realize. She wasn't ready to have a child. She wasn't prepared for the move across the country. She had a hard time being alone when your father was away from home for the FBI. Marq was punished for it. Marq was beaten. He was just a baby."

My father knew but never intervened. It would become my parents' dark secret.

I think Dad tried many times, in small ways, to make it up to us for all the trouble at home. I remember mentioning once how much I'd love to have a leather basketball. I wasn't asking him for one, just saying how great it would be. That same day he put me in the car and drove me all the way into town, to Dillard's Sporting Goods, where I picked out my first leather roundball, a Spaulding, the model the college players used, the one I'd seen in all those *Sports Illustrated* photographs.

On another day, he surprised Marq and me with two glistening football helmets he'd bought at the sporting goods store on his way home from work. Mine was red with two white stripes down the middle. "There ya go, Jonny," he said. "A genuine official Falcons helmet, straight from Atlanta. I told the coach you're a star split end, and he sent you this helmet."

Marq's was blue with three gold stripes. "What team is mine, Dad?" he asked.

"Green Bay Packers. I told the coach you are a hard-hitting linebacker, and he said he wanted you to have this helmet. Said he wants a look at you when you get older and bigger."

My helmet didn't have a Falcons logo on it, and it was unlikely that a team from a place named Green Bay wore blue helmets, but these quibbles never came to our minds, or if for an instant they threatened to take form, we swiftly dismissed them. Our need to believe in our father was overwhelming. Even later, when I realized he'd been lying, making up tales on the fly, I never felt duped. I felt only gratitude that he had wanted those helmets to seem special.

When we were smaller, he would play with us on Saturdays without any urging, usually starting up the game himself. Now, however, he'd lie on the couch watching the ball game and drinking beer, sometimes a lot of beer. Getting him off that couch was hard work. We'd tug at his arms and beg him, and when he finally gave in and got himself going, he'd enter into it, spending hours with us, orchestrating and officiating our football clashes. Marq was always the defensive back; I was always the flanker back; Dad was always the quarterback. He started each game with the traditional coin toss. "Call it in the air," he said, just like the referee on TV. It never struck us as odd that he always got the ball.

I basked in Dad's attention as we huddled to devise each play. "Okay, Jonny, we're going for pay dirt," he would whisper in my ear. We went for pay dirt on every play. The play was always the same, a long bomb aimed at the end zone. The only things we had to deal with in our huddle were how I would end up there and exactly when and where I was to look for the ball. "Ten yards and cut to the post," he would say. Or, "Eight yards, cut middle, go long."

Or, his favorite, "Banana, on one." The banana pattern was a full-speed run that followed the shape of that fruit.

I lined up to the right every time. Dad always called the signals with a high-pitched shout, as if he were straining to make his voice heard over the roar of 70,000 cheering fans. "Blue, green!" he cried. I never knew what the colors were for, but it sounded like what we heard on TV. "Set! Hut, hut!"

I'd shoot from my three-point stance and streak down field, hitting my fake at eight yards, cutting behind my defender, and turning to see the ball. It was right on the mark almost every time, just high enough and far enough to force me to leave my feet, extend my arms, and make an amazing grab.

Marq knew where I was going. He'd seen me run those patterns hundreds of times. The understanding was that he would cover me closely enough so that we both had an equal chance at the ball. My father had an uncanny knack for throwing the football in a perfect spiral, tight and true, every time. He knew how to float the ball right where he wanted it to go, just far enough to make us leap and extend ourselves to make the catch, yet never out of reach. On most plays, Marq and I dove flat-out to snare his passes.

We craved the sound of Dad's cheers. When I made the catch, which was about half the time, he'd yell, "Touchdown! Touchdown! The crowd goes wild!" When Marq made the grab, he'd yell, "Interception! What a catch!" Hours passed as Marq and I streaked back and forth across our front yard, chasing those perfect spirals. His cheers echoed in our ears and inspired us.

My father knew how to make his sons feel good about themselves. He convinced me that I could do anything. "You keep this up and someday you'll be good enough to go pro," he kept saying. He started me thinking at an early age that the sky's the limit. I got that from Dad.

Dad's approach to Daryl was entirely different. He'd be rough-and-tumble with Marq and me, but he'd hold Daryl on his lap and cuddle and rock him and call him "my sweetheart boy." He gave Daryl a golden retriever puppy, which Daryl named Red Man and loved with rare devotion. For Red Man's first six months, Daryl carried the dog around in his arms everywhere he went. Daryl invented a companion for Red Man, a dog he named Road Man "because he goes on the road with us." Daryl and Red Man shared fantastic imaginary adventures with this invisible pup. Daryl sang a special song to them:

Red Man and Road Man, walking along the river.
They were very good friends.
They were very good friends.

He'd sing those lyrics over and over, until either Marq or I punched him in the arm and told him to knock it off. Then he'd run to Dad and crawl up in his lap, and Dad would stroke his brow and tell him that people didn't understand him because they weren't as smart as he and that someday, Daryl would be bigger than his older brothers, and he'd be able to push them around.

Daryl was often alone. Marq and I would go off in one direction, and Mom and Dad in others, and Daryl was left to himself. He tried to keep up with his older brothers, but he couldn't. On hikes through the woods, we rapidly outpaced him, leaving him to find his own way back. If Marq and I dragged him along when we camped overnight by the lake, he would never last. Every time, around midnight, he'd start whining, "I want to go home!" He'd cry until Marq or I walked him back to the warmth and safety of the house. He loved to go watch the convicts who were mending a road near our property. He talked to them as they worked, and they talked to him. They asked him if he'd like to go back to jail with them. "Yeah!" Daryl said eagerly. "Sure!" Not until the convicts left for prison at the end of the day did Daryl go home. My parents knew about Daryl and the convicts but didn't mind. Road gangs were part of the scene in those parts, and they were heavily guarded.

One of Daryl's misfortunes was that he'd grown rapidly and now was much bigger than any of his classmates. In a southern town like Anderson, a big kid—even a big kid who was only eight—was expected to play football. Dad, Mom, Marq, and I pushed Daryl onto the Little League field. Crying and complaining, he went. I remember the look on his big, round face the first day of practice.

"Come here, son," the coach shouted. "I'll put you in at guard and tackle— both at the same time!" The coach roared at his own joke, to Daryl's bewilderment. He didn't know what a guard or a tackle was.

If his body was large for his age, his head was enormous. None of the Little League helmets would fit it, so the coach had gotten the sporting goods store in Anderson to get a helmet from a supplier that sold gear to Clemson University. On the field, Daryl stood way above the rest of the kids, his large orange helmet bobbing along over all the little white ones.

Daryl's mass wasn't muscle. He was a fat boy, and slow. On the first play of the first game of the season, he had a hard time getting down in a three-point stance. There he was, in the middle of the defensive line, bending over, pointing his finger at the ground but not touching it. When the ball was snapped and the play started and all the other boys leaped from their stances to block each other and run their simple routes, there was Daryl, still bent over, trying to stand up straight so he could see what was going on.

On the second play, two boys hit him from the front, and two of his team-mates hit him from the back, trying to rush through the line and tackle the boy with the ball. Daryl just stood there in pain and confusion, wondering why so many boys were bumping into him, wondering why we'd lied and told him football would be fun. He trudged to the sidelines, pulled the huge helmet off his head, and threw it to the ground, then sat on the bench and cried.

✤ ✤ ✤

CHAPTER FOUR ❧
Stolen Potato Chips and a Daryl Sandwich

My brothers and I were sitting on the couch in the living room of our basement halfway house when we witnessed the first unmistakable sign that our family was falling apart. Daryl was 8, I was 11, and Marq was 13. We were watching television, talking to Mom, waiting for Dad to come home. It was a Saturday evening, and my mother hadn't seen him since he'd gone to work Friday morning. He hadn't even phoned.

We heard a car on the gravel driveway. When the car door slammed, my mother sat up straight and rigid. Finally, my father appeared and slouched his way across the living room toward the kitchen. His hair was mussed, his $700 navy-blue pinstriped suit was wrinkled and dirty, and there was a wet spot on one lapel. His shirt collar was unbuttoned, and his tie was loosened halfway down his chest. His eyes were bloodshot, and beneath his drooping lids hung reddish sacks.

I assumed he was doing one of his comedy routines, so I watched without saying a word as he shuffled across the room; I didn't want to interrupt the act. But then Marq started giggling, and that made me and Daryl giggle, too. We were too young to recognize a full-blown hangover. We didn't realize, either, that Dad's absence the night before had been unexpected and unexplained.

He stopped when he got to the middle of the room, turned to us, and barked, "What, goddamit?" We boys waited for the punchline to the joke. "Just leave me alone!" he yelled. That struck us as funny, and we laughed. I looked up at my mother, thinking she'd be laughing, too, but her lips were trembling, and tears were dripping from her cheeks. Her face was aflame. I'd seen her angry many times before, but now she was also hurt.

Her composure broke. "Why you dirty *bastard*!" she screamed. "How dare you come walking in here like this! Where the hell have you been?! You filthy *drunk*!"

"I'm drunk because I live with a *bitch* like you!"

"You *sonofabitch*! I've had the police looking for you. I should have them throw your ass in jail! I won't let you come in here and defile this house!"

"This is my house, you ungrateful bitch, and I'll come here any time I want!"

Spit flew from their mouths as they flung out their hateful curses. My brothers and I were terrified. My ears began to buzz so loudly I could hardly hear the yelling.

We were sobbing now, utterly confused and scared. Marq stood and ran from the living room into the bedroom we shared. Daryl and I followed him and slammed the door behind us. We fell in a heap on Marq's bed, burying our faces in his pillow and soaking it with our tears. We cried until our throats were hoarse and our bodies limp. As our parents raged on, we called out things like, "Please stop" and "Don't be mean" and "What did we do?" We cried until we were spent and all we could do was moan and mumble.

As the oldest, Marq tried to comfort Daryl and me. "Don't worry," he said. "It'll be all right. Someday we'll get out of here, and it'll be all right."

No one came into the room to comfort or reassure us. We fell asleep huddled on Marq's bed; it would be our sanctuary during the years to come.

There was a lot of shouting from that night on. I don't remember my dad ever hitting my mom or my mom ever hitting my dad, but a lot of plates and glasses and pictures and records and furniture were thrown around, and there was plenty of swearing. My brothers and I used to lie in bed at night and hold each other's hands as our mother and father fought on the other side of the partition. We idolized our father, so it was confusing and painful when he turned into a belligerent drunk. It shook our whole world.

"Don't worry," Marq would say. "It'll be over soon. Don't worry." But Daryl would start crying, and that would make me cry, and when I cried, then Marq would cry, too.

"Let's just go to sleep," he'd say. "We don't have to listen to it if we're asleep."

Over the next few months, Dad grew bolder, and his absences became more frequent and more conspicuous to us boys. He seemed ill or tired most of the time. Mom's explosions became more frequent and more violent. We never knew what might set her off, which made it hard to be in the same room with her without being nervous or scared. She became too depressed to get up in the morning to make sure we were bathed and dressed and fed and sent off to school on time. And since these duties certainly weren't something our father was going to take on, we had to do them ourselves.

We didn't hold any of this against our parents. We didn't know how to resent or place blame. We loved them, and after a while, we began to think that this was what you were supposed to do when you got to be our ages; you were supposed to get yourself up and make your own breakfast. Eventually we developed a routine. We woke each other up, and Marq and I would help get Daryl dressed. There never was anything for us to eat but Carnation Instant Breakfast, if my mother remembered to buy it. It was a chocolate powder you mixed into milk. No juice or cereal or eggs or toast.

Eventually my father would drag himself out of bed to drive us to school and himself to work. We'd rush out of the house holding our plastic cups of Carnation Instant Breakfast and clamber into Dad's tan Mercedes. It was a diesel, and he had to wait 90 seconds for the engine block to warm up before he could give the starter a yank. That meant we had 90 seconds to drink our breakfast. Sucking on his cigarette and pumping the accelerator pedal, he counted us down.

"Finish your drinks, boys. I don't want that stuff spilling all over my car when I start rolling." I sat on the back seat shivering from a belly full of cold milk, sliding back and forth on the slick leather upholstery and rubbing my stomach to make the cramps go away. I hated Carnation Instant Breakfast, but more than that, I hated being late for school. As hard as we tried to hurry, we were almost always an hour late. It was embarrassing to be that late. Everybody would look at you when you walked in.

The little country schoolhouse that Mom and Dad had transferred us to after the Tyrone incident had closed down over the summer, and they'd transferred us to other schools in Anderson—Marq to McCants, the junior high, and Daryl and me to North Anderson Elementary. I knew nothing about my new school, didn't know any kids there, and on my first day I was jittery. I held my breath as I walked toward the sixth-grade room. I was the new boy, this was the first class, and I was an hour late.

The door creaked as I opened it and stepped in. Thirty-two heads turned and looked at me. I froze in the doorway. No one said a thing.

"May we help you, young man?" A small white-haired woman was speaking to me. She wore a print dress and a pink cardigan buttoned all the way up to the collar, and she was examining me over gold-rimmed reading glasses.

She turned her head slightly, as if to reach for my answer with her good ear. No answer came. "Young man?" she tried again. I looked down, then back up. I forced my mouth open, but nothing would come out.

She held up her clipboard and flipped a page. "Are you Mr. Du Pre?" she said, consulting a list. "Mr. Jon Mason Du Pre?" I learned later she always addressed her students by their surname, as a sign of respect.

"Yes, ma'am," I answered through a parched throat.

"Well, Mr. Du Pre, do you have an explanation for your late arrival to our class?"

My gut cramped a little tighter. How could I tell her that my mother and father had been screaming at each other half the night, and that Dad was too hung over and Mom too depressed to pull themselves out of bed and get us ready for school? I looked down at the floor again, painfully conscious of the stares of my classmates. I forced myself to answer. "No, ma'am."

The kids began to stir, about to laugh at the anxious boy standing at the door looking stupid.

"Settle down, everyone," she said in her dainty yet commanding voice. "It looks as if we saved the best for last. Let's make Jon Mason Du Pre feel welcome. Mr. Du Pre, I am Miss Casey. We're glad you could join us. Your place is right over there." She smiled and held out her hand to show me where I would sit. On the desk was a white card with "Jon Du Pre" written on it in Magic Marker.

I breathed a sigh of worshipful relief, profoundly grateful to my new teacher. Miss Casey had sensed my distress. She had read my face and known I had no acceptable explanation, and she had made sure I sat down right away and blended into the class. Perhaps she'd heard of my parents' marital problems; my father was well known in Anderson. Although I showed up late for class most days that year, she never questioned it again.

Miss Casey was the oldest teacher at North Anderson Elementary and as small as most of her students, small enough to look us straight in the eye, which she always did whenever she talked to us. For more than 25 years, she had held her classes in that second-floor room on the northeast corner of the old, red brick rectangle. Almost every week, one of her former students would drop in and say hello to their favorite teacher. She always remembered their names, every single one of them. Every visit ended the same way, with the former student stooping to hug our little teacher, then turning to our class and saying something like, "You kids are very lucky to have Miss Casey as your teacher."

Miss Casey could give me the discipline I needed without ever singling me out or letting me be ridiculed. I never resented her scolding, not even the time I got in trouble for sopping my pea juice.

Most days, my only real meal was whatever they served in the school cafeteria. I made a practice of pestering the girls in my class for the scraps they always left on their plates. They'd just walk away and leave their trays for me to clean up. One day I grabbed one of the girl's leftover rolls and used it to soak up the pea juice from my empty plate. Mary Lou Price, a shrill, skinny girl sitting on the other side of the table, was horrified.

"That's rude, sopping your pea juice! I'm going to tell Miss Casey on you!"

I ignored her and cleaned my plate and two others. But when I got back to the room, I saw Mary Lou standing at Miss Casey's desk. "There he is, Miss Casey. There's Jon. He sopped his pea juice at lunch today. Near made me sick."

Miss Casey looked at me and said, "Mr. Du Pre, is that true?" I put my hands in my jeans pockets, shrugged, and nodded. I sensed that she wasn't really cross but was going through the motions. "Well, Jon," she continued—I was astounded she'd called me Jon; she'd never done that before, "I know you're growing fast and you need lots of energy, but I expect good manners from my students. We do not sop our pea juice in the cafeteria. Do you understand?"

"Yes, ma'am."

"And Miss Price," she said, turning to Mary Lou, "nobody likes a tattle-tale. Do you understand?" Mary Lou looked surprised that her squealing had earned her a rebuke. Our classmates snickered. Once again, Miss Casey had taught me my lesson without embarrassing me.

This was sixth grade, a nourishing, stimulating year when I needed encouragement. When I was in class, I could forget the worries I had at home and be a normal boy. The best time of all came near the end of each school day. Miss Casey was a teacher with a vision; she wanted to introduce us to special things we wouldn't otherwise encounter in school. Just as all the other kids in the building were getting restless and noisy, and all the other teachers began shouting at them to sit down and be quiet and wait for the bell, Miss Casey would gently close the door, move to her desk, and open a volume of C. S. Lewis's great allegorical adventure series, *The Chronicles of Narnia*. We students sat back in our seats to listen. I closed my eyes so I could see the pictures that Lewis was drawing in our minds. Miss Casey's voice was like the magic horn that summoned Pete, Susan, Edmund, and Lucy from the dreary train station and back to a magical place where they had once ruled as kings and queens. My teacher spoke in a slightly brushed tone as she led me time and again through hidden portals—in Digory's Uncle's closet, in the stone wall behind the gym, in the back of the professor's old wardrobe—to the mystical place called Narnia.

No book could have been better crafted to speak to my own situation than the second in Lewis's series. *The Lion, The Witch, and the Wardrobe* took me along with Lucy, Peter, Susan, and Edmund who, as they wait out the World War II air raids at an old professor's country estate, grow terribly bored and begin to explore, discovering that the back of the professor's closet is really a door to an enchanted world, blanketed in beautiful snow. They take coats from the wardrobe and put them on and step through into the land of Narnia. There they encounter a kindly, peculiar little fellow, half man, half animal, the first of many wonderful creatures they will meet on their adventures that lead them to a magnificent lion called Aslan, who symbolizes goodness, and who, ultimately, sacrifices his life for the children.

To me, a boy whose parents were in the process of sacrificing not their lives but his, the Aslan story was poignant and therapeutic. Like Lucy and her playmates who were escaping boredom as they passed through the wardrobe, I was escaping the sad and tense life I lived in the basement of my parents' dream house.

As my family unraveled and I couldn't depend on my mom and dad anymore, I unconsciously began looking to other grown-ups for emotional support. At school, my powerful Aslan was the diminutive Miss Casey. After school, I found my lion at the Anderson YMCA.

My father enrolled us in the YMCA not because he was concerned with developing us as athletes, but because he needed somewhere to park us until he could pick us up after work and his after-work activities. He knew he couldn't depend on my mother to get us; she was pouring everything she had into her dance studio and had nothing left for anything or anyone else. For the time being, she'd given up on all of us and turned all her attention to the only thing that gave her any sense of accomplishment or worth. "When I wasn't teaching class or planning the next day's lessons," she told me years later, "I was at home in bed. That's the way it was for most of the years we were in Anderson."

The YMCA proved to be a godsend for us, in the person of its director, Jim Gentry. Mr. Gentry coached a number of the Little League teams, and I saw a lot of him. He was a rugged man, and he looked it. He was tall, maybe 6'2", wiry, and powerful. The other kids had nicknamed him "Cabbage Calves" because of the way his calf muscles bulged when he walked, and he was the fastest walker anyone had ever seen. He'd lean forward, prop himself up on his toes, pump his arms, and take off. My buddies and I grew so fond of him that we made a sport of trying to follow him on his swift rounds through the building. Jutting out our jaws, popping up on our toes, pumping our arms, we'd do "the Gentry walk" down the halls, through the gymnasium, past the swimming pool and the billiards room. Sometimes as many as five or six boys would fall in behind him and tiptoe quickly along in his wake. He'd be walking, and we'd be running. Every few minutes he'd slam on the brakes and turn and say, "Don't you clowns have a circus to go to?"

We may have laughed about him, but we also wanted to make him proud. Whenever our teams went on the road to play those from other towns, we were playing for Mr. Gentry, and if we got a trophy, we'd run straight for his office in the back of the gym when we returned.

If you passed him in the hall without saying hello, he'd say, "Hey, boys! Aren't you happy to see ol' Mr. Gentry?" He'd poke us hard in the ribs with his big thumb.

"Ow!" we'd cry. "Hi, Mr. Gentry."

It was his way of keeping the connection, a rough, manly way acceptable to adolescent boys. But underneath the toughness, he was a sensitive man who cared for the young people under his stewardship and wanted to see us succeed in sports and in life.

During our time with Mr. Gentry, Marq and I became leading athletes at our levels. We played football, baseball, and basketball, and we competed on the swimming team. Marq was strong and rough and intensely competitive. His aggressiveness became Little League legend in Anderson the day he squared off against Clay Evans.

Clay was no regular football player. He was the 14-year-old star running back who had the high school coaches panting for his arrival. But then, Marq's tackles were no regular tackles. Marq, also 14, was playing linebacker because his coach enjoyed watching him take a running start and slam into the ball carrier.

The mythic clash occurred when Clay took a handoff and lumbered through a gaping hole in the line, not paying much heed to the skinny kid coming at him from the outside linebacker position. Clay lowered his head toward this nuisance, confident that he'd shed the tackle and keep right on going.

But the force behind Marq's hit was extraordinarily hard, harder than Clay had ever been hit, harder than anyone in our town had ever seen a Little Leaguer hit. The explosive crack brought a gasp from the coaches and the parents and kids on the sidelines. Clay Evans was knocked off his feet and sent flying through the air five yards sideways. The collision knocked Marq off his feet, too, sending him sideways through the air in the opposite direction. The two boys landed and stayed there, flat on the ground in the middle of the field, both of them stunned.

Nobody moved for a moment; it was as if the crash had knocked out the spectators, too. Then the coaches dashed onto the field. By the time they got to the boys, both of them were rolling over, moaning, trying to sit up. That's when Clay's coach noticed what had happened to Clay's helmet. It was split from its crown to its rim. The coach unfastened the chin strap and lifted the helmet from Clay's head. You could see daylight through it.

"Good God!" he said. "Somebody call an ambulance."

"Look what I did!" Marq yelped.

It was easy to guess that it was frustrations at home that powered Marq's aggressiveness on the football field. Or a death wish. His willingness to take drastic physical risks was that of someone who had written off not just safety, but the future. In Anderson, people began looking at him in a new, slightly uneasy way.

❧ ❧ ❧

My father spent his evenings in a bar somewhere, and sometimes it wasn't until midnight or so when his car appeared. Every day it was the same routine. After classes, Marq would come over from the junior high across town, and we'd meet at the Y. We'd play basketball, usually for three, four, five, six, seven hours at a time. At first there were other kids to play with, but toward supper time, their parents would pick them up and we'd play on alone. We never did homework; our parents never told us to. We just played until the building closed.

Closing time was seven o'clock, but I could tell that Mr. Gentry was reluctant to kick us out. He had observed what was going on with us, and he knew that we had hours to wait for our ride. There was a men's club in one section of the building with a massage room where a masseur worked on the men. This area didn't close until nine, and Mr. Gentry arranged for us to stay indoors, out of the dark and the weather, until then.

That helped with one problem, but there was still another: hunger. We had no food and no money to use in the vending machines by the main entrance. So every evening between seven and nine, we raided those machines. We'd been playing basketball all afternoon and into the night with nothing to go on but a glass of Carnation Instant Breakfast and whatever was on our trays at the school cafeteria at noon that day. This was our dinner.

We'd figured how to untwist metal coat hangers and stick them up through the open trough at the bottom of the machines and pull the bags of potato chips and peanut-butter crackers and pretzels off their clips. We got so skilled at this that we could snag the bottom two rows of bags. Sometimes in trying to hook the bags, we just tore them, and the food would fall down loose, and we ate it out of the trough.

Hunger is one of the most insistent memories from my childhood. I was hungry all the time. The irony didn't escape me, or fail to hurt me, that even though my father was successful and influential, pulling six figures in the early 1970s and building a large home, my brothers and I were hungry almost all the time.

Marq and I had attended Our Lady of the Rosary school in Greenville for a couple of years. I was fascinated by the ritual at the Tuesday mass and particularly by the way Father John carefully placed the flat, white, circular wafer on each outstretched tongue. Once two girls giggled at me, and I realized my mouth was opening with each passage of a wafer from hand to tongue. Not being Roman Catholics, Marq and I didn't take communion, and I couldn't help wondering how the wafer tasted. It must have been sublime, I thought, noticing how the sixth-graders seemed uncharacteristically reverent as they returned to their pews, never chewing the wafer, just holding it behind their tightened lips.

That was the way Marq and I ate the potato chips we managed to yank out of the vending machine. Not the way I eat chips now, crunching a bunch at a time in my mouth and then swallowing. That would have ended the enjoyment too soon and left us with our hunger longer. Instead, we took one chip at a time and carefully placed it flat on our tongue. The taste of the chip made me feel something like reverence flow through me. The first chip always caused my salivary glands to respond so strongly that they cramped below my ears. It was a spiritual experience, carnal pleasure of a high order. I sucked each chip until it was drained of salt and oil. The barbeque-flavored chips lasted even longer. Only after I'd gotten all the taste out of a chip did I chew it, slowly and gently, until the chip was mush. My tongue swished the mush around inside my mouth as if to say good-bye. Only then did I swallow. We boys could make a two-ounce bag of Tom's potato chips last about an hour.

Every so often, Keith Hooper offered me a delightful reprieve when my little friend invited me to his house for supper. He lived in one of the poor parts of town with a woman he called his mom but who was far too old really to be his mother. I rejoiced when I went home with Keith, because his "mother" always served a big, steaming supper.

"Don't rich people come around this house too much," Keith would say, beaming. And I would nod politely as I sat there stuffing my mouth full of beef stew or chicken and dumplings, noticing that the old woman always stared at me with an expression of intense curiosity, and thinking that if this was what it was like to be poor, I'd be happy for Keith and his so-called mother to adopt me into their poverty.

It was a wonder that Marq and I never got into trouble for raiding the vending machines. Looking back now, I'm sure Mr. Gentry allowed it. Every morning the bags were missing or torn, and he had to have known who did it, but he never put a stop to it. I have to believe that he, like Miss Casey, somehow knew what we were going through. Every evening the machines were full again.

Marq and I tried everything we could think of to avoid being put out at nine. When the masseur, a fat old blind man named Kevin, waddled down the hall to close the building, we'd hide in a corner, lying on the floor as quiet and still as we could, hoping he'd pass us by and lock us in; at least we'd be warm there.

Kevin always appeared right on schedule, tapping with his cane, softly whistling, and we'd hold our breath. It never worked. His senses of hearing and smell were so acute that it was as if he could see us in broad daylight. He'd pass us by and stop at the door.

"All right, boys," he'd say. "Get up, go home."

"*Please* let us stay, Kevin."

"Out you go, boys, out you go."

As he left, Kevin always slammed the door harder than he had to, to shut it tight. Then we'd hear the deadbolt sliding into its socket. The scrape of the deadbolt signaled the beginning of our nightly exile, when we were stranded outside the YMCA, waiting for Dad to come.

As we sat on the curb, keeping our lonely vigil, time was our enemy. We desperately sought any diversion from the long, long wait. First we skipped pebbles across the street, competing to see who could get his pebble closer to the far curb without touching it. In the dark, it was hard to see across the street and determine the winner, and the pebble-skipping usually led to an argument. Arguments usually ended with Marq winning with a punch to the middle of my chest.

In summer, Marq and I prowled the nearby area, but we were never out of sight of the driveway. We sneaked as close as we could to the little house next door to the Y and peered into the window, where an elderly couple sat watching television. "I wish we were their grandchildren," Marq would say.

The nights it rained were the most tedious. All we could do was sit on the doorstep under the concrete awning over the entrance of the Y and stare at the driveway. We knew Dad would turn in there, eventually. Spring and fall weren't so bad, but in the winter we got cold, so we'd curl up as close as we could, sharing our body heat. Marq, at some point, found that one spot on the brick wall was always warm because on the other side was the steam room in the men's club. On cold nights, that wall was our salvation. We pressed up against it until the warmth was gone.

Daryl spent many of those evenings with us. He would wedge his way between his bigger brothers and take shelter. Suddenly Marq would shout, "Daryl sandwich!" That was my cue to grab Marq by the arms as he gripped mine. We pulled our bodies together as close as we could, squeezing Daryl between us until he could hardly breathe. "Stop it!" he'd squeal. "You're squishing me."

Marq and I loved to hear that squeal. As the game went, we'd fake sympathy and apologize, patting Daryl's red curls and hugging him tenderly until he was calm and comfortable again. We'd sit quietly for a few more minutes. Then "Daryl sandwich!" and the game would start all over again.

The last hour of our vigil, from 11 until midnight, was unbearably long. Every set of headlights shining from the direction Dad would come offered the promise that our wait was over. As I realized the headlights would pass, disappointment swelled in my throat. Many nights, Marq and I just sat there crying during that last hour. "Please, please, *please!*" we begged when a new set of headlights appeared. "No! No!" we whimpered through our tears as the car passed. When at last we heard the clacky grumble of Dad's Mercedes diesel, the relief was overwhelming.

I grew closer than ever to Marq during those nights. We were indispensable to each other, but the waits were devastating. To this day, I hate waiting for anybody, even for five minutes. I did my share of waiting when I was a kid.

Those close to me, when they hear that story, invariably ask, "Where was your mother? Why didn't she rescue you from those desperate nights?" Only now, after years of thought and several conversations that only an adult son can have with a mother, can I answer. Mom was deeply depressed, barely able to cope with the challenge of caring for herself, let alone seeing to details of family life such as taxiing her children around. My brothers and I never asked her about it when we were young, just as we never complained to Dad when he showed up past midnight. A child's mind didn't work that way. With our limited perspective, it never occurred to us that we might be able to effect some change if we complained to our parents. Grumbling about something to get what you want was a luxury not enjoyed by many of our peers. My brother and I simply went along with the program, whatever it was or was not. We adapted. We kept our heads low and our mouths shut, and we survived.

This was the period when Dad took me along on his visits to his mistress, Miss Tilly. Years later, I learned that he owned that little brick house she lived in. He had arranged for Miss Tilly to move out of the tarpaper shack she'd been living in on the south side of town, where the poorest blacks lived, to this rambler on the east side. "Hell, I owned quite a few houses," he once told me in passing, almost bragging. That was what he had been doing with his money—buying houses for his mistresses, receiving the rent in "services." His perverse boast helped explain why my brothers and I were always hungry as children, why our clothes seldom fit, and why it would take so long to build the dream house.

Long afterward, I also learned that Dad had often taken Daryl with him to Miss Tilly's house, and to the other houses where he'd stashed girlfriends.

Unlike me, affable, easygoing Daryl wasn't self-conscious around Miss Tilly's children. He played with them, and they became his friends. Dad made the little boy his confidant, teaching him how to lie to Mom for him. In return, Dad would give him money and freedom.

Daryl, now nine, had a whole *lot* of freedom. He hated sports and refused to go to the YMCA, so he went almost completely unsupervised during this period. There were times when no one remembered to pick him up after school. Until someone noticed he wasn't home and went looking for him, sometimes as late as two A.M., he'd roam the town or the Anderson Mall. Soon he and a friend began to shoplift. They started with toys from K-Mart. Daryl eventually had every Hot Wheels car that Mattel made, about 50 of them, and nobody at home asked him where he'd gotten them. It wasn't long before he moved up from cars to clothes; the idea was to see how much they could carry out of the stores without getting caught. Once they got to the parking lot, they'd dump the stuff and take off. It was a game to them, a game they always won.

Daryl's stealing might be seen as something a neglected little boy desperately does to attract some attention—from his parents, from anyone—and ready to go to any length to do so. But there wasn't any way to get their attention during those years, and Daryl knew it. I think that Daryl's petty crimes were his way of asserting control over a small part of a world that, for him and the rest of us, was spinning out of control.

❧❧❧

One of the distinct memories I have of my father was that he was always at odds with something or someone. Let a righteous provocation wander by, and he'd embrace it with frantic passion, courting self-destruction. And no provocation was embraced as frantically as the righting of a wrong done to one of his sons.

I found out what it was like to be at the center of one of Dad's passionate engagements the summer I was 12 years old. Mr. Gentry had decided to move to a YMCA in another city. We were all upset about this because Mr. Gentry was such a good coach and such an inspiring guy, but we were impressed that his successor, Bill Vickery, had been a minor-league baseball player. He may have had that going for him, but he struck out when it came to working with young people.

I was sitting on the bleachers by the baseball field one slow, lazy summer day watching a T-ball game. The T-ball players were the youngest kids in the Little League program, eight and nine years old. I was playing fast-pitch ball by this time and thought I was a big shot. I noticed Vickery striding toward the field from the gymnasium. I thought nothing of it until I realized he was headed right for me, glaring. He came up and grabbed me by my shirt and jerked me to my feet. Then he seized my jersey by the front and back and yanked it off my body.

"You're suspended for a week, you little thief!" he bellowed, then turned and strode back toward his office, grasping the jersey in his fist.

The jersey had been mine during football season. We'd been instructed to turn in our jerseys after the Dogwood Bowl game, but I'd forgotten, and then I'd decided that no one would miss mine. Somehow I figured I'd sort of earned it because I'd scored a touchdown in the game.

My buddies, along with about a dozen parents in the bleachers and most of the kids on the field, were gaping at me, the boy who'd just been branded a thief. I realized I was shirtless. I desperately wanted to hide my naked upper body, but I had nothing to cover myself with. I wanted to run, but I didn't dare. I felt keenly ashamed and embarrassed. I sank back to my seat and looked out at the field, silently begging the people staring at me to turn their attention back to the T-ball game.

Before the inning was out, I sneaked away, first walking, then running at top speed. In back of the gym, the weeds grew high, and I hid there until dark. When I was sure everyone had gone, I came back out and walked to the spot where my father picked us up to take us home. I stood there for several hours before I saw his Mercedes turn into the drive.

"What are you doing standing around with no shirt on?" he demanded when he saw me up close.

I didn't know what to tell him. I ran around, opened the car door, threw myself in, and burst into tears.

Dad threw the gear into neutral, jumped out, and came around to my side of the car. He opened my door, pulled me out, kneeled to my eye level, and asked, "What happened, Jonny? What happened?"

"Mr. Vickery . . ."

Once he'd pulled the story out of me, he got back in the car, slammed it into gear, and sped away from the Y. Instead of heading out of town to where we lived, he drove straight to Bill Vickery's house. He didn't stop in the driveway, but tore into the middle of the front yard, skidding to a halt 20 feet from the front door of the tiny home.

"Daddy, don't!" I shouted, as he bounded from the car and stomped toward the front door. "Daddy, please! Let's just go home!" I was dismayed. I didn't want to be in the middle of what was about to happen. I didn't even want to witness it. My father was out of control.

"Vickery!" he boomed. He was a powerful shouter. "Vickery, get out here, right now!" He pounded the door once, so hard that I thought he would break it down.

The door swung open, and there was Mr. Vickery, four inches taller than my father, 20 pounds heavier, 15 years younger . . . and frightened to the depths of his soul.

"Come on out here, and take this shirt off my back, Vickery!" my father bellowed. "Are you man enough to take my shirt from me? Let's see if you're man enough, Vickery." His rage seemed to rattle the windows of all the houses in the neighborhood. "Fall out here where my son and all your neighbors can watch me whip your good-for-nothing ass!" And they *were* watching. They'd all come out of their homes to see what the ruckus was about.

"Listen, Bob," Vickery began, "you have no right disturbing—"

"The police will read me my rights when they haul me off and book me for ripping your head off your shoulders and shoving it down your neck, Vickery! Now get out here and take your punishment!"

My father's tirade lasted about five minutes. I sat in the car and quaked. Vickery stood in the doorway and shook along with me. He didn't come out. After one or two more feeble attempts to shout something back at my father, he just stood there, holding the door, ready to slam it shut if he needed to.

Then Dad delivered his valedictory: "If I ever hear that you've come within a hundred yards of Jon or any of my boys," he declared, "so help me God, Vickery, I'll burn down your house, run you out of town, and make sure that no YMCA in this country will give you a janitor's job."

With that, he turned, stomped back to the car, and drove me home, saying nothing to me except, "No one lays a hand on my boys, Jonny. No one, ya hear?"

He never mentioned the incident again, and neither did I. That night, I was impressed and grateful for what he did, but over time, the incident became just another instance in the series of contradictions surrounding my father. It confused me that the man who went to battle for me that night could ignore my brothers and me in so many other times of need.

My father practiced law in the same way he dealt with Bill Vickery. From the very beginning of his career, he had jabbed at the limits of what strong adversaries would put up with before they'd turn and clobber him. In whatever he'd done, he'd been asking for it, but now, it seemed, his behavior was becoming more extreme. Without quite forming the idea, I sensed that he was directing his steps toward some emotional precipice.

To get his new law practice going, my father had accepted the post of public defender for the Tenth Circuit Court. He soon came up against Circuit Court

Judge James Spruill, who was dismayed by the number of indigents, accused of all manner of crimes, who were pouring into his courtroom and aggravating his work load. He simplified things by processing them right through to trial, without the customary preliminary hearings. No one seemed to notice or care until April 17, 1970, when Robert Du Pre stood up in court and objected.

"Your honor," he said, "I wish to enter a motion on behalf of my client, Mr. Darby. We move, Your Honor, that Mr. Darby be granted a preliminary hearing, in which he should have the ability to fully examine, with his counsel, the state's case against him." The judge's face reddened, an omen my father ignored.

"You are out of order!" the judge thundered down from the bench. Then he slapped my father with a contempt-of-court citation.

My father pressed harder. "Living in Anderson County does not make Mr. Darby or any of my clients a second-class citizen, Your Honor."

"One more of those outbursts and you'll spend the night in jail with your clients, counsel. Two more and I'll bring you up for review!"

The judge's threat to my father's license shut him up, but cannily, my father converted his muzzling into a tactic. He decided to stay mute through all of his cases in Spruill's court. His objection would take the form of silence. No examinations, no cross-examinations, no jury addresses. My father had gambled that without the vocal participation of a defense counsel, the judge would be forced to declare mistrials.

Over the next three days, he said almost nothing in court. Spruill saw what was happening. He knew he couldn't allow mistrials in more than 300 cases; he'd be a laughingstock. But he was helpless. He had been able to make my father stop talking, but he couldn't make him speak.

Throughout this legal drama, a young reporter from the *Greenville News* was sitting in the back row, observing. The young attorney's brash challenge to a powerful judicial figure was newsworthy, and the next day the paper ran the first of a series of three reports casting Dad's act as an assault on Goliath by a courageous David.

My father knew he couldn't fight this battle all by himself. For perhaps the first time in his life, he set aside his ego and called for help. The ACLU sent two of its best lawyers to stand beside him as he took on the Tenth Circuit Court. They helped him file petitions to dismiss charges against scores of clients who now faced trial. Those petitions represented a fraction of the total number of cases, but they were far more than Judge Spruill's court could handle. The judge was forced to adjourn in disgrace, reporting to his superiors in Columbia that he had disposed of fewer than half the cases on his docket.

Du Pre's cases would be remanded to another judge, one who would ensure the defendants the ability to defend themselves properly.

In later years, my father would speak of this standoff as the best thing he had ever done as a lawyer. It brought reform to South Carolina's Tenth Judicial Circuit, but it also publicly humiliated Judge Spruill, giving Dad a potent enemy and winning him the hatred of segregationists in western South Carolina.

There was also one tragic consequence. In this battle, Dad's right-hand man was assistant public defender Dan Castles. Castles shared Dad's high principles, but not his appetite for confrontation. He was frightened by Spruill's threat to drive my father out of the profession; it could have happened to Castles as well. He was caught between his boss and a vengeful judge. One night during the battle, he went out on his front porch, drank a quart of whiskey, and shot himself in the side of the head. No one ever knew whether it was personal problems or the pressure he was under that had caused him to snap. In any case, his death greatly raised tensions in Anderson County.

Those my father hadn't managed to offend with that case, he proceeded to enrage with another. His client, Larry Watt, had been charged with an armed robbery on Anderson's west side. He would have been just another doomed indigent defendant except that my father, the public defender, now had the luxury of preliminary hearings. The hearings allowed him to see the prosecutor's case against Watt and to interview Watt thoroughly. Watt spilled his guts when my father met him in the visitation cell at the county jail.

"He said he couldn't have done that armed robbery," Dad told us afterward. "And he was telling the truth. He was 42 miles away, in Greenwood, breaking into a furniture store at the exact hour the robbery went down in Anderson. It checked out: I found the guy he did the burglary with, sitting in the Greenville County Jail."

My father knew that this was more than just an everyday false arrest. Billy Newton, the detective who made the arrest and wrote the report, was a bad apple. So he played a hunch.

He probably could have disposed of the case in the judge's chambers by confronting the prosecutor with what he knew. But, impelled by his lust for the theatrical, Dad let the court empanel a jury, then sat back and waited to spring his shocker.

The trial began with Detective Newton's confident recounting of Watt's arrest. Then my father stood up to cross-examine.

"Detective Newton," he said, "what's your father been up to these days?"

"I don't know what you mean."

"What I mean, detective, is that your father has been moving a lot of product around the county, hasn't he?"

The question was incendiary and was meant to be. Insiders knew that Newton was the illegitimate son of a man named Fletcher who had made a small fortune running drugs—or "product." Fletcher had been untouchable because his supplier was none other than his illegitimate son, the police detective. Newton, who was respected in town as a cop who'd earned medals for bravery, had been stealing drugs from petty pushers, selling them through his father's operation, and splitting the proceeds.

Fletcher routinely shook down the small dealers in town. But one night, it went bad. He broke in to a pusher's house, and neighbors heard the noise. Officers responded. Someone had to take the fall. Detective Newton arbitrarily picked one of Fletcher's legmen, one he thought would keep his mouth shut—Larry Watt. Encouraged by the public defender, Watt ratted them out.

While the assistant county attorney yelled out objections, my father relentlessly pressed his attack on Billy Newton, baring his shameful secret. Newton folded on the stand, recanted his testimony against Watt, and the case was thrown out.

The shamed hero inflicted a punishment upon himself far harsher than anything the court would have meted out. He drove to a remote spot along the Pickens Highway southeast of town and blew his brains out—yet another suicide linked to my father's zealous pursuit of justice. Many in Anderson blamed him for both. Once again, my father's actions, though admirable in motive, were erratic and destructive in their consequence. We had almost grown accustomed, during those years, to threatening phone calls—it went with Dad's practice. But Newton's death brought his enemies out of the woodwork. The phone began ringing at all hours, angry callers making frightening threats.

I answered one call. "Son," said a gruff voice, "you tell your nigger-lovin' daddy we've had enough of him. He better get his family out of here or we'll *burn* him out!" I was petrified. From that night on, white-robed Klansmen, terrible in their ominous silence, regularly marched their black stallions through my nightmares.

Two months later, my father came home from work early and called an unprecedented family meeting. "Guess what?" he said in the same voice he used to announce the visits to Miss Tilly's house, the voice he used to make bad news sound like a cause for celebration. "We're going to California to visit your grandparents. In fact, we're going to live out there near them."

Marq raised his fists in the air and shouted, "We're moving to California! We're moving to California!"

Daryl and I raised our fists, too, and repeated his cheer: "California!"

We remembered our trips to Grandma and Grandpa's house. California was paradise as far as we were concerned. The sky was always blue, the winter always warm, and we could hike to the beach any time we wanted.

"And that's where the hippies are," Daryl said, quietly and to himself.

I looked over at Mom. She was smiling as I hadn't seen her smile in years. Whether or not she was happy to be going back home, near her parents, she was relieved to leave this place where, despite all her efforts to be sociable and to build a successful business, she was still looked down upon by nearly all the women in town.

I was struck by two strong thoughts in a row. The first was wonderful: We'd be escaping the black horsemen and their threat to our family. The second was disappointing: I'd be losing my beautiful room.

Six months before, after dragging on for six years, the construction on the dream house had been completed. We had climbed up out of our basement apartment and moved into the main house, and I'd been given my own bedroom, upstairs at the end of the hall. I was 14 by this time, and I finally had my own domain, complete with my own closet, my own desk and chair, and my carpet that I had picked out myself at Pete Vrontikus & Sons furniture store, with a pattern of crescent-shaped swishes in red, orange, yellow, and black. I spent many hours sitting on the edge of the desk in the corner, my back to the wall, so I could see every inch of my room, admiring the colorful carpet, gazing out the big bay window at the lake below, just savoring the fact that this room was mine.

When Dad told us we were moving, I mourned the loss of my room. I'd waited so many years to have one, and now I was leaving it. But after a day or so, I got caught up in the general euphoria that the announcement had brought to the house. We hadn't felt anything like that in more than eight years. I yearned for a better life, and this trip promised a new start.

Many years later, I would learn that it wasn't just the Klan behind the move. The banks were after my father for bad checks and defaulted loans; they'd threatened foreclosure on the dream house. Car dealers were nipping at his heels. The drinking had begun to take its toll, and Dad had started to lose his grip on his law practice. Clients were pestering him to finish the cases he'd started. Lawyers could get away with lying, cheating, and stealing, but not failing to make court appearances.

The cure for those miseries was the classic American remedy: Go west.

✤✤✤

CHAPTER FIVE
California, Here We Come

For hundreds of years, the Du Pres had stood fast in South Carolina, but now my father was breaking off his branch of the family and taking us far away. In December 1974, we climbed into his yellow Pontiac Grand Prix, which he'd crashed while driving drunk and had repaired, and left home. My brothers and I, in the back seat, were eager to see what this new adventure would bring. In the front seat, my parents fixed their gaze on the road ahead, afraid to look back at what they were fleeing.

I was 15 now, Marq was 17, and Daryl was 13. During the five-day drive to Southern California, we occupied ourselves by "calling cars," a game of no skill and no purpose except to annoy grown-ups. Whoever spotted a cool car on the highway and was the first to shout out his claim on it, "calling" it, became the owner. The player with the sharpest eyes and quickest mouth accumulated the biggest make-believe fleet of cars.

"I call that Mustang!" Marq would yell.

"I call that Corvette!" I'd cry.

Marq and I amused ourselves by holding our hands over Daryl's mouth so he couldn't call any cars at all. He'd squirm and squeal until Dad's right hand released the steering wheel and reached back, groping for a boy to slap.

"If I hear Daryl complain one more time," he'd growl, "I'm pulling over and cutting the first switch I can get my hands on!" At that, Daryl would sit up and grin that maddeningly smug little grin of his, knowing he had the might of the law on his side. Daryl's protection, however, and his grin, disappeared on the third day of the drive, when we reached the barrens of West Texas where there were no more switches for Dad to threaten to cut.

Our other diversion was talking about what our new California house was going to look like. This discussion kept us occupied for hours each day. Like little architects, we sketched every detail we could imagine, right up to the shingles on the roof. We'd gotten pretty good at that sort of thing, having watched our parents do it for the eight years it had taken them to partially build their dream house on Lake Hartwell. We were unconsciously mimicking their own excited conjectures when we'd moved from Mauldin to the lake shore in Anderson.

Daryl said our new home would be a replica of that house and suggested using the same blueprints. He said that instead of seeing the lake outside our windows, we'd see the ocean. "Only this time, it won't take so long to build it, because there won't be any rainy days."

Marq envisioned a tall, narrow house. "Mama and Daddy, your room will be on the top floor, the penthouse suite!" He looked at them, expecting them to turn and smile in approval, but they stared straight ahead. "Jon's room will be right under that," he went on, "and Daryl's under that. And *my* room . . . mine will be on the first floor so I can hop on my bike and ride right out the door to the beach."

My own California dream house was Spanish adobe-style, inspired by photographs of movie stars' houses I'd seen in magazines. It was one-story, with arched windows and doorways, and topped with a ceramic tile roof. "And there's a bell hanging in the archway that leads to the front porch. Mama can ring that bell when it's time to eat, and we'll come running from the beach!" No response from the front seat.

We didn't give a thought to our parents' silence during our spirited five-day discussion. They must have grieved to hear us fantasize about delights we'd never experience. They had made such a big thing about our Carolina dream house, and implicit in their enthusiasm was a promise that this house would be the place where we'd all be happy again. This was the setting we needed to be the kind of family we were supposed to be. How bitter the ironic aftertaste of their words must have been as they listened to us, knowing the disappointing reality that awaited us. How horribly my mother must have dreaded her shameful return to California.

Our destination was San Diego's north county. As Interstate 5 rushed past the beach towns, I could see the ocean gleaming a mile to the west, and my excitement swelled. But when we reached Santa Fe Boulevard, Dad didn't turn toward the beach. He turned east, away from the water. I felt a stab of apprehension; something was wrong.

No one spoke. Up the hill we went, into a mass of lower middle-class housing—stucco, flat roofs, each little place crammed up against its neighbor. This was Encinitas, our new home.

Eventually we came to San Dieguito Union High School, a cloister of pale yellow stucco buildings. It looked like an abandoned Tahitian village. I watched for a big sign hailing the school's football team. Back home my school had had a banner shouting, ***T.L. Hanna High School—Home of the Yellow Jackets!*** Here, no banner, just a little wooden plaque with a horse on it, something somebody had made in shop class—badly. It all seemed disturbingly alien. I looked at the buildings with foreboding, slowly beginning to realize that I might have to go to that school.

At the far end of the campus, Dad swung the wheel and entered a small street. It was not a major thoroughfare; Dad was obviously getting pretty close to where he was going. We were going to live in this seedy neighborhood. The street, inappropriately named Bonita Drive, Spanish for "pretty," ran around the back of the school, where its auto shop was. There were broken-down cars up on racks, piles of junked tires, and a stench of exhaust. This was precisely where Dad pressed the brake pedal. He pulled to the curb in front of a low building divided into two apartments, one of which would be our new home. I wanted to leap from the car and start running—where I didn't know, just to some place that looked like the California I'd imagined.

"Look," my father said as we climbed out of the car, "the high school is right across the street." My immediate concern was whether I'd be able to go back and forth to school each day without my friends noticing where I lived. "And we're only five minutes from Grandpa and Grandma"—my mother's parents. That thought must have caused my mother to wince.

The apartment house was stuccoed, and long ago it had been latexed white. Out front was a wooden awning painted an awful mint green, the kind of color they use on warehouses. Our apartment was a cramped, dingy, two-bedroom affair on the ground floor. The yard behind the building was tiny and scorched by the sun, and it wasn't even ours; there would be no more football games with Dad.

Marq got his wish; his bedroom was on the first floor, but he had to share it with Daryl and me. Dad had sold off a good part of our furniture before we left South Carolina to raise cash; what remained had arrived the day before, and Dad crowded our three beds into the room and lined them up side by side. It looked like the triage ward at a public hospital—appropriate for three wounded boys. The first time I walked into the room, it was dark, and I looked for the light. As I was about to touch the wall switch, I saw that the switch plate and the wall around it were covered with a mottled gray shadow, the accumulated fingerprints of the unnumbered people who had lived in the apartment and slept in the bedroom before me. For the whole time we stayed there, no one ever washed off that switchplate or painted those walls. Whenever I went to touch the switch, I tried to remember to pull the sleeve of my sweatshirt or pajamas down over my fingers so I wouldn't have to touch it with my bare hand. The gray shadow always reminded me that the place wasn't ours and that we couldn't afford a place of our own anymore.

Soon after we unpacked, we drove over to see Grandpa Marquis and Grandma Marie. The atmosphere was strained. This was not the homecoming my mother might have wished for, the handsome young matron attended by her prosperous husband. She was returning in mortification, the ill-used wife of a disreputable failure.

"How did the car hold up on the drive?" Grandpa Marquis asked, straining to seem interested in the trivia of our trip and ignore what all the adults knew—we were refugees from a home that was a war zone.

After some small talk, Mom and Grandma went outside to the back patio where they feigned interest in Grandma's potted exotic flowers. Dad went out the front driveway and pretended to give the car a checkup without removing his hands from his pockets. Grandpa, the stern but sweet patriarch, let Daryl climb on his lap and let Marq and me leaf through his scrapbook and chuckle at the old photos of him posing in his Army and police uniforms.

Grandma served one of her famously delicious meals that evening. She and Grandpa did a masterful job of making us boys feel positive about our sudden transfer to a new place. During our time in Encinitas, Grandpa and Grandma's house was a sanctuary for my brothers and me, if not for our mother. We spent many Sundays at their small house, where the air was almost always sweetened by something baking in the oven. As adept as they were at making my brothers and me feel welcome, my grandparents, especially Marie, were judgmental and hurtful toward our mother. She hid her feelings from us, but Mom resented her mother's lectures about the shame of a failed marriage. As for our father, they rarely spoke to him after our arrival, and he took great care to stay away from their house. There seemed to have been an unspoken agreement between our parents and grandparents—as harshly as they disapproved of their daughter dumping the refuse of her spoiled marriage on them, they would try to help make this unseemly situation as pleasant as possible for their grandsons.

One of the first things our parents did was to trade in the Grand Prix, which was now beaten and road-weary, and replace it with two much more modest cars. Dad's was a charcoal-gray Chevrolet Impala with a gray interior. It didn't have the style of the Grand Prix, but it was new and clean and exciting to see, sitting in our driveway. "I'll need a big, fast sedan to make that commute downtown to my office every day," Dad announced, ignoring the fact that he didn't have an office downtown, or even a job for that matter.

Mom drove up in a brown Ford Pinto, the dullest of cars but, like the Impala, clean and new and welcome.

One Saturday afternoon a few months after we moved in, Marq was sitting by the window, staring out at nothing, when he suddenly shouted, "Dad! Someone's towing the Chevy!"

We all rushed to the window. There was the Impala, hanging tail-high from the end of an orange-and-blue wrecker. One of the tow operators, a big-bellied, muscular man with long sideburns, tattoos on his forearms, and a cigarette pack rolled into each sleeve of his T-shirt, was checking the cable connection; the other man, just as imposing, was about to climb back into the wrecker's cab.

"Whoa!" Dad yelled out the window. "Get your goddamn hitch off my car!" The men never bothered to look in our direction. Marq and Daryl and I kept up the clamor while Dad raced out the door. He was just in time to see his car, drawn by the wrecker, rolling backwards down Bonita Drive.

He ran after the wrecker half a block, waving his arms and cursing as it receded into the distance. Then he stopped and stood there, gazing after it, wheezing. "That son-of-a-bitch dealer!" he gasped when he got back to the apartment. "I knew he was a crook. I ought to call the cops." But we noticed he made no move toward the phone. Instead, he stomped back outside to the end of the driveway, where he lit a cigarette and watched the sun set over the ocean. I knew that his loud eruption had just been for show. The repo man's visit had been no surprise to my father. Like the apartment, the cars weren't ours either.

The loss of the Impala wasn't nearly as disheartening as the sight of my father standing in the street shaking his fist at the tow truck, helplessly trying to prevent the two men from driving away with it. The image stayed in my mind when I crawled into my bed that night. I lay there, staring at the ceiling, trying to make sense of something that had never before occurred to me—that my father wasn't the all-powerful, all-knowing superhero I'd always thought he was. No longer could he shake his fist and growl at people and say things like, "Do you know who you're dealing with?!" and make them do whatever he wanted them to. We were in California now, a place where nobody knew Bob Du Pre—and nobody cared.

My father began his search for work soon after our arrival. He took it as a humiliating and demoralizing chore. Every day he dressed in one of his classic, somewhat threadbare $700 suits. Late every afternoon, he came home rumpled and cranky.

I was walking out the front door one afternoon, on my way to watch guys ride skateboards along the concrete paths in the park next to the high school. The skateboarders, not the football, basketball, or baseball players, were San Dieguito High School's most prominent athletes. Dad was walking in the door just as I opened it to go out. It was only about three o'clock in the afternoon, and I was surprised to see him.

"Daddy!" I shouted, happy as always to see him. "What are you doing home so early?"

Uncharacteristically for him, he didn't have a quick, glib answer. He walked past me into his bedroom. I followed him, still expecting an answer. I stood at the door and watched as he slowly, wearily, kicked off his brown oxford shoes without untying the laces. "Well, Jonny," he said, breathing a heavy sigh, "I guess I just got tired of beating my head against the bricks." He said it without looking at me.

I was stunned. Here was my father, the world's greatest lawyer, the smartest man in the universe, telling me that he couldn't get a job. No other revelation could have shocked me more. Two disturbing emotions flooded my mind: pity—pity, of all things, for the man who was my hero. And something like anger: It occurred to me that he wouldn't have had to look for a new job at all if he and Mom hadn't been so strangely anxious to get out of South Carolina.

❧❧❧

One day a few weeks later, Dad came home and told Mom that he'd found work. "A big firm . . . 20th floor of the Home Federal building . . . a pack of ambulance chasers. They've got me doing grunt work . . . investigating evidence . . . writing briefs."

"Hallelujah," Mom said with a sneer. "It's about time."

"Fuck you," Dad muttered.

"To hell with you," Mom replied, not even looking up from the pan where a few pieces of chicken sat in oil, slowly frying.

It had seemed for a while, when we first reached California, that my parents were on better terms, but the truce had disintegrated. My mother complained about being stuck in that little apartment. My father complained about being stuck in a low-level job. She lost her temper. He drank. The fighting started again and grew worse. Marq and Daryl and I tried to ignore it, but it was impossible, living in that tiny apartment.

And then the fighting petered out. Our parents were tired—not just winded, but fatigued all the way to their core. The spirit had gone out of them; they were slowing down, giving in, resigning themselves to their plight. The feeling in their home now was so different from what it once had been. The energy and urgency that had accompanied everything they did was gone. No longer were they rushing to get somewhere, hustling to accomplish something. Instead, they sat at opposite ends of the old swirly-striped orange-and-gold couch in the living room, not doing much of anything. They had no feeling left for each other, not even anger or hatred. They hardly seemed to notice their sons.

We boys stopped hoping, stopped talking about reconciliation. We too were burned out. Our recourse, we knew, was not in the present but in the future. Marq kept saying, "Don't worry. Someday we'll be old enough to get out of here."

Grandma Marie and Grandpa Marquis were our only solace. We spent Christmas at their house, and they made it a holiday for us. They wrapped presents and stacked them under the tree. Grandma prepared her famous family favorite, crêpes suzette, piled high on a huge platter. We drowned them in maple syrup and ate until we couldn't fit any more in our bellies. Being in the warmth of my grandparents' home comforted us, but it seemed to embarrass Mom and Dad, who couldn't hide the obvious—that their marriage was in a shambles and that Dad's career was over.

I like to think, seeing the coming troubles, that my father had done the wise and right thing—putting us near our grandparents so they'd be a stabilizing influence in our lives when our world turned upside down, as he knew it must. But Marquis and Marie weren't disposed to meddle in their daughter's life. They would not offer help that wasn't requested, and Mom was too proud to ask for assistance from a mother she hadn't been particularly close to in the first place.

My brothers and I seized any excuse to get out of that apartment. Daryl and I took to following Marq wherever he went. But the trouble was that Marq had run out of places to go. He was 17 now, 6'2" inches tall and 185 pounds. His thin waist flared up in a V to a set of broad shoulders. He had brown hair, curly like Dad's, a square jaw, a prominent nose, and bright green eyes that flashed mischief and uneasiness. A boy his age couldn't indulge in the kind of mischief that had entertained him when he was younger—that is, not without getting into real trouble. And that's what he started doing.

Just when it looked like Marq had gotten good work, a night janitor's job at the La Costa resort hotel, he got busted for shoplifting a pack of bologna in a grocery store. "I wasn't even gonna eat it," he said, almost bragging. Huck Finn just wanted to see if he could get away with it.

"The guy behind the counter looked like he was slacking off, so I grabbed it and walked out just to show him he should stay on his toes." The guy behind the counter was on his toes after all. He called the cops, and the next thing Marq knew, he was under arrest.

The following week, dressed in a dark suit and tie, Dad took Marq to his juvenile court hearing. The rest of us stayed home and waited.

Three hours later, they were back. Dad was exasperated. "I sat in the back," he said, "just to make sure everything went smoothly. That judge was about to let Marq off with a lecture when the boy opened his big mouth. It was all over."

The judge had read over Marq's file, saw that it had nothing in it except a stolen pack of bologna, and then had done what judges do when they're ready to let a minor offender off the hook—he gave Marq a chance to apologize. "Well, son," he said, looking down over his bifocals at the tense, muscled teenager before him, "what do you have to say for your silly mistake?"

Marq's lips thinned and he stuck out his chest. Dad knew what that meant. "I could tell he was about to say something really stupid," he said. He was right. "I did it," Marq declared in the toughest manner he could affect. "I admit it. And I'll probably do it again. *And,* don't call me 'son,' 'cause I'm not your son."

"I just sank in my chair," Dad said. "I didn't know what in the world the boy was trying to prove, but he managed to piss off that judge."

In truth, Dad must have sunk in his chair that day because he knew exactly what was going on. His eldest son was acting out what he'd seen in his father— stubborn defiance.

We all looked at Marq on the other side of the living room and waited for him to start explaining.

"Stop lookin' at me!" he cried out. He dashed for the bedroom and slammed the door.

Early the next morning, Dad took our belligerent thief to the federal penitentiary in downtown San Diego, where he would spend the next four days and three nights camping out with real criminals. Daryl and I pushed our three beds together and enjoyed our king-sized sleeping accommodations all three nights. We didn't worry about our big brother. We figured he'd known what he was letting himself in for and that he could handle himself well enough.

Four days later, when Mom drove down to pick up Marq, Daryl and I eagerly went with her. We were the children of a criminal trial lawyer, after all, and we'd met lots of criminals over the years. We were curious to see if our older brother would look and smell and talk like them. We wanted to see if his hair would be greasy and slicked back on his head, and whether he'd walk with that forced gait that criminals used to try to make themselves bigger than they really are. We wanted to sniff him, to see if he'd carry the smell of stale body odor masked by cheap after-shave that my father's clients had always seemed to reek of when they'd visited his office.

It was already nightfall when we got to the prison. We parked in a loading lane outside a gray steel doorway in the 15-story prison. To Daryl's and my disappointment, there were no guards, no barbed wire, no searchlights blazing down from watchtowers.

The designated pick-up time was five o'clock. Right at five, the gray steel door slowly swung open, as if it could move all by itself, and out slunk San Diego's newest ex-con, his head bowed. If he'd had a tail, it would have been tucked between his legs like a dog that had just been swatted hard with a newspaper. He almost ran to the car.

"Open the door and lift the seat," Mom told him in a pleasant voice, trying to keep the moment from getting too heavy. Marq threw himself into the back seat next to Daryl and sat there staring straight ahead. Mom pulled the car away from the tower, turned around, and headed up the block toward the I-5 northbound on-ramp.

The suspense was enormous. I was dying to ask, "What was it like in there, jailbird?" but I didn't get the chance. Marq burst into tears and began sobbing.

"It was terrible!" he cried out. We braced ourselves for Marq's horrific revelation. "They fed us liver for dinner every night!" Liver? We wanted stories from Alcatraz, and he was giving us liver. "And there was this huge guy. He told me he liked liver, and if I didn't give him mine, he'd cut me when we got back to the block. So I had to give him my liver every night. And I was so hungry and nervous I couldn't sleep!" He sobbed some more.

Mom tried to comfort her traumatized son. "Let's stop and get something to eat on the way home," she said. "Would you like that?"

"Yeah," Marq blubbered.

Then Daryl did it, just as he had back in Mauldin when he was three and we were trying to surprise Mom on her birthday. He blurted out the very thing we didn't want him to say. "How about a baloney sandwich?"

Silence. Then Mom burst, and I did, too, and then all three of us were roaring with laughter. "Stop it!" Marq screamed, and he cried some more. For several days, Daryl and I pressed him for details about his prison stint, but Marq never would speak of it. He looked so miserable when we raised the subject that we finally stopped.

Marq's stonewalling was an unsettling experience for me. Until this time, he and I had shared every secret; now, suddenly, there was something he was refusing to share. An intimacy that, without thinking about it, I'd taken as a given was suddenly lost to me, and cold was coming from a place where there had always been warmth. I was introduced to a sensation entirely new to me—feeling alone. Marq felt it, too, and he was saddened. It was at the time of this unutterable prison experience of his, I think, that Marq's growing inner tragedy became apparent. And it was the beginning of our eventual estrangement.

We would remain close friends for a while, though, and he would continue as my defender, which was a very good thing for me. I needed him.

We both went to San Dieguito Union High. It was a strange new environment for us, which required a difficult adjustment. The kids on campus seemed more sophisticated, more worldly. Even though they were spouting the same meaningless babble as teenagers everywhere, they spoke in crisp syllables that made them sound a lot smarter than we drawling southerners. Shy and in dread of seeming different, I immediately began studying the way they talked. They didn't say a soft "ah" for "I," but a staccato "eye." They said their "o's" without letting their jaws slacken or their lips do that pouting Elvis Presley thing that made an "o" sound more like "o-u." I began learning to speak with tighter lips and a more controlled mouth. I monitored my speech for any hint of a southern accent, and I began to lose it rapidly.

Marq, on the other hand, didn't seem to care that he sounded different from all the other kids. He was cutting away now from everyday congeniality. He relished his status as an oddball and challenged anyone who dared to mock him. He wore construction boots and overalls over a referee shirt almost every day. This brought on no small measure of ridicule from the school tough guys, the football players in particular.

"Hey, technical foul, Farmer Brown!" they would jeer. And each time they did, Marq walked right into their faces.

"You better be ready to back up that trash talk, beach boy," he'd retort. He'd dare them to bang it out right then and there, in the middle of the cafeteria or the phys ed class or the hallway.

They all learned, one by one, to think twice before messing with the new kid. They knew that even if they could whip him, they'd end up getting bloodied and looking foolish in the process of trying to entertain their friends. Marq, the southern boy, was tough in a way that these kids who had grown up frolicking on the beach couldn't possibly be. The scorn soon subsided, and one afternoon it was silenced forever.

The incident involved me. I was walking home from school when I heard a voice from the direction of the auto shop. "Hey, country dude! Wait up, man!" I cringed. Despite my best efforts to hide my southern accent and replace it with instant California, there were those who still noticed I was different.

I knew whose voice it was. The guy was in my grade, but only because he had flunked a couple of grades and stayed in school a lot longer than he should have. He was bigger than my big brother. And he was moving my way.

I kept walking and tried to pretend I hadn't heard him, but he had the angle on me and cut me off, stepping in front of me just before I made it to the chain-link gate that opened onto the street.

"Hey, dude!" he barked. "I said wait up, man. Are you tryin' to ditch me or what?" He cocked his head and threw his long, curly, greasy red hair off his face and back over his shoulder.

I tried to seem friendly and unconcerned. "What's happening, dude?" I answered.

"What do you mean, 'What's happening'? Maybe I should kick your ass right now, country boy. You want me to kick your ass right now, or what?" He grabbed my sweater at the shoulder and pulled hard, stretching it taut as he lifted me nearly off my feet. He pulled me up to his face. He was smiling a mean smile, and his teeth were yellow and crooked.

I resisted by pushing into his chest. That gave him the excuse he wanted. His right fist cocked and started for me. Suddenly his wind emptied from his mouth and his eyes widened in shock and confusion. He released me and went down hard onto the hot pavement.

There stood Marq, blowing anger out his nose. He stepped over my attacker. The giant who had looked so menacing seconds earlier lay face-down, clutching his ribs with one hand, pushing at the asphalt with the other as if he was trying to roll himself over and take breath.

"Get up!" Marq screamed down at him. "Get up and try to touch my brother!"

Then, remarkably gentle for someone who had just knocked the wind out of a 230-pound person, my rescuer put his arm around my shoulders and said, "Let's go home."

Once again, my bodyguard had protected me, the way he'd protected Tyrone years earlier. I knew that thanks to my big brother, I had nothing to fear from anything or anybody. It let me walk the world with confidence. If only Marq had had a Marq.

❧❧❧

Daryl had nobody, not even me. Marq defended his younger brother, but I, lost in my troubles, failed to defend mine. As for Dad and Mom, Daryl was all but invisible to them. He went off to school at the junior high every day, and they never asked how he was doing. That's the way things had gotten with them. Neither one of them dared ask us any questions for fear we might ask for their help with our problems. They simply had no help to give. They were two people whose unstated objective was just to get through each day without incident. The person this affected the most was Daryl. If they'd been paying any attention to him, they'd have seen that he was making unwise friendships.

When we arrived in Encinitas, Daryl's main escape was still the one he'd always had, his imagination. He'd sit in the parched yard—on a soft, cool pile of vegetation called an ice plant—and play games with his make-believe pets. He'd talk to them for hours; sometimes he'd just hum to them. But slowly things changed. The world outside seeped into Daryl's private world and extinguished it.

Now, for the first time, he had friends his own age, and he wasn't at all particular about them. Anyone would do. Every so often, he'd drag home some scraggly-looking kid. The boy would wait outside while Daryl changed into torn jeans and his dreadful black T-shirt with the insignia of an acid rock band on the front. He soon started to look like those kids he brought home. After a lifetime of being immature for his age, he was now ahead of his time, jerking to the jagged beat of hard music years before it was popular. It was the '70s, and only the hardcore drug users knew about acid rock.

One day my mother went to heat up some food in the oven. Under the steel tray she saw what at first looked like dirt. No, it was leaves of some kind, and seeds. Marijuana. Daryl, it turned out, had been curing his crop. He was substituting artificial fantasy for that wonderful imagination of his. Years later she said she had thought of calling him to task, but she didn't. Let him have his comfort.

❧ ❧ ❧

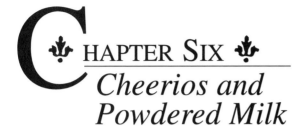

CHAPTER SIX ❧
Cheerios and Powdered Milk

As the months went by, life in the little apartment on Bonita Drive kept getting quieter. We stopped talking to one another. What I'd mistaken for tranquility had been a welcome respite at first, but the quiet was becoming stifling. It was as if we were on a sinking ship and everyone knew it, yet no one could say, "Hey! Let's all grab hold and help each other stay afloat." To mention our troubles was to acknowledge them. We were a once-respectable family, too proud to admit we were disintegrating.

Daryl had his escapes—roaming with his scraggly friends and smoking weed that made his head buzz—and I'd developed one, too: sleep. On weekends and vacations, I'd sleep more than half the day away, hoping that when I woke up it would be the day after tomorrow. No one ever bothered to wake me up.

One hot and humid Saturday in the spring of 1975, I slept right through the morning and into the afternoon. What roused me was the heat. I was too sweaty to lie there any longer, so I dragged myself up and stumbled into the kitchen and found a box of Cheerios, a rare treat. But there was no fresh milk so I mixed some powdered milk. I hated powdered milk—not only because of the taste, but because it reminded me that it was all we could afford. I was sitting at the kitchen table and had just eaten a few spoonfuls of cereal when my mother came in.

"Well, your father's gone," she said. Just like that. I stopped and waited. She sighed and said, "We decided it would be best if he just left, so he's moving back to South Carolina." Nothing more. She went on to the living room.

I sat there, stunned. This was something more than my teenaged intellect could process. I couldn't begin to imagine how this event had instantly redefined me and already changed the course of my life. I had no way of knowing how such a profound loss would transform my personality and cause unimaginable suffering for loved ones I hadn't even met yet. In that instant, without realizing it, my identity changed. I was no longer a member of a family. I was an individual. My parents' marriage was over. Dad was gone, and Mom was giving up. I would forevermore be on my own. It was too much to think about, so I concentrated on the cramping sensation in my stomach. My gut knotted. I couldn't swallow the partially chewed cereal in my mouth, so I just opened wide and let it splash back into the bowl.

Mom didn't pull up a chair next to me, put a loving arm around my shoulders, squeeze me to her, and tell me that my father had left us. She didn't even pause as she walked through the room. She just made the crushing announcement as she passed, as matter-of-factly as if she'd said, "Looks like a cloudy day outside." The quiver in her voice, ever so slight, gave her away. I knew she was coming apart inside. I also knew she was afraid to look at me, afraid that if she saw the expression on my face she'd burst into tears and make a big scene of it. In a way, I actually appreciated her restraint, having endured so many of her screaming fits in my earlier years. I'm sure it was all she could manage just to tell me the bad news without breaking down. Then I wondered whether she'd told her parents. The thought of how humiliating that would be for my mother made me forget myself in that moment. I riveted my emotions so as not to make this any more difficult for Mom.

At night I cried, very quietly. I got good at clamping shut my mouth and gritting my teeth and letting the tears flow from my clenched eyes without making a sound my brothers could hear. Crying was the only comfort that allowed me to fall asleep and forget the yearning. I still loved my father. His faults had crept up on me; I'd gotten used to them before I could perceive and judge them. He'd been wonderful so long that I kept on thinking of him that way even after he wasn't. No matter what he'd done, I still needed a man in my life.

I was lying in bed one night staring at the blotchy plaster ceiling, and it occurred to me that I should say a prayer. My parents had taken us to various churches when we were little, mostly because that was what you did on Sunday in the South—you went to church—but we'd had nothing you would call religious training. No one had ever taught me how to pray, so I improvised. I folded my hands across my chest and looked at the ceiling and started talking.

"God, You know where my dad is. Please take care of him. Please tell him we love him. Please help us all get back together again. And also, please stop all the wars and help all the poor people. Thank You, and good night."

Marq and Daryl, in their beds a few feet away, chuckled the first time they heard me talking to the ceiling. I didn't mind. In fact, it made me feel good to make them laugh. There was something about laughing in the dark that was contagious. Sometimes, Marq could get the whole room laughing just by making a scuffing sound with his nose, like he was trying to hold back a laugh. Laughter gave us a feeling of relief. In a sense, it was a form of prayer. Marq, who seemed to be able to make himself burp or fart at will, would let out a clap of wind in the dark and make Daryl and me laugh until we could hardly breathe. In the spirit of our bedtime solidarity, my prayers caught on. One night, Daryl spoke up in the darkness.

"God, we're trying to be good boys. Please don't be mad at us if we get in trouble. Please help Daddy and Mommy to not be mad at us. Please tell Daddy we love him, and we hope he comes back soon. In the name of the Father, the Son, and the Holy Ghost. Amen." Daryl's prayers, so innocent and pure, touched Marq's heart and moved him to tears. We could hear him quietly sniffling after Daryl finished. Then one night, he uttered his prayer.

"God, our heavenly Father, we miss our dad and wonder what happened to him. We hope he is safe. Please tell him we love him. You can do miracles. Would You please do a miracle for us? Would You please bring our father back and make us a family again? I'll do anything You want. Amen."

Our prayers became a nightly ritual. Marq first, then me, then Daryl. We were begging God to let us finish our childhood.

In those few minutes before falling asleep each night, I built a vision of better times. Piece by piece, from observations I'd made in the homes of friends, I assembled an image of the life that would be mine when I grew up. I imagined what my wife would look like. I could almost see her face and hear the voices of bright, happy children playing on the living room floor. Over the years, that vision became steadily sharper, and I lived in growing confidence that it would someday be real.

❧❧❧

Long before Dad left, it was clear that the money had run out. He had no license to practice law in California. He'd done some clerking for a local firm, but not much. He obviously wasn't going to pay anything to help us once he left—no child support, no alimony. Mom never bothered to make it an issue. Once Dad was gone, she sat Marq and me down at the kitchen table. "Boys," she said, "you've got to get jobs."

A buddy of mine worked at the Union 76 station about a mile away on Santa Fe Road, and I got work there pumping gas. What I earned I mostly used to buy dinner at the Jack In The Box on Santa Fe Boulevard. It took some of the pressure off my mother to keep us fed. Marq got a job as a night janitor at a hotel. Daryl was too young to work.

But the money Marq and I brought home wasn't nearly enough for the four of us to live on. For months we depended on welfare and what Mom could bring herself to ask for from Grandma and Grandpa. And then, with the last remnants of her emotional reserve, my mother once again started a dance studio. It was what she knew how to do, and the continuation of her old dream. She rented an 800-square-foot space above a sandwich shop in Cardiff-by-the-Sea, about five miles from the apartment. With a little venture capital from her parents, she installed mirrors and ballet bars along the walls and bought a portable tape player. With those simple tools and her charm, energy, and recaptured enthusiasm—the result no doubt of having gotten my father and his degeneracy out of her life—she turned an empty office space into the reborn Marquise Du Pre School of Dance. Within a few weeks, she had a dozen students tiptoeing around the room; and in another month, a dozen more. They were all girls. This time there would be no embarrassed boys in leotards scowling in the corners. She didn't even attempt to recruit us.

I'd noticed changes in my mother almost as soon as my father left. She spent less time in bed and more time clothed, and when she dressed, she wore regular clothes, not just her bathrobe. As the months went by and her shame over her marriage eased, she drew closer to her parents. She'd drive us over to their house, and while she chatted with Grandma Marie; we'd follow Grandpa Marquis around as he changed the oil filter in his car or pulled weeds from his tiny vegetable garden. My mother's parents had never been particularly warm, but they weren't hardhearted. They were sorry about their daughter's disappointment, and they tried to help. Just being back in touch with them meant a lot to her. For the first time in many years, Mom had someone to talk with.

If she empathized with us boys and understood the grief we felt over the loss of our father, she never once showed it. Like her parents, she was not affectionate. We'd never experienced the ordinary maternal expressions of love—hugs, kisses, caresses—so they didn't matter to us. What did matter was the change in her behavior. Gone was the volatility and the screaming we'd been conditioned to fear. She had been through her hell, and now she seemed to be looking for peace.

She threw herself into her work at the dance studio, and did everything she could think of to attract new pupils. It was tough going, and over the months, the strain began showing in her face. "We're breaking even," she would say at the dinner table, trying to make it sound hopeful. It sounded good to us. To break even after our family's string of losses was a major moral victory. To see our mother believe in something again was a miracle.

One day I found her in her bedroom, sitting on the edge of her bed, head down. I said, "Mom?" She lifted her head but didn't turn and look at me.

Her face was haggard again, the new vitality gone. "What's wrong, Mom?" I asked her.

"Oh, nothing," she said and then started to cry. I wanted to go sit next to her but suppressed the impulse and stood in the doorway, waiting for the crying to stop. "There's no way around it," she finally said. "I'm going to have to close the studio."

"But Mom!" I said. "You said you were breaking even!"

"I am. But breaking even isn't good enough. I've got to make a profit. I've got to bring some money home."

"Maybe in a few more months . . ."

"I can't wait a few more months. It's been a year. That's long enough. It wouldn't be right to keep on taking welfare when there's no real hope." She sat up straight and looked ahead. "No. I've got to pay my own way. I've got to shut down the studio." She started to choke up, then brought herself under control. "I've got to get some kind of job," she said, not so much to me, it seemed, as to herself. "We'll be all right."

One thing was clear. She was not reaching out to me for whatever comfort I might give. She was a woman alone. With tears in her eyes, she closed the door on her dancing school and her dreams. That day, I think, my mother let go of any hope she had that she'd ever accomplish anything worthwhile. That day, I believe, she also gave up on *herself.* Soon she found work at a fabric store, at more or less minimum wage.

I wanted to believe that, as she said, we'd be all right; nevertheless, I began to form a survival plan of my own. It was woven around a man back in South Carolina named Jim Wyles. Wyles coached basketball at Anderson Junior College, and his teams were almost always nationally ranked. From time to time during my years in Little League and junior high basketball, Coach Wyles would drop by for a look at the young players, and occasionally he said something encouraging about my progress. Those few words of his now became my best chance. I prayed he'd meant them. If I could just get Jim Wyles to give me a try-out, maybe I could get a basketball scholarship.

When we'd left Anderson two years before, I'd been six feet tall. Now I was 6'4". I was gawky and spindly, and my body looked jumbled. On the basketball court, I was slow, too slow to be taken seriously by any big-college scouts who might have caught a glimpse of me during those long afternoons at the Anderson YMCA. But I'd been working hard on my game at San Dieguito High, and what I lacked in speed, I now made up, I hoped, in craft. I was cunning and deft with the ball. I could dribble through a crowd and hit my jump shot with defenders hanging all over me. I figured I had something to offer, but was it enough?

It would have to be. A basketball scholarship was the only way I'd ever attain my unspoken goal, which was to go to college. My father had filled me with collegiate fantasies during those afternoon football games long ago. He'd told us bright, brave tales of his own college days and passed along that essential American dogma that I could achieve and obtain what my mind could imagine if I was willing to work for it. I could imagine myself in college—I couldn't imagine it otherwise—and I was more than willing to work. My determination was as much a part of me as my right arm.

Basketball was already changing my life. I made the team at San Dieguito High, which brought me some acceptance and even attracted the attention of a few girls in my class. Until then, I'd been too broke to do more than dream about girls—no money, no wheels, and not much to wear. And, I lived in fear that one of the girls I liked would see me walk home from school and learn I lived in one of those scruffy apartments behind the auto shop. Now, however, being a varsity athlete seemed to offset those problems.

One day a friend of mine named Richard Kozlowski sat down next to me in the cafeteria. "You going to the prom?" he asked.

"You know I'm not," I replied, resenting what I took to be a mean joke.

"Well, yeah, I know," he said, "but what I mean is, would you like to go?"

"I can live without it," I said, refusing to admit I wanted what I could never have.

"But what if I told you that Christy Carroll is looking for a date? What if I told you she wishes you'd ask her?"

"I'd say you're a lyin' asshole."

Christy Carroll was the kind of beauty that the actress Heather Locklear would soon become when she was in her pin-up poster queen stage—sparkling eyes, plump cheeks, ash-blonde hair, long thin legs, and a pert little butt that swung with confidence. Christy was the girlfriend of Richard's older brother, Mike, a muscular, good-looking, mature young man. He'd graduated from San Dieguito the year before and was now tailback on the football team at the University of Colorado. Asking Mike's girl out on a date seemed like the formula for personal annihilation.

But Richard kept at it. Mike couldn't take Christy to the prom himself, he said, and didn't want her sitting at home that night. It was okay with Mike if some no-threat like me escorted her.

The prospect of taking out adorable Christy Carroll was so thrilling that I let myself be persuaded. The next time I saw her, I ambled over and said, "Say, Christy, I was thinking of going to the junior-senior prom but never got around to asking anyone. Waddayasay you and I go together?" It was amazingly easy, and I had to conceal my surprise.

She smiled and put her arms around me. "That'd be cool, Jon," she said.

Using money I'd earned working at the gas station, I went in with a buddy of mine and made it a double date. We borrowed his parents' sedan, rented cheap tuxedos, and made dinner reservations at Tom Ham's Lighthouse on San Diego Harbor. The evening was the best I'd ever had. Before it was over, Christy gave me a sample of what all my male friends had been dreaming about. After a few polite kisses, she deftly stretched out her shiny, pink tongue and stuck it in my well-scrubbed ear, making me twitch as if I'd been electrocuted. Then, after thoroughly soaking my ear with her saliva, her slippery probe licked across my right cheek, parted my lips, and plunged into my mouth. This was the "mashing" I'd heard so much about and only pretended to understand. It lasted well over an hour—Christy, without saying a word, coaching me through all the various head angles and tongue positions a good make-out artist should know about.

I knew she was just being nice, showing routine appreciation, but I was happy to take it on any terms. It was a first-rate introduction to the marvels of gender difference. Whenever we saw each other on campus after that evening, she always smiled at me and patted my arm. We both knew it would never happen again. She was attached, and I was broke. But being Christy Carroll's friend brought me other friends and transformed my senior year of high school.

❦❦❦

All the winter and spring of that year, I fretted over the pitch I'd make to Coach Wyles. Should I play it cool? Should I beg? I had to get it right the first time. Jim Wyles was the only card in my hand.

Two months before graduation, I placed the call. His secretary took my name, and Wyles came right on the line. "Jon Du Pre?" he asked in a sharp, quick voice that tensed me up. "Jon? Where'd you get to, boy?"

"I'm in San Diego," I said, figuring that would sound more impressive than Encinitas. "I'm about to graduate from high school."

"That's wonderful, son," he replied.

"I want to come play for you, Coach," I said in a rush.

"You must be a pretty big fella by now."

"I'm 6'4" and weigh about 180."

"You got game in you?" Wyles was a hip coach who could talk the players' language.

"I've been scoring about 20 points a game, I can handle the ball, and I can shoot the lights out." I knew I should stop there, but I raced on. "I could have done better if my coach had built the offense to get me the ball more,"

I added, instantly regretting it, recognizing that I was beginning to sound like a loser.

"How are your grades?" he asked.

"B-plus average." That was true enough, but I'd exaggerated my weight and scoring average a little. I allowed myself the overstatements. I was desperate for a try-out. I knew that if I got even a small chance, I could make it by sheer determination, if nothing else.

The coach considered for a moment. "Come on down, Jon," he said at last, with what I hoped was enthusiasm. "You come on back after graduation, and we'll give you a try."

With those words, a wonderful new life seemed to open up before me. From then on, through the end of the school year, I had a hard time thinking of anything but the chance Coach Wyles was giving me. I did everything I could to prepare. To build up my legs and endurance, I went down to the beach every day and spent hours sprinting in the soft sand. I spent my weekends on the beachside basketball courts, alone on the cracked concrete under the ragged palms, dribbling and shooting my worn rubber ball, beating imaginary defenders to the rusty iron hoop, and launching jump shots that quietly dropped through, hardly touching the tattered net that hung off one side of the rim. And all the while, I imagined that Jim Wyles was watching me.

❖ ❖ ❖

My mother did get one lasting benefit from her failed studio. Before taking their daughters off to other dance schools, several of the mothers invited her to attend church services with them. I'd never known my mother to be religious, so I was surprised when she came home one Sunday afternoon gushing about the church she'd just discovered. "What a friendly group of people! So warm, so down to earth! I want you boys to come with me when I go next week." But she had lost most of her authority over her sons. We were becoming more independent as we grew, and less inclined to listen to anything she said. We ignored her invitation.

One morning at eight, she roused us out of bed, saying something about getting in the car and helping her pick up groceries. That word *groceries* woke me up. We hadn't seen much in the way of food in our cupboards or our refrigerator in a long time. Full of excitement, the four of us piled into the Pinto and took off toward San Diego. Mom had directions written on a piece of notebook paper, and they led us to a two-story warehouse about the size of an average supermarket. It bore no neon logo, however, and seemed to have no name.

"Where *are* we?" Daryl asked.

"This is the Mormon Church's welfare warehouse," she said in an almost reverent tone. That word, *welfare,* repulsed me, and I wanted to leave right then.

"The women I go to church with told me to come here. The congregation has offered us help during our crisis, and I accepted their generosity. I wanted you boys to come with me so you'd appreciate what they're doing for us." As she spoke the last few words, her voice broke and she started crying. For the first time, I saw our family's plight not just as my problem, but also my mother's, and my heart softened toward her. At least she was trying to do something for us.

I was sitting in front next to her. I wanted to put my arm around her but felt too embarrassed, in front of Marq and Daryl. The three of us sat in the car and waited for her to get back her composure and wipe her eyes. Then, reluctantly but quietly, we followed her in.

The place was full of provisions; they were stacked on shelves that rose ten feet high along every aisle. Mom had a long list of items that we would take: canned meats, canned vegetables, yeast and salt and sugar and flour and, oh no, powdered milk. None of the stuff was brand name, and there wasn't any flashy packaging. It was all generic and bland and looked awful to me. I hated being there. I felt ashamed to take anything off the shelf and put it into Mom's grocery cart, knowing we weren't going to pay for it when we passed the checkers at the exit.

The overloaded Pinto strained all the way back up I-5. For the many months that followed, we would subsist on the odorless, colorless, tasteless food we got from the church warehouse. We ate out of necessity rather than enjoyment. But slowly, my brothers and I developed gratitude for the gift of survival that had come from these people we didn't know.

One evening, Marq and I were watching a Lakers game on TV when we heard a knock at the door. I opened it and saw two very clean-cut guys standing on the front porch. They were wearing white shirts and dark neckties. I thought they were recruiters from the Marine base at Camp Pendleton in Oceanside, about half an hour to the north.

"Save it, fellas," I said. "You're wasting your time here." I still had my ambitions, and they didn't include being a Marine. I was skinny and slow, but I dreamed of going to college.

"Are you Jon?" the taller one asked.

That surprised me enough to keep me from slamming the door. "Yeah. How'd you know my name?"

The two guys very politely and professionally introduced themselves as missionaries. "We're from the Church of Jesus Christ of Latter-day Saints," they said proudly. It seemed odd that two guys practically as young as I was would want to wear shirts and ties and stand on a stranger's doorstep talking about religion. "Your mother invited us to drop by and talk about our church and about how you can find . . ." It was something about true happiness. I didn't hear what they said, but their raw sincerity (and no doubt a need I didn't know I had) made me pause a couple of more beats before closing the door.

"My mother isn't around right now," I said. "You might want to try back some other time."

"Jon!" Mom's voice cut through the thin walls. "Who's at the door?"

I just shook my head, and the young missionaries smiled, looking embarrassed for me. "Two guys," I called back. "They're from some church."

"Let them in!" she ordered as she scurried out from her bedroom. She greeted them warmly, offered them cold drinks, and ushered them to the couch in the living room. Marq got up and walked off into the bedroom. Daryl came out of the bedroom and stood by the door to see who had visited us.

"Boys," Mom said to us in a voice more stern and resolute than I'd heard in a long time, "I want you to sit down and listen in on what these young men have to say."

Daryl, who had great curiosity and was open to anything weird, sat down, and so I sat, too, but way over in the corner, where I could be present without being part of the conversation. Marq reappeared at the bedroom door. I pretended to listen to their introduction but kept my eyes mostly on the Lakers game.

"Jon!" Mom said. "Turn off that TV and pay attention." I stood and shuffled toward the television set.

"We'll talk fast," the shorter one said, smiling at me. "I promise we won't stay more than a half hour."

"Nonsense," my mother politely argued. "You'll stay as long as you wish." Marq huffed and went back to the bedroom.

I didn't pay much attention to their pitch, but as they approached the end of it, Daryl moved his chair across the room; he seemed interested in what they were saying.

"How's that with you, Jon?" They caught me daydreaming.

"Uh . . . how's what?"

"How's Tuesday of next week, same time?"

"Uh, sure," I answered, not focusing.

When they showed up the next week, smiling and poised, I cursed myself for forgetting they were coming. Again I ignored most of what was said, wondering why Mom and Daryl, the big bad punk rocker, seemed so intrigued by it all.

"We've got a movie to show you," one of the guys said, "if that's okay with you." They unpacked a movie projector and set up a screen and asked if it was all right if they turned off a few lights. I saw a figure at the bedroom door. It was Marq, edging out into the living room so he could see the film.

After it was over, the taller one, whose name was Aston, gave a little talk. He was trying to explain the concept of eternity, and he picked up the first thing he could find to write on, a cardboard box on the floor next to his chair. Using it as a prop, he drew three circles. "These are mankind's big questions," he said. "Where did we come from? Why are we here? And where are we going?" As he spoke, he drew three circles on the side of the box. The circles were meant to represent the place we'd come from, the earth-life we were now in, and the place we might aspire to go to after our life was over, heaven.

The questions struck a chord with me somehow. These were questions I'd thought about, lying in my bed at night. Aston went on sketching out something that was meant to represent the answers to the three questions. I was impressed with his apparently absolute conviction. I was also intrigued that someone about my own age, an evidently normal guy, could know such things and make them sound as though they would apply to my life. As he talked, I began to listen, and soon his words were registering. They seemed to express how I had always thought things should be.

After he left, I picked up the cardboard box and studied the sketches he had drawn on it, and I thought over what he'd said. I felt as if I'd found something that I hadn't even known I needed but that was valuable to me, something that was filling me with hope. For what, I didn't precisely know, but it felt right. My spiritual conversion had begun.

Three weeks later, my mother told the missionaries that she wanted to be baptized and join their church. She strongly urged my brothers and me to be baptized with her. It was unusual for her to ask us to do anything. I was so impressed with her enthusiasm that when the day came, I joined her and Daryl at the baptismal font.

That event was the first thing we'd done more or less together, the first thing that had brought any sense of unity to our family since our move to Encinitas. However, Marq stood off. He still had questions about this mysterious new religion we'd never heard of until four weeks earlier. I was satisfied that the people I'd met in Sunday services and during the youth activities were the kind of positive-thinking, caring, and trustworthy people I wanted in my life.

Almost immediately, friends started popping up everywhere, friends who didn't care about the traces of my southern accent or the fact that I wore the same shirt three times a week. Richard, our high school's star football player, took me under his wing and made sure I had someone to hang out with during lunch break and after basketball practice. Randy saw to it that I knew about all the activities at church and that I understood what they were talking about in Sunday school. Laura appointed herself as my social secretary. She made sure I was introduced to all the girls in the district. Daryl had similar experiences. He followed his newfound church buddies to their Cub Scout den meetings, where he was surrounded by boys who liked him even though he was huge and fluffy-haired and his breath smelled like pot.

Marq watched closely and soon found himself very much at home among the people who had taken us in, practically as members of their extended family. This was a totally new experience for all of us. We felt vital and significant again, as we had been more than a decade earlier.

Two of these people emerged as the kind of role models Miss Casey and Mr. Gentry had been for me back in Anderson long before. Their names were Ted and Maryann Jensen, and they invited Marq and Daryl and me to their home every week. We'd join them in whatever they and their four kids were doing. Sometimes they'd just be watching a Padres game on television or shooting hoops in the backyard or going out for hamburgers, or, as was often the case, making the biggest, sloppiest, gooiest hot fudge sundaes I'd ever seen. I could never finish one of those super-sweet concoctions, but I had fun trying.

"T.J.," as Mr. Jensen was known, was a 275-pound auto insurance salesman who insisted he wasn't fat, just too short for his weight. He showed up regularly at the San Dieguito High basketball games. That struck us hard; our father had never been around to watch us play basketball.

T.J. always sat on the bottom bleacher and yelled instructions to Marq and me. "C'mon!" I heard him shout a thousand times. "You're loafing! Pick it up! Pick it up!" It would have been annoying except that we were so touched that someone had taken the time to come out and watch us play. And he didn't show up just once in a while. T.J. somehow found a way to make it to every home game we played that season. We came to count on seeing him on the bottom bleacher when we jogged out for warm-ups.

He watched everything we did and saw things even the coach routinely missed. "Relax and play your game," he shouted at Marq over and over again. "Relax!" We didn't know why this middle-aged man with six children of his own had decided to take a remarkably keen interest in us, but we didn't ask questions. His presence made Marq and me play with a purpose and effort we would never have otherwise mustered.

"I saw a little potential in you two guys," he told me years later. "I didn't want to see you waste yours the way I wasted mine because I took it for granted." T.J. often spoke of what might have been if he'd played minor-league baseball.

People like the Jensens and others, who reached out to make us feel welcome in a place where we were outcasts, helped our wounded family heal a little.

Thanks to T.J., a near stranger who went out of his way to encourage me, I salvaged my childhood determination, fostered by my father, to get into college on a sports scholarship. Indeed, after two years without any contact or financial support from my father, I knew that making somebody's basketball team would be my only way of pulling off what at the time seemed impossible.

I didn't know why I was so determined to seek a higher education. My parents hadn't encouraged it, specifically. Neither of my brothers seemed interested in continuing their education after high school; Daryl wouldn't even graduate. For many of my classmates, graduation was just the natural conclusion to hanging around for four years without getting pregnant or arrested. But I just had this opinion of myself, and it seemed to me that I should go to college.

❧❧❧

Encouraged by her newfound friends, my mother decided to start dating again. This time, she thought, she'd do it right. No more flashy FBI spies or fast-talking lawyers. And no more drinkers. She'd only associate with men who were well mannered and sober. She'd find them, she believed, at church-sponsored dances. Her friends said she'd have her pick of San Diego County's eligible Mormon bachelors. They were right. She met dozens of polite, middle-aged men. We hadn't even known that she and my father were divorced, but we knew she needed company and another chance, and we didn't give her a hard time. When she came home from her first dance, beaming like a prom queen, she found her sons waiting up for her.

"Young lady," Marq said, pretending to scold, "where have you been at all hours of the night?"

"We've been worried sick about you!" I chided.

"Check her neck for hickies!" Daryl howled.

We collapsed into laughter, and Mom laughed along with us.

At her third dance, she met a man named Bill. "I noticed him right away," she said years later. "He was by far the best dancer on the floor." My mother, the dance instructor, would naturally spot the best hoofer in the hall. She'd gone right over and asked him to dance. "Wallflowers my age were wilting!"

Bill was the one. He was overweight, but he stayed light on his feet and led with a sure hand. Mom was impressed from the start. "He was a charming man, very courteous and quick to laugh." Bill said all the right things and made all the right moves, on and off the dance floor. And why not? He'd had plenty of experience; he'd already been married *four* times.

When things got serious between them, Bill disclosed his track record, but my mother was unconcerned. She was impatient, and she was flattered by his attention. Despite her age, she was fairly new at this sort of thing. Bill, after all, was only the second man who had ever courted her. She would come to regret not having looked into the reasons behind her suitor's multiple marriage failures.

The first time Bill walked into our apartment, he smiled nervously, his hand grasping Mom's. His cheeks were flushed. He was a big, burly, white-haired man with a high-pitched voice that made him sound as if he were whining. He worked as a high school math teacher eight months of the year, with a sideline in driver's ed, and during summers he was a draftsman at the gigantic Convair aerospace plant in San Diego. He had never fathered a child. I sensed, as kids can, that he detested young people. Marq and Daryl and I were wary, and it showed. We forced smiles and stood back and said nothing.

Our mother's fondest wish was to have a man in the home, someone who would provide the leadership she felt her sons needed. She hoped that maybe a father-figure-in-residence would keep her boys around the house a little longer. She could tell that my brothers and I had our sights fixed on the door. She wanted to finish raising us before we left the nest. Maybe Bill would make us a family again.

One evening, the two of them sat on the couch and told us that they were getting married and that Bill would be moving in with us. We'd known that this was coming. It seemed so strange, seeing our mother holding hands with a stranger, professing love for him. We nodded and smiled as best we could.

I was surprised that I felt almost nothing upon hearing this announcement. I was even pleased—in a detached, mature way—to think that Mom might be happier now that she'd found someone. Somehow I knew that this marriage would have no direct effect on me. I had plans, I was on my way out. But Marq and Daryl had no plans, and they saw Bill as an intrusion into this family they still depended on, although it hardly existed any longer.

"We already have a father," Marq complained as we lay in our beds that night talking about Bill.

"No one can take Dad's place," Daryl declared.

The wedding was at the Mormon chapel on Lake Drive. There were about 30 guests. My mother cried, and Bill stood there with a giddy grin on his face, as though he'd never done this before. My brothers and I sneaked out and wrote "Just Married" across the side of his green Ford LTD with a bar of soap. We tied streamers to the antenna and tin cans to the rear bumper. When Bill and his bride emerged from the chapel, he was not amused. He stood on the top step frowning, his face turning pink. Mom poked him and squeezed him and said, "Don't be grumpy on your wedding day." He smiled and helped her in, and the two drove off for a three-day honeymoon.

When they returned, Bill moved in. He'd filled the trunk and the back seat of his car with his belongings, and he told us to carry the stuff into the house.

His first act as stepfather was to call us to the dining room table for a "family meeting." For a moment, he said nothing, just looked portentously from one face to the next.

"Boys," he began, "you don't know me, so let me tell you a few things. I'm tough. I'm fair, but I'm tough. Don't even think of trying to put anything over on me, because it won't work and you'll be sorry." He smiled in satisfaction. Out of the corner of my eye, I could see Marq's hands clenching and unclenching in his lap, his forearms almost imperceptibly trembling.

"I'm also big on responsibility," Bill went on in his little, strangulated voice. "Very big on responsibility. I teach math, yes, but what I really teach my students is responsibility. You can't learn responsibility young enough, that's what I always say."

He looked to Mom for endorsement. She tried to seem supportive, but her expression was artificial.

"So here it is," Bill said. "From this day forward, you boys are going to pay rent. No more freeloading. No, sir. You're going to make a positive contribution in the family. No better way to learn responsibility."

Pay rent in our own home? I couldn't believe it.

Mom's eyes widened. I could see her trying to summon the courage to inform Bill that both Marq and I already contributed a good part of what we earned from our after-school jobs. Her lips parted, but nothing came out.

❦❦❦

Marq had always said, "Don't worry. Someday we'll be old enough to get out." When I walked across the stage at San Dieguito Union High School and collected my diploma from the principal, Mr. Morris, my bags were already packed. Although just 17, younger than my classmates thanks to my early start in school 12 years before, I was now old enough to leave home. I was getting out.

Ted and Maryann Jensen came to the ceremony; Bill did not. After it was over, Mom and my brothers and I got into the Pinto and drove to the bus in downtown San Diego. I sat in the back with Marq, our long legs folded up to fit in the cramped space. It was hard to imagine Marq not being there to guide me. I'd been following him since I was old enough to crawl, but now, leaving home, I'd be following him no more.

He had graduated from high school the year before and had gone on to a local junior college where he had unsuccessfully tried to make the basketball team. Now he was moping around campus, trying to keep from flunking out, and holding down a job as a night-shift janitor. I'd miss him very much, and I knew he'd miss me, too.

With Mom it was different. I knew she loved me, but I also knew that she was worried about the tension between her difficult new husband and her resentful sons. My absence would make life simpler for her. She would wish me well and breathe a very quiet sigh of relief, I was sure, when I got on that Greyhound.

The four of us stood close in the middle of the busy station waiting for the bus to be announced. We boys had our hands in our pockets and nervously scuffed our feet on the blue-and-gray linoleum floor. We chuckled at Mom. Her eyes were welling with tears, and she'd run out of tissues. She was folding her moist ones inside out to wipe the streaking mascara from her cheeks.

To see me off, she had made herself up and put on a silk maroon blouse and a pair of dressy pants. As I studied her face, trying to memorize it before I left, I noticed how she'd aged. The strain of a 20-year bad marriage showed—in the loose skin under the eyes, the thinning hair, and the pallid complexion. My mother's beauty had not been erased, but it had been eroded.

Marq looked at Mom and then back at me. "Give her a hug," he said gruffly, nudging me toward her with his elbow. Hearing that from rough, tough Marq caught me off guard and snapped the chain I'd wrapped around my feelings. I turned to my mother.

She put down the plastic bag full of snacks she'd prepared for me. Then she hitched her purse strap over her right shoulder and held out her arms. "Come on, you big lug," she said gently. "I won't bite."

I dropped my adolescent self-consciousness and pose of indifference and put my arms around her. I was shocked to see how much taller I'd grown since the last time I'd hugged her, whenever that might have been. My little mother pulled me down and squeezed me tight. This hug was meant to last.

"Mom," I complained, "you got makeup on my shirt!" Marq and Daryl laughed.

"Oh, you'll live," she said, and playfully swatted me on the arm.

An announcement crackled over the terminal's loudspeakers: Greyhound Coach Number 305 was ready for boarding.

It was time to say good-bye to Marq and Daryl. "All right, you punks," I said, "let's get this over with." I stepped up to Marq, not knowing exactly what to do. We had never done this before, never separated from each other, never shown each other open affection. Once again it struck me that for the first time in my life, I'd be out from under the wing of Marq's protection. It scared me.

Marq made the first move. He held up his right hand and said, "High five, bro."

"High five," I said, a lump in my throat. Our right hands met with a clap above our heads and he held tight, squeezing my hand in his.

Sweet Daryl pushed closer, eager to say his farewell. "Good luck, Jon," he mumbled, his voice breaking. We looked downward, too bashful to let our eyes meet. Our handshake was long. I looked up. Daryl's cheeks were puffing and turning red, and he was starting to cry. I pulled him into me and held him in the only hug I'd ever given him.

"You be good, Daryl," I said.

"I will," he said, his voice quavering, his head still bowed.

My brothers and I had supported each other when there was no help from any other source. We had been everything to each other. Now we were separating. I was going, they were staying, although soon they too would go, disappearing down their own paths, and none of us would know where to find the others.

I boarded the bus. My seat was on the wrong side of the bus—not the platform side, but the other one. Between the bodies of the other boarding passengers, I caught only glimpses of my family as they stood there searching for me through the blackened glass. Mom was wiping her eyes. Red-faced Daryl crossed his arms and squeezed as if it was all he could do to contain his emotions. Marq stood tall, almost at attention, his open hand still waving, as if he wanted it to be the last thing I saw as I departed. I closed my eyes and felt the bus move under me.

The driver backed the bus out, then put it in forward, and my trip began. I was bound for South Carolina. That's where Dad was.

CHAPTER SEVEN ⚜
Humpback Jack from Across the Track

Getting an education wasn't the only reason I was desperate to get into Anderson Junior College. I knew my father had moved back to South Carolina, and I longed to see him again. He had phoned a few times during the previous two years, just to say hello and ask how everyone was doing. We hadn't talked much, but he did say he'd hung out his shingle in Walhalla again and had started a new law practice.

I called directory assistance to get his number. They didn't have one for him, so I called his younger brother, Jimmy.

Uncle Jimmy was one of the best friends my brothers and I had when we were growing up. At least one Sunday a month, Dad loaded us into the car and drove us the 30 miles to Walhalla, where we played with our cousins. Jimmy's eldest son, Ronnie, my age, could run rings around Marq and me on the basketball court, both of us at the same time.

Jimmy was a younger version of my father. He looked the same, with his sizable nose, his sculpted jaw line, his Paul Newman eyelids, and his curly hair, a lock of which he was always twirling between his thumb and forefinger. Like my father, Uncle Jimmy could make us laugh until we begged for breath. He had a gift for making amiable fun of whoever or whatever happened by. Laugh at Jimmy once, and you'd hear the same joke in 12 more versions as he milked it for every giggle he could get. Both Dad and Jimmy stuck out their tongues to help them concentrate.

That's where the similarities between my father's behavior and Jimmy's ended, though. Jimmy was a careful drinker with a level head and a conservative approach to life. He had married his high school sweetheart, a tall, slender, soft-spoken woman from the other side of Oconee County. He and Aunt Connie still lived in the same house they'd built shortly after they were married, a little brick rambler at the foot of my grandfather's hill.

I hoped Uncle Jimmy and his family would be as eager to see me as I was to see them. I thought of Aunt Connie's great southern-cooked meals—chicken fried in yesterday's grease, just like Grandma's, with all the fixings. Maybe Aunt Connie would invite me to their table.

Jimmy seemed delighted to hear I was coming east, but he didn't give me a number for my father. I got the feeling that Dad didn't have a phone. Jimmy said he'd make sure Dad got my message and that I should call back that evening about seven.

At seven, my heart thumping, I made the call. "Hey, great, Jonny," Dad said when I told him about the try-out. "You come on back. We'll have a hell of a time, just the two of us cruising around." He spoke in that familiar tone, the one he used when he was trying to put a spin on something, trying to disguise some fact. But my guard was down, and I clicked right into it. My only thought was that I was going to see my father for the first time in three years.

I was so absorbed by that prospect that I was hardly conscious of the bus trip across the country. As the bus neared Anderson, traveling the familiar route my brothers and I had taken to school every morning in the back of the old beige Mercedes, my nose was pressed to the window. I remembered every bend in Clemson Highway. We crossed the bridge over the narrow arm of Lake Hartwell; Marq and I had spent countless summer days diving from the guardrail into the murky waters.

The gas station where I'd sneaked my first taste of beer when I was 13 was still there, with the same "Out of Order" sign on the same pump. Grocery carts still littered the parking lot of the Winn-Dixie supermarket. Nothing had changed, nothing at all, except the building that used to be the Marquise Du Pre School of Dance. It was now a nightclub. Despite the sameness, Anderson looked entirely different to me this time. It wasn't the center of the universe. It was just another Appalachian town.

Dad met me at the depot. I ran to where he stood and wrapped my arms around him. Neither of us let go for several minutes. We had a reunion right there in the terminal, and as we stood talking, I took a good look at him. He seemed much older, badly worn, unhealthy. He'd lost a lot more hair. I could see he'd been drinking heavily, and it had hurt him. On the bus I'd wondered if he was a successful trial lawyer again with a brand new practice or down-and-out. Now I saw that he was neither. He was hanging around, hoping to get lucky. That was what he'd been trying to disguise.

I thought of asking him the question that had burned inside me those two years, the question not even God had seemed able to answer: Why had he left us? I realized I didn't want to get into that. I was focused now on my future. More than that, I was seeing him, along with Anderson, in a different light. He wasn't my father so much as a man. He had changed for me, and I had changed, too. Two years of taking care of myself and helping Mom take care of us and getting through school by hook or crook had made me independent. When he'd left, he'd cut the cord. I didn't look to him anymore; I'd learned to rely on myself.

Coach Wyles had invited me to stay at his house the first night, and Dad said he'd drive me there. We tossed my bags—a khaki Army duffel I'd found in a high school locker and a blue gym bag I'd borrowed from Marq—into the trunk of his white Chevy Vega. There I was, sitting next to him in a car again, going down the streets of Anderson as if on our way to school or a Klan rally or Miss Tilly's. Memories hazed my thoughts and made me feel like a child again. It was an uncomfortable sensation.

When Dad pulled the car to the curb at Coach Wyles's house, I could see he was hoping to come in with me. I didn't pick up on it. I wanted to see the coach alone and start my new life. I was going my own way.

"Give me a call when you can," he finally said.

"My try-out's tomorrow night," I said. "We'll probably scrimmage in the gym about seven o'clock."

"I'd like to come by for that."

"That'd be great." I wanted him to come. He had never once seen me play basketball in high school, and I wanted to show him what I could do. Although I couldn't have thought of it at the time, I wanted my father to see me in a new context. I wanted him to see how I'd grown and matured. I wanted him to see me as a man. We said good-bye, and I grabbed my two bags and headed up the walk.

The next day, I was busy settling into an empty dorm room, which the coach had arranged as my sleeping quarters for the rest of my three-day stay, when my father showed up. I could tell he was just killing time. *Doesn't he have anything to do?* When I finished unpacking my bags, I set out to explore campus, using a little map the coach had given me. Dad followed along, continuing the one-sided conversation he'd begun the day before, stories I'd heard many times.

"So I hung my shingle in Walhalla. All the lawyers in that county will shit a brick when they find out Bob Du Pre is practicing law again." It had been chatter until he said that. I stopped in front of the student union and turned to him.

"Nobody knows you're practicing law again?" I asked sharply. For the first time in my life, I spoke down to my father. I don't mean I spoke disrespectfully; I mean I physically spoke from a higher position. I was now taller than he. And immediately, he was as uncomfortable looking up at me as I was looking down at him. My height and my terse question had stopped him in his tracks. His response revealed that he felt threatened.

"What the fuck kind of smartass question is that?" he snapped back, jutting out his chin and opening his eyes wide. It worked. I backpedaled.

"Naw, I'm not trying to be a smartass. It just sounded like you said you just barely opened a law practice. I thought that's why you came back here in the first place."

"If you listen like that in the classroom, young college smartass, you'll flunk out of this school. What I said was the lawyers in *that* county will shit a brick when they find out I'm practicing law again, leaving open the possibility that the lawyers in *this* county already know I'm practicing law again. Got it, hotshot college boy?"

"Got it. Got it. I understand now, professor." And I did. He'd slipped and tried to cover his tracks, but I saw where he was going. I knew enough to know Oconee and Anderson Counties were part of the same judicial district. If he'd been lawyering in Anderson, they would have known in Walhalla. Hell, everyone in the South Carolina's criminal court system would have heard about it by now. Three years earlier, he'd walked out of our little Encinitas apartment. I guess we boys just assumed he'd returned to his homeland to go back to work. We should have known better. He hadn't sent back a dime. And now that I was back, he was on the spot to make it look good. He'd either just rented office space in Walhalla and hung out a shingle, or he was feeding me a line of crap. I had a feeling it was the latter. *What the hell has my father been doing for three years?* My head started spinning, and it scared me to think about it.

I found out years later that Dad had already begun slipping into a sort of occupational limbo. He hadn't held a steady job since he'd left us in Encinitas. Part of the reason he'd stayed stubbornly unemployed stemmed from the false pride that had become his hallmark; the rest of the reason had to do with his realization that he was almost unemployable. After nearly 15 years of practicing law, Bob Du Pre was not only too proud to apply for a menial job, he was too specially trained to be able to learn new skills. The once-revered and hated litigator was left to grovel for odd clerking jobs with the few lawyers in South Carolina who weren't afraid to be associated with him. Dad picked up a little cash here and there, but mostly, he survived by relying on his relatives' strong southern sense of obligation.

What *did* occur to me was that this might be the biggest day of my young life so far, and I couldn't afford to let myself get distracted. Suddenly, I was irritated by the fact that my father was oblivious to the importance of what I was about to do—that is, try to get in to college. All he could think about was making himself look good. I turned away and continued walking, trying to get the feel of this place. Dad followed again, this time without speaking. After a couple of hours, he decided he'd had enough.

"I can see you're all set here," he said, trying to make it sound as if he was my one-man orientation committee. I saw him differently now. Smaller, somehow. A petty manipulator, always on the make. "I'll be back around seven."

"Yea. See ya then," I replied, hardly looking back at him. He disappeared.

This was not the way I had envisioned our reunion. I thought about all those nights, laying in bed, begging for another chance to see my father. And now that we were back together, I'd brushed him aside. It seemed perversely disloyal that I should be distracted by selfish interests at a time like this. On the other hand, what was I doing here, anyway? I was trying to fulfill a promise made years earlier—a promise made to my father and myself during all those hot summer afternoons under the rickety basketball hoop in the dream house driveway, and all those long nights at the YMCA gym—that someday I would be a ballplayer. In that light, maybe it was my father breaking a promise—the promise that he would help me.

❖❖❖

Tall trophies gleamed with confidence behind the glass of the display cabinet that dominated the gymnasium lobby. They advertised Coach Jim Wyles's teams' many accomplishments during his ten years at Anderson College. There were tournament championships, a top-five finish in the national finals, and a slew of junior college all-America standouts. There was Barry Isom, the hometown product who'd gone on star at Virginia Tech. It had only been a few years earlier that Marq and I had sneaked into the gym to watch the Trojans play. We always scanned the crowd for middle-aged men who looked like major college scouts. There were always a smattering of them, watching studiously, taking notes. It was a surreal feeling to be walking into the same gym again—this time, to play.

The low rumble of bouncing balls told me that I was not the first to arrive. I parted the "Trojans" logo painted on the double doors and walked onto the court. The sight was startling. These people were bigger and much more menacing-looking than the Trojans of a few years earlier. Under the near basket were four of the blackest guys I'd ever seen, all of whom stood 6'7" or taller. Under the far basket was a giant of about 6'11"; he must have weighed 275 pounds, solid muscle. I suddenly felt a long, long way from San Diego County, where basketball was, for the most part, played by undersized white guys, though fast and well organized. These Anderson College guys were enormous and strong and appeared serious . . . and very, very black. Thankfully, nobody had seen me enter.

I picked up a ball and went to a side basket and started shooting, half hoping that no one would notice me. It had been a few months since I'd played any serious hoops, and I felt rusty. Another ball rolled my way. I picked it up and instinctively flipped it behind my back, in the direction of the four medium-sized giants under the near goal. My pass had a little too much pace on it, and it caught one of the guys off-guard, slipping through his hands and hitting him on the chest. The others chuckled. That directed their attention my way.

The group, four guys, walked over to my basket. "You with us?" one of them said.

"You mean, tonight?" I asked, unsure.

"I mean, are you the 12th man?"

"Oh. I don't know yet," I said. "I guess we'll see what happens tonight." I gathered from his question that there was one more open spot, the 12th on the roster. Coach Wyles had been vague about the details of my try-out.

"Wass yo name?" one of them asked.

"Du Pre."

"Pre? Wutt kinda name is that?"

"*Du*," I said. "*Du* Pre. Jon Du Pre." They all shrugged, an indication that they weren't impressed because they hadn't heard the name, meaning Coach Wyles hadn't mentioned that I was coming. For basketball players, reputation is half the game.

"I'm Kevin. . . Dunbar High School. . . Baltimore." Then he just peered down at me.

"Great," I responded politely. "Nice to meet you."

"What, you ain't heard of Dunbar High? The number-two high school team in the nation?"

I paused. "No, why?" More laughter.

This try-out was not getting off to a wonderful start. Already I'd hit one of the giants in the chest with a ball, and disrespected another in front of his teammates. The last thing I wanted was for one of these mammoths to want to humiliate me once the scrimmage started.

It wasn't that I was afraid of them. They weren't at all hostile. Mostly they seemed curious, as though they were studying an animal in a zoo. I was a white guy, one of two in the gymnasium that evening. I had a bronze tan, and my hair flowed long and blonde. Instead of a silky mesh tank-top jersey bearing the logo of some basketball camp or all-star game or high school champion, I wore an old white T-shirt with holes in it and a "Pepsi" logo steam-pressed on the chest. It had been Marq's. He'd let me take it from his drawer, and I wore it because it was like having him there with me. All in all, I added up to strange. To these kids from Alabama, Georgia, and the Carolinas, I was a novelty.

Besides Kevin, I met Reggie and also John, whom everyone called "Moose" because he was as big as one. Also Winbush, who had the biggest hands I'd ever seen dangling from the ends of a human being's arms. "My homies call me 'Nutbush,'" he told me.

"So, what do *I* call you?" I asked.

"I'll let you know," he said with a wry smile. "And for now, I won't call you nunudat *'Du-pee'* shit, o whatever the fuck yo name is. How 'bout yo name be *Humpback Jack from Across the Track?*" They all cackled. Winbush was poking a little fun at the way I slumped when I walked, still uneasy with my height, five inches of which I'd gained during the past year and a half. I pretended to laugh along with the others. What else was I going to do?

It was a relief to start the scrimmage because it took their attention off me. But now there was a new, more unsettling scrutiny. I could practically feel Coach Wyles's eyes following me. He had already seen the others perform. I was the reason for tonight's assembly. As the game got under way, with my future now on the line, I replayed in my head the advice T.J. had given me:

"Stay loose. Don't force it. Let the game come to *you.*"

The coach put me at point guard. My job was to bring the ball up the court and get some kind of improvised offense going. The first few runs up and down the court, I handled and distributed the ball without incident. I soon saw that the four other guys on my team, one of whom was Kevin, knew when and where to post up—to take their positions close to the basket—which made it easy for me to pass the ball in to them for a score. Kevin turned and scored three times in a row. Things were going well.

Then they got better. The other team's point guard, the one who'd been heavily recruited out of high school, a speedster from downstate named George, was bringing the ball up the floor. I waited for him at half-court, noticing that he seemed a little lazy with the ball. He'd probably sized me up and decided I'd be no threat. I decided to try and take him by surprise. I darted at him before he reached the mid-court stripe. He put his left foot down to change direction, and began a spin move, intending to wrap himself around me and keep going. His mistake was that he carried the ball around the spin with his outside hand, leaving the ball exposed for a fraction of a second. It was a ball-handling error Coach Wyles himself had preached against when I attended his summer camps as a boy. I reached behind George's back, and during the middle of his dribble, picked off the ball.

The east end of the court was empty. I pushed the ball ahead of me and sprinted along behind it. Planting my foot, I jumped at the basket. To my amazement, I rose high, higher than I ever had, holding the ball well above the rim. There was a sharp impulse to dunk it, but I'd never done that and didn't know how. So I laid it off the glass and let it softly drop in the basket. When I turned around, I saw George still standing at half-court, stunned, staring at me as if to see through my white skin and find a black guy, since no white kid could ever have picked him off like that.

"Go, Humpback, you skinny muthufucka!" Winbush squealed. "White boy got game," I heard someone else say. I wanted to glance at Wyles, just to make sure he'd seen the play, but I resisted the temptation, trying to appear unimpressed by what I'd just done—I'd found a new identity, and just maybe, a slightly open back door to college.

It was then that I heard an all-too-familiar voice from the bleachers: "Attaboy, Jonny! That's kickin' some ass!"

I groaned. This wasn't the kind of shouted encouragement Dad had bestowed during all those front-yard football games of my youth. This time his shout was gravelly and slurred. It was my father's drunk voice.

Oh God, no. Not tonight.

He was plastered, just arriving, stumbling into the bleachers. He plopped down about halfway up and began barking out instructions to me as if he were my personal trainer. "John Roach, John Roach! Drive and dish, drive and dish!" he barked. The stale reference was to the endless backyard games we'd played on the dirt court behind the dream house. We'd devised the play when I was 11 years old while watching John Roach on television. He was the all-America guard at my father's alma mater, the University of South Carolina, and known for his ability to drive the lane, draw the double-team, and dish the ball off to his big man. The reference was horribly outdated, a reminder of the years we'd lost.

As if he were auditioning for an assistant coach's position, as if this night were about *him*, my father was trying to make it look as though he'd taught me everything I knew. He was taking credit for what I'd learned during those endless hours in the gym at the YMCA, stranded, waiting for him to pick us up and take my brothers and me home. Rather than an encouragement, his presence was a terribly distracting frustration. I found myself playing the game while keeping one eye on the indigent and irritable fan in the stands, all the while stealing glances at Coach Wyles to see if he had noticed my father. I was grateful for the noise of the game, the squeak of rubber on lacquered wood every time anyone started or stopped or changed direction, the rumble of floor every time anyone jumped and landed, and the constant shouting between players . . . "Ball!

Ball! I'm open! Hit me!" "Pick right! Pick right! Help side!" "Rebound! Outlet! Outlet!" "Yeah, baby! In yo face!" "Git that weak stuff outa here!" It all helped drown out the drunken heckler—almost.

The scrimmage ended at last. "Come over here, boy," Dad called out, waving me to him. "Come on over here." He wanted to analyze my game, tell me what I'd done wrong and what I'd done right. At the same time, Coach Wyles was motioning me over. I made a beeline for the coach, who was standing at the half-court stripe in his well-creased slacks and golf shirt, his hair perfectly parted. He looked like the clean-cut middle-aged men who model men's wear in the Sears catalogue. "I like what I saw, Jon," he said. "We'll get together tomorrow and talk."

I was so preoccupied with embarrassment about my father, I hardly noticed that the coach had just told me I'd passed the test. My attention was focused on how I would get out of the gymnasium without the players noticing that the drunk in the bleachers was mine. I didn't go over to him but stood around talking to some of the other guys. "You play point guard in high school, Humpback? California boys got game or what? Why you come all the way back here, Humpback? Why you didn't stay on the beach and play at Long Beach State or somewhere?" I had won a small measure of respect from these players who'd intimidated me at first sight. But rather than feeling a sense of euphoria over my accomplishment, I could only think of making my exit.

Dad had to stand to the side and wait. That made me edgy. I remembered well that when he was drunk, he was touchy about things like that. I didn't want to talk with him for fear he might explode at me for running to Coach Wyles instead of him. I couldn't let that happen in front of the guys I might be spending the next two years with. I jogged to the sidelines and picked up my sweatshirt and motioned for Dad to meet me outside.

"Wyles said he liked what he saw," I told him. "We're going to talk tomorrow."

"Well, hell yes, he liked what he saw," Dad said. "I always knew you had the stuff to play college ball. This'll be your tune-up for big-time NCAA competition. I always knew you had the talent." He went on and on, self-importantly. I patiently nodded my head, looking around for someone who might interrupt the conversation. I wanted to say something about his showing up drunk, but I didn't dare. Even though, at 6'4", I was three inches taller than my father, I was still a child in his presence. I didn't know how to scold a parent. I didn't want to anyway. And I was still afraid of how he might react. I couldn't let him blow up on me. Not here.

"I'd better hit the showers," I said. By the time I'd dressed, it was almost ten o'clock. He waited outside the locker room. We walked to his Vega, and he opened the door. This time, instead of a hug, we gave each other a quick handshake, and he drove away. Our reunion was over. I had found the reason for coming back to the South, and it wasn't my father. My growing sense was that if I wanted to make something of this stroke of great fortune, selfish and sad as it seemed, I would be better off avoiding him.

I met Coach Wyles in his office under the gym the next afternoon. "I'll take you up to Dean Stanley's office," he said. "He's the dean of student affairs. He has the scholarship forms you need to sign." I heard him say the word *scholarship*, but it took a few seconds for it to register. *Scholarship*, I thought. *He said scholarship!* It was all I could do to keep from screaming and jumping for joy. I'd done it. I'd realized a childhood dream—to get into college on a basketball scholarship. No matter that it was a junior college. I might just as well have been signing a letter of intent to play at UCLA or Indiana or North Carolina. Suddenly there was an unfamiliar but exhilarating sense of freedom and relief. At long last I was on my own. I was taking care of myself.

Careful attention to the coach's instructions, plenty of hustle in practice, and surprisingly good speed to go along with my marksmanship made me the seventh man on the squad, the first guard off the bench. It was a high-powered team, at one time during the year ranking seventh among the nation's junior college teams. I played a backup role to two junior college all-Americas, so I was happy to be getting in the game at all. I made the most of it.

I lived in the dorm and ate in the cafeteria—breakfast, lunch, and dinner. For the first time in years, maybe ever, I was eating a regular, nutritious diet. I gained a lot of weight, filling out my frame, growing into myself. More important, I was growing into a new self-image. It wasn't long before I had a circle of friends—teammates, dorm-mates, girls—and was having a wonderful time. Teammates would call out my new nickname when they saw me on campus— "Humpback! Wassup, Jack?" They didn't know how well their pet name fit me—the boy from across the track, or just across from the auto shop behind the high school, as the case might be. I'd left Encinitas far behind. I was still the kid with no money and no car, but so was everyone else who mattered to me. The worried expression on my face slowly disappeared. Here, nobody knew my background, nobody knew my parents. I was an equal.

During the course of the year, I made four especially close friendships, the kind of relationships that gave me a comforting sense of belonging. Al, our team captain and a first-team all-America guard, was a handsome, mild-mannered, intelligent guy from deep in South Carolina's rural peanut farming country, who seemed intrigued by the idea that I'd come from California. "I know about black folk," he would say. "It's you white people I haven't figured out yet." This was Al's good-natured way of under-explaining his preference for socializing with people he could relate to rather than people he was expected to associate with. There was Ken, Al's roommate, a sharp-shooting guard from suburban Chicago, a bright kid with unruly red hair and a wit to match. Millie was a petite dark-haired, brown-eyed girl with soft, pouting lips and a pert little rear end, who rarely spoke and only then in a whiny voice that somehow made her seem irresistibly cute, in the true Southern tradition.

Fond as I was of these three, they were merely the supporting cast to the director of our social stage play, Kathy. Killian, as she insisted we call her because the commonness of her given name betrayed her extraordinary personality, was the freckle-faced, chipmunk-cheeked, blue-eyed daughter of a Baptist minister and the head cheerleader for our basketball team. Nobody was paired with anyone romantically, although Al and Ken and I sometimes spoke in private guy-talk of what it might be like to lure Millie up to our dorm and make her whine with delight. On weekends, while other kids were getting drunk at fraternity parties, Killian would rally us to some expedition, always a pursuit of harmless fun, whether it was a movie or a hike or a panty raid or a trip to a forbidden nightclub. Oh yeah, I remember that place.

One Friday night during the fall semester, she called us together and announced, "All right, you guys, we're going to The Whip!" Everyone had heard of the place, but none of us had ever been there. The five of us piled in to Ken's car, joined by a cute little blonde girl named Annie whom Killian had invited so we'd be an even number of people and everyone would have a dance partner. Navigating from the back seat, Killian took us to Greenville, an actual city about a half hour's drive from Anderson.

"Take the 291 bypass," she ordered.

"Wait a minute!" Ken shouted. "There's nothing on the 291 bypass!"

"Trust me," she insisted.

Five miles along 291, Killian chirped, "There it is!" We spotted a small, slatted, tar-shingled roadside structure. There were neon beer signs in the tiny windows on either side of the big steel entrance door, and the dirt parking lot was jammed with cars, mostly dented old Cadillacs on skinny tires with fat white sidewalls. Painted on the door of the building was its name: "The Whip."

"Oh, no," Al protested from the back seat. "Killian, this time you've gone too far, girl! You ain't gittin' me in there." This was an all-black bar and dance hall, and our African-American friend Al wasn't about to be seen walking in with five lily-whites. Killian didn't give him a chance to resist. Her enthusiasm was far stronger than Al's fear. Head bowed and hands in pants pockets, Al slunk in.

The lighting was dim. The air smelled of cigarette smoke and malt liquor— richer and nuttier than the sour scent of beer—mixed with the unmistakably sweet tinge of "Afro Sheen," the greasy hair care products black people slathered on their heads in those days, when it was fashionable to straighten and smooth their thick, kinky locks. Once my eyes adjusted, I saw dozens of dark faces floating in the smoky haze, nearly all of them looking at us, but none with a threatening expression. They seemed more curious than anything. My compatriots didn't dare look up, so they didn't notice whether the crowd appeared angry or apathetic.

"My red 'fro doesn't exactly fit in here. Maybe this wasn't such a good idea," Ken said softly.

"Killian, let's get out of here," Millie muttered.

"I'm a dead man," Al moaned.

I couldn't help but enjoy the moment. I'd been in the company of black people most of my life—in school, on playgrounds and in gymnasiums, in friends' homes, in the rear waiting room of our family doctor's office, and particularly, at my father's law office as he worked with clients, most of whom were African-Americans. If there was one thing I knew about them, it was that I was safe in their presence. They weren't at all like southern whites—crudely judgmental, standoffish, and segregationist. My experience had been that I was almost always made to feel welcome whenever my brothers and I found ourselves surrounded by black people. Someone would always say something like, "What da fuck yawl Unca Remuses doin in the black 'hood?!"

The question was never meant as a threat—rather, an expression of genuine astonishment. "Unca Remus" was what southerners of the 1960s and '70s called whites who associated with people of color. It was supposed to mean the opposite of "Uncle Tom," the nickname tagged on black people who kept the company of whites. Whether any of my black friends and neighbors in the South had ever read the classic American novel *Uncle Tom's Cabin,* I didn't know. We surely had never seen the book in English class at the junior high school. But it was generally understood that the book told the story of a slave who sympathized with white people. Where Uncles Tom's opposite, Uncle Remus, came from, that I can't say. What was clear was that black people used the term somewhat affectionately, in contrast to the way they sneered when they called someone an "Unca Tom." I took it as a compliment, especially when it was followed by someone else saying something like, "Don't worry, Remus, ain't nobody gonna fuck wit cha 'round here." I was confident that our little group of interlopers was safe at "The Whip."

At that moment, especially to Al's relief, the show began. "Ladies and gentlemens!" the announcer called out in his best James Brown imitation. "The Whip proudly brang you . . . the one, the only . . . The Plattas!"

Out strode four skinny old men in powder-blue tuxedos, gaudier than the rented one I'd worn to the junior-senior high school prom. They spun in unison and shuffle-stepped up to their microphones and started their show. And what a show it was. They belted out the great Motown hits of the '60s: "What I Say" and "My Girl" and "How Sweet It Is," substituting falsetto voices for the women's parts, along with their signature hit, "Under the Boardwalk." Whether they were the "One and Only" Platters or a crude knock-off of the Motown recording stars, no one seemed to notice. And neither did anyone seem to care any longer about the five white intruders and their friend.

Killian, who was at least a foot shorter than I, grabbed my hand and yanked me out to the middle of the dance floor. Ken and Millie and Annie and Al joined us. We quickly forgot our surroundings and let ourselves cut loose. We hooted and whistled and cheered as the old men on the stage sweated and grinned and worked the crowd with every number. Before the night was over, we were imperishable fans of the Platters, and welcome guests of The Whip.

I'd never had fun like that. I'd never had the time, the money, the clothes, the self-confidence, or the maturity to enjoy companionship on this level. I'd never been able to permit myself to be carefree, even for a few hours. One night at The Whip had opened up new realms of joy.

But the old unhappiness continued to dog me. Dad came to a couple of games during the year, always drunk. I knew when he was there, because when they'd announce the starting lineup and I wasn't on it, I'd hear that voice from about halfway up the bleachers yelling to the coach. "Come on, Wyles, put my boy in! He's better than the nigger you got out there!"

Drinking made him nasty. Words he would have detested when he was sober flew from his mouth when he was drunk. Just as I had cringed when I heard him say degrading things to my mother during their fights, I now shuddered as I sat on the sidelines trying not to hear his tirades from the bleachers. I felt ashamed. How could I tell the crowd that Dad had put himself on the line for black people for years and that they should make allowances? How could I tell *myself*?

For three long years after my father left us, I'd wanted to be reunited with him, have him be part of my life, and to be part of *his* life—the two of us enjoying each other's successes. I'd had visions of finally getting to show him how well I could play ball. This was a critical time for me. Every high school ballplayer wonders if he'll be good enough to play college ball, and now I was doing it. Yet when Dad showed up at the games, he was so drunk he didn't even know what was going on.

He made a spectacle of himself. But now, unlike the time of the first scrimmage, I had friends in the crowd, and here was this drunk standing up and shaking his fist at the referee, cursing the coach for not giving me enough playing time, and cursing me when I passed the ball instead of shooting it.

The first game he came to was a nightmare. He wore a suit, one of his $700 specials left over from the glory days, but it was stained and wrinkled. His boozy tirades were endless. I tried hard to concentrate, to keep my mind on the game, and to never look up into the stands. All those years I'd been waiting for him to come watch me perform, and now I'm playing college ball, getting some good time, scoring some points, dishing out a few assists, and making a few good defensive plays. I'm playing for Jim Wyles's team, and we are good. Then Dad shows up, and he's drunk.

At the end of the game, the players' parents and friends started coming down onto the floor to congratulate them, and the guys whose parents weren't there began gathering to jog down to the showers together. I wanted to be with them, but I knew I would have had to trot in front of the section of bleachers where my father was sitting, and I didn't dare let him see me. I grabbed my sweats and ran to the opposite side of the floor and disappeared down an exit, taking the long route to the showers. Sitting in the locker room alone, I felt ashamed that I'd sneaked away from my father after the game. At the same time, I was angry that he'd shown up drunk and ruined what could have been such a thrill for both of us. Two emotions that had become familiar to me, guilt and rage, visited me again.

When they came, then and for years afterward, they always came together. I'd be enjoying life, the simplest pleasures, and suddenly I'd think of my father, where he was, what had happened to him, and I'd feel guilty, and then angry. *Why am I beating myself up over this?* I'd ask myself. I knew the answer to that question: I still loved the guy.

For the most part, that first year at Anderson was wonderful. By spring, Coach Wyles was telling me I was going to start next season at the number-two guard position. That was exciting. Both the guys I subbed for that year were being recruited by a dozen different four-year schools. If I followed in their footsteps, it might happen to me, too. It was the pot at the end of the rainbow, and I was halfway over that rainbow. But ambition wasn't more powerful than obligation.

One day during my first-year final exams, Dad came to my dorm. "Jonny," he said in his hustling, coaxing way, "we're going back to California, you and me. I've got some things going for me out there, a great job with a big firm in L.A."

"But Dad—" I began.

"Aw, come on now," he cut in. "I need you with me. You're my travel companion."

"Dad, I've got—"

"Son, *please*."

It is astonishing to me now that I actually went along with what he asked of me. He told me he needed me. He called me Jonny—that had always been his affectionate name for me when I was a boy, and nobody else used it. Now I knew he was using it to soften me, and the hell of it was, it was working. Even at that point, I was willing to believe in him. I've never known where I got that cast-iron sense of obligation to my father. Somehow, I felt obliged to go with him. There was also the guilt factor. I had all but ignored my father since returning to Anderson eight months earlier. I'd sensed the emptiness of his existence. Once I got over the disappointment of realizing that my father had been bumming around since leaving Encinitas, I should have reached out to him. Instead, I shut him out. Maybe, I figured, I could help him get started again by accompanying him back to California. It meant sacrificing my summer vacation, but I was willing to pay that price. I told him I'd go.

I dreaded the thought of what Coach Wyles would think when he heard I wouldn't be staying for the summer. He had told me he was planning to put me in the starting lineup the following season. I knew what that meant. It meant I should stay on campus over the summer, work hard in the weight room, and put in as much time on the hardwood as I could. Coaches make all sorts of promises to athletes all the time. Wyles didn't mean I had a lock on the position. He simply meant the opportunity was there for me to earn it. Wyles would surely bring in hot new recruits from all over the region, and I would have to compete for my starting position. My coach, a gifted motivator, was simply telling me that he expected me to win it.

It frightened me to forfeit the crucial summer-long workout. Beyond that, something scared me about going with my father. I knew him too well. I had a sick feeling that going with him meant putting my fate in his hands. Would he break my heart again? I had so much more at stake now—college, friends, newfound self-esteem. Would he find a way, whether he intended to or not, to screw it up for me? It was too late to back out.

He was a master at playing on my emotions. He had found a way to trap me in a choice between what was good for *me* and what was good for *him*. He knew what I would do. He was the one, after all, who had taught me the rightness of making personal sacrifices for people in need. He was twisting it all around now and using it against me. And I could hardly do a thing about it.

News of my sudden departure right after final exams caused a small stir within the group of friends. Killian organized a vigil. We sat up all night in the dorm, talking, laughing, the girls crying a little. The others took turns roasting me and then eulogizing me, pointing out my quirky personality traits.

It was incredibly flattering to realize that these young people had noticed me. I had an identity: Humpback Jack from Across the Track. I loved it.

The sun was rising when we heard the squeal of worn brakes from the parking lot outside my dorm room window. I drooped. "It's my father's car," I moaned. We listened as the engine shut off and the door slammed. Al and Ken helped me carry my bags down the hall and out to the parking lot in a funeral-like procession.

"Hi, kids," my Dad said merrily. "How you guys doing?"

They helped me put my bags in the trunk, and everybody hugged everybody. Even Al gave me a hug, a surprising expression of emotion from that bashful guy.

I hadn't known how to tell Coach Wyles; I couldn't bring myself to go see him. That summer I wrote him a letter telling him what had happened. As we pulled out of the parking lot, I looked back and saw the others—Killian, Al, Millie, and Ken—still standing there. For the first time in a couple years, I cried. Turning away from my dad, I closed my eyes and clenched my teeth and silently let the tears flow. That quiet crying skill came in handy right then.

❦❦❦

CHAPTER EIGHT
California, Here We Go Again

Dad was doing one of his numbers. "Sand, sun, and all the beach babes you can feast your eyes on," he said with a leer. "You're gonna love this spot, Jonny."

The strained joviality and phoniness of that pitch made me want to reach over from the passenger seat of the Vega and punch him. I'd done my duty to father and family. I'd gotten in his car and let him drive me away from the best year of my life. To sit there and have him insult my intelligence by pretending this trip was all for my benefit stretched my forbearance.

Dad's destination was Manhattan Beach, which, I had to admit, was not the most dismal place in the world. It was what people thought of when they pictured Southern California. The Boulevard dropped like a roller coaster, terrace by terrace, down the steep hill to the beach. Clean white sand spread 200 yards to the water's edge. Along the boardwalk, there were joggers and skaters and bikers and walkers and weirdos and, as my father had foretold, the most fabulously beautiful women I'd ever seen wearing practically nothing—oblivious to anything but their own private celebration of paradise.

Manhattan Beach was just a two-hour drive from Encinitas, but it might have been on the other side of the ocean. I was completely involved in the quest to save my father. I was in his world now, and it had nothing to do with my mother's. I didn't even tell her that I was just up the coast. And it wasn't as if she was anxious to know where I was. I'd set out on my own a year ago, and as far as she was concerned, that was that.

Dad had found a studio apartment right on Manhattan Beach Boulevard, but location was all it had. It consisted of one small room, 20' x 12', and a tiny bathroom. There was a primitive kitchen in a closet.

"I got a good price on this one," he said; $350 a month was the rock-bottom price for an L.A. beach rental in 1977. "I'll sleep here," he said, pointing to a single bed, more like a cot. That left me to sleep on the floor and hope he wouldn't step on me when he got up to go to the bathroom at night.

The first thing I set out to do was find a job and scrape together a few dollars to live on. I hit all the usual places—the groceries and the restaurants, a sporting-goods store that sold mostly surfboards, and the local bicycle shop. "We'll review your application and see how it meshes with our business's needs," was the typical pretentious response, as if hiring a college student to perform their mindless, meaningless tasks required careful deliberation.

Two blocks off the Boulevard, hidden at the end of an alley, I noticed the warehouse of a ceramics factory and went in.

"Who's in charge of hiring?" I asked the woman sitting at a desk by the time clock.

She didn't answer. She just picked up her telephone receiver and pressed a button. "Manny, front desk. Job applicant to see you."

A big Latino man appeared, wearing a dark blue shirt and a black necktie. He didn't ask about my job experience; he just looked me over. "What's that on your arm, man?" he asked.

"That's my birthmark." I was born with a wine-red discoloration on my right arm. It ran from the tip of my thumb to the top of my shoulder. Once it had been a source of shame for me. When I was a little boy, I hid it under long-sleeved shirts. I hated explaining to the other kids that I hadn't been burned. That all changed in my eighth year. My father noticed my embarrassment and resolved to do something about it. "Son," he said, "why not just think of it as a racing stripe? Maybe that's the reason you can run so fast, because you've got a racing stripe on your arm." I told that to my friends, and soon I was the envy of them all. Suddenly and forever, I was no longer ashamed of my little physical oddity and didn't mind people noticing it.

When I was 14, my father used my birthmark to help me get my first job. He took me into the Baskin-Robbins ice cream shop in the Anderson Mall to talk to the manager, Enzo Barone. Mr. Barone had hired Marq a month earlier, and I had been pestering my father ever since to help me get a job there. "Mr. Barone," my father said, "this is my second son, Jon. He's reliable, he's punctual, he knows how to count change, and he's very well behaved. But that's not all." He turned to me and said, "Roll up your sleeve, Jon." I did. "Now, notice the red stripe on his arm. There's extraordinary strength in that arm, Enzo. That boy can scoop ice cream with the best of 'em." I went to work, convinced that it was my stripe that had won me the job.

Manny lost interest in my birthmark and turned to a more important matter—hefting clay. "Can you lift okay?" he asked.

"Yeah," I answered. "How much would you want me to lift?"

"About a ton a day," he said. "Fifty pounds at a time."

"No problem," I said. The job paid $6.50 an hour, 40 hours a week, and it was within walking distance of our apartment.

Starting at six every morning, I moved 50-pound clay blocks from the clay room to the potting room. It was back-breaking work, but I could handle it if I paced myself. I noticed that other workers much smaller than I hardly seemed to strain under the weight of the blocks. They'd cinched belts or towels around their waists to support their backs, and they'd found a way to move blocks without ever bending over. They'd do a squat that got them close to the floor, roll the block onto their shoulder, and carry it about a hundred yards through the plant to the potting room. It was pretty good exercise, and it didn't injure my back. That would have been all I'd needed—to show up for basketball practice in the fall with a wrenched back.

Every afternoon when the blocks had all been moved, we'd report to the drying room. This was the skill work. I had to carry long, heavy planks with clay pots on them from the drying shelves to the glazing room. If I didn't place my hand under the shelf exactly in the middle when I lifted it, the plank would tip and the pots would go crashing to the floor. I got pretty good at finding the balance point, but never as good as the two Mexicans I worked with. I dropped at least one plank a day, always expecting that Manny would show up and boot me out onto the street.

Nobody else in my wing of the plant spoke English, so I got to do a lot of thinking. I missed Anderson College. I worried about Coach Wyles's reaction to the letter I'd sent him trying to explain why I couldn't work out with him that summer. I kept hoping he'd reply, assuring me that he understood, that everything was okay, that my place was secure. I tried to think of this California interlude as a service project: My father needed me; I didn't know exactly what for, and he never came right out and specified why, but he needed me. As I hefted those 50-pound blocks of clay, however, I began to feel that I'd made a terrible mistake coming with him.

Dad spent his days looking for work at law offices in the city, finally landing a job "doing investigations," as he put it, for a Beverly Hills firm. He took me there one day to show me around and introduce me to his bosses.

It was uncomfortable, walking into that suite of offices with Dad. I half expected someone to call the police and have us arrested for loitering. He never took me to an office or a cubicle to identify it as his own. He showed me common areas of the tenth floor, places anyone could go. He didn't seem to have an immediate supervisor. He smiled and waved at clerks and secretaries but didn't interrupt any of the associates as we passed by their offices. Most people in the halls didn't seem to know him, but one man in a suit did acknowledge him.

"Hey, Bob, what are you up to, old man?"

"Just cracking a big case, Joseph," Dad answered with a nervous laugh. If he worked here at all, I thought, it must be as a freelancer, a go-fer of some sort.

As we left the building, he said: "Wait and see. I'll be working bigger and bigger cases. And then, when I take the bar exam and get my license to practice law in California and they see what I can do, these lazy bastards will be scrambling to clear a corner office for me."

My father was still putting on a pathetic play for me.

❧ ❧ ❧

I was driving southbound on the 405 freeway late one Saturday afternoon when thick black smoke began pouring out from under the hood of Dad's Vega. He'd let me borrow it to do a little sightseeing, but 170,000 miles was all she could give. I pulled the car over to the right side of the freeway near an off-ramp and ditched it in the ice plant. I quickly put about 50 yards between me and the old white clunker, then turned and watched it burn. It was a blackened shell by the time the first fire engine arrived. I told the highway patrolman he would have to get registration information from my father and gave him a false address and phone number. I was fairly sure my father wouldn't want to talk to a law enforcement officer.

Dad was surprisingly calm when I finally got home that night and told him his car was just a cinder. "No great loss," he said. "Hell, I stole it anyway."

"You stole the car? How did you manage that?"

"I just borrowed it from a dealer friend. He used to be a client. I just never brought it back." He noticed my dismay and tried to soften his story. "It was more like he gave it to me."

"Some friend," I replied. "You steal a car from a guy and call him a friend? How do you figure the guy is your friend, let alone your client?"

That hit a raw nerve. "That car got you out here to Southern California, smartass. How I obtained the car is none of your lousy business. You should just be grateful and keep your mouth shut, since you don't know the first thing about how I conduct my business affairs."

"You call car theft a business affair!" My anger with my father for suckering me out of Anderson was boiling over. "No wonder you don't have a business anymore. The fact is, Dad, you don't have any business affairs. So don't try to con me about your so-called business affairs. And while you're at it, don't try to con me about your so-called job at that Beverly Hills law office. And while you're at *that*, don't try to fool yourself into thinking you did me some kind of favor by dragging me all the way across the United States for no reason except that you wanted somebody to listen to your drivel!"

The moment I stopped talking, I saw that my father was hurt. My tirade cut him deep, and I felt terrible for unleashing it on him. It was as though I had driven my knee right into his belly and knocked the wind out of him. He couldn't defend himself against a beating like that, by his son.

He opened the door and quietly walked out. I stood in my tracks for several minutes, thinking about what happened. I was astonished at how easy it had been. All I'd done was state the obvious, and it had crushed him. I felt like a bully. I was ashamed of myself.

I lay on my bedding on the floor that night, waiting for him to come back, until eventually I fell asleep. When I awoke the next morning, he was sitting on the metal folding chair, drinking a cup of coffee, reading the *L.A. Times,* whistling.

"I fixed you some breakfast," he said pleasantly. "Sausage, biscuits, and orange juice, just like the old days." There, on the tiny end table by his bed, was a McDonald's bag.

"Thanks," I said, and left it at that.

My father didn't go long without a car. The next day, a Monday, I got home from work at about 5:30 to find a shiny, black, used Chrysler Cordoba in the driveway, Dad's new wheels. He was eager to show the car off to me. I had to get in and let him take me for a ride right then and there. He drove me around for about an hour, then pulled into a gas station and asked, "You got a few bucks for gas?" I filled his tank.

There were moments when I acknowledged to myself that my father was using me—for rent money and fast cash, not just companionship—but I pushed those suspicions away. I couldn't bring myself to leave him during a time when he seemed to be vulnerable. I kept telling myself that maybe he was on to something good. Maybe he could turn his freelance gig into steady work. Maybe, I thought, I would be the one to help him get back on his feet. I hadn't even begun to understand the way he used his skills to keep me tied to him and that awful apartment. I did sense that living the way he did was steadily eroding my self-respect. I didn't feel good about myself anymore.

What prompted me to take action was the prospect that my dreams were fading away. I hadn't played ball or worked out since I left college, and I was afraid that even if I could somehow find a way back to Anderson, I might be so far off my game that I'd be a disappointment to Coach Wyles.

Worse, I'd seen almost no sign that my efforts to help my father were working. There seemed to be no end to his dependence on me. So long as he continued to slide, I was stuck. I could feel his failure pulling me down.

One night in July, just as Dad and I went to bed, I got up my courage. "I need to get back in touch with Wyles pretty soon," I said, trying to sound practical and matter-of-fact. "I have to figure out how I'm going to get back to campus." I waited. He said nothing. Soon, the snoring began.

A few days later, Dad came home beaming. "Oh, Jonny," he said. "Oh, Jonny. Let me tell you what your old Dad has done for his ungrateful son. You definitely don't deserve it, but you're going to get it anyway." I was dumbfounded. "She's classy and she's gorgeous, Jonny. She's the receptionist at my office. Her name is Linda."

My father had set me up with a blind date. I'd spent most of the summer in a ceramics factory, holed up in that tiny apartment. The idea of going out on a date sounded like welcome relief.

Linda turned out to be a bombshell of a woman, a redhead wearing dark, almost black lipstick that unnecessarily called attention to the ampleness of her mouth. The shortness and tight fit of her black skirt left most of her thick, shiny thighs exposed. Her sheer, lacy, white blouse cradled two mighty breasts that she held high by strenuously arching her back. At 28 or 29, she was older than I by ten years, and obviously far beyond my league. The rookie league. I could practically smell the sensuality emanating from her, and it scared the hell out of me.

I drove the Cordoba—it was my gas, anyway—but my date was in charge. She took me to a party at some rich man's house in Sherman Oaks. I just followed her around with a glass of ginger ale in my hand and pretended to be pleased to meet all the middle-aged Southern Californians who told bogus stories about movie deals. None too soon, Linda made her exit and we got out of there. I drove my date home, relieved to have the night over with—almost. When we got to her apartment, I stepped out of the car and came around and opened the door for her, unaware of how ridiculous my well-mannered conduct must have seemed to a woman of Linda's sophistication.

"Get back in the car," she said with lots of breath, and so I got back in. "I want to show you something," she purred as she easily unbuttoned her white blouse. Opening it as though she were parting the curtains to a Broadway play, she revealed her chest, about half of which was tightly tucked inside a black lace bra. She smoothly reached behind her back and with one hand, popped a clasp that allowed the black silk to fall to her lap and reveal her attributes. She looked at them and then back at me, proudly displaying perfect, round breasts that glimmered in the unreal orange light of the streetlamp. "Do you like them?"

"Yeah, sure," I mumbled. She was right to be proud.

"Don't you want them?" she invited in a whiny voice that suggested she didn't think she should have to ask. She cupped her hands beneath her gleaming mounds and gently lifted them, then dropped them, allowing them to bounce and settle back into position. I was so close to them, and so attentive, I could see how the bouncing action, and perhaps the anticipation of a full-grown virgin sucking them, made her nipples shrink and tighten. Viscerally stimulated as I was, I didn't plunge my face into this woman's chest. Instead, I was secretly revolted. This was sex, beckoning me to take my first taste, and all I could think of was the vulgarity of it all—so many guys in so many locker rooms bragging about their conquests in the crudest terms possible. Mostly, I remembered my father's rantings: "Your mother is frigid. Her pussy might as well be stapled shut!" And my mother's complaints: "Your father's idea of foreplay is rolling on top of me. He's never even tried to bring me to orgasm." I'd heard all this talk at such an early age that it was all sickeningly strange. When I contemplated sex, I felt dirty, the way I'd felt dirty during those long nights when my dad made me wait in the living room of his mistress's house.

"No, thanks," I mumbled apologetically, as if I were skipping dessert. It wasn't that I wasn't fascinated and attracted. It was just that I didn't have the first clue what to do with those enormous breasts, or for that matter, this horny woman. She made me feel dirty again. I got out of the car again and went around and opened the door for her. I had severely offended my date, who was obviously accustomed to having her way with men, and who had employed her heaviest weapons in a failed attempt to conquer me. Without bothering to reattach her bra strap or to button her blouse, the busty redhead awkwardly emerged from my borrowed car and stalked up the path to her apartment.

She must have complained about me to my father the next day at the office, because when he came home, drunk and agitated, he chewed me out.

"I knock myself out to set you up with a good-looking woman," he groused, "and you don't even know what to do!" The way he saw it, he'd gone to a lot of trouble to get me laid. He'd told the woman that he had this son who was a strapping young athlete who needed some action, and she'd been more than willing. To him I was spurning a rite of passage. It was his responsibility as my father to get me my first sex. Then I'd be a man. I'd failed him. Worse, I'd offended someone who gave him access to the office where he pretended to work.

It was a calculated move on my father's part to either get me interested enough in Southern California so that I'd stay, or to keep me distracted enough so that I would miss my chance to go back to Anderson College in time for the fall semester. The blind date had backfired. But he didn't stop there.

It was the next Saturday morning, my most coveted time of the week, when I got to fall on Dad's cot and sleep in as long as I wanted. "Get up, Jonny. I've arranged for you to meet a very important person today."

"No more of your blind dates," I moaned.

"Not this one," he said, smiling with glee. "This one's the head basketball coach at Santa Monica City College. Strap on your sneakers, boy. I got you a tryout."

"A tryout?" I said. "What do I need a tryout for? I'm going back to Anderson."

"Listen, what would it hurt to meet this coach and show him your stuff? If he likes what he sees, he'll put you on his summer league team, and you'll get to sharpen up for your sophomore year." It sounded good.

Once again, my father, using devices he knew would work, had manipulated me. He had read my fears about going back to Anderson College unprepared, and he'd persuaded me that this tryout would help. What I didn't see, because I was so easily influenced, was that he was desperately trying to keep me nearby. He had grown dependent on me for cash and companionship and couldn't let me go. He was my very own demon, and he had whispered in my ear. I'd listened and given in to temptation, and I would spend a year in hell for it. We got in the Chrysler and drove to Santa Monica.

When we arrived, I half expected to find that my father didn't know the coach at all. But when we entered the gym, Dad walked right up to the small man with big teeth who was obviously the coach. "Dave, this is Jon," he said. I held out my hand.

"Glad you could come down, Jon. How ya feel? Good? Feel like playing a little pickup with us this morning?"

"Sure."

"Well, then, what I thought we'd do is just let you and Ronald here run a little two-on-two against Joe and Terence over there. We'll go to 21 by ones and take a breather."

I didn't like the situation. I hadn't touched a basketball in two months. I hadn't even warmed up. I almost felt as if I'd been set up. It bothered me and got my adrenaline pumping.

It turned out to be my Anderson tryout all over again, another one of those once-a-season days when I just couldn't miss. I heard the coach say, "Whew!" after I buried my fourth or fifth 20-foot jumper in a row. Ronald, a recruit from Texas, and I beat the homeboys (both starters who'd gone on to star at UC-Santa Barbara) three straight games before the coach called it off. He took me aside and laid the hard sell on me right then and there. "Jon, I've been looking for a point guard, and baby, you're it."

He went on to tell me how I could run his offense, and how Ronald and I could provide the bulk of the scoring, and how we could win the conference championship again, and how we could make a serious run at the state title, and how we could get great exposure playing right next door to Los Angeles, and how we'd be seen by all the scouts.

"Hey," the coach went on, "I'm personal friends with coaches at UCSB and Loyola Marymount and Pepperdine and Cal State Northridge. And listen, buddy, I know Coach Cunningham over at UCLA. . . ."

That's what got me. *UCLA,* I thought. Could this be true? Could this guy really know the coach at UCLA? Could there be, in my wildest dreams, a remote chance of a spot for me at the end of the UCLA bench?

Suddenly, my plan to go back to South Carolina disintegrated. I had loved Anderson College, and I loved Coach Wyles. But no coach from UCLA would ever see me play in Anderson, South Carolina. This fast-talking coach had me by the throat. I agreed to play on his summer league team.

The rest of the summer went by quickly, and hardly a day passed without Dad saying something about his having gotten me the tryout. He didn't want me to forget that I was obligated to him.

My plan was to move out of that stuffy little studio apartment and into a place of my own. Coach Wagner had promised to set me up in an apartment near campus, and that sounded great to me. I yearned to return to college life. I knew it was bad for me to be around Dad. Still, I felt guilty for being so eager to leave him behind.

The apartment the coach found for me was off Pico Boulevard, one block from campus—just right. I waited until the day of my move to tell Dad I was leaving. I'd been afraid that he might get emotional or try to talk me out of it.

"Well," I said, "I'll be leaving today." It sounded eerily similar to the way my mother had informed me of my father's abandonment years earlier.

Dad said nothing. He didn't even look my way, but kept his eyes on his newspaper. I could tell he was thinking, though—thinking about what he'd do next, thinking about how he'd get along without his sidekick.

He offered to drive me and my luggage over. When we arrived, I got out, and he stayed in the car. "Go get 'em, Jonny," he said. "I'll drop by to check on you every so often after work. Beverly Hills is right next door."

"Sure. That'd be fine," I said, trying to sound pleased. I waved as he pulled away from the curb, then carried my two duffel bags into the building. The apartment was clean, and although it wasn't large, it had all the space I needed. I fell on the couch and exhaled a loud, happy sigh. Could it be that I was really alone in this place? I was! I let out a yelp. My liberation would be short-lived.

Two weeks later, on a Sunday night, I heard a knock at the door. I opened it, and there he was, standing on my doormat, weeping.

"Jonny," he cried. "I need your help, son." He rattled off a story about how the landlord at the Manhattan Beach place was a crook. He'd gotten into an argument with the guy, he claimed, and he desperately needed to stay with me for just a few days. "I'm starting to get more work at the office, and the money's coming in. I just need to crash here for a night or two, son. Until I find a new place."

My spirits sagged, but I didn't dare let him see disappointment on my face. "Of course you can crash here," I said. "Come on in." I had a sinking feeling that he'd be staying for more than one or two nights. One or two weeks, maybe, or one or two months, more like it. But I'd be busy with school and basketball and whatever social life I might fall into, so how bad could it be to have a boarder?

The first thing he did was persuade me to pick up his car payments. "Without my wheels, I don't have a prayer." Even now, after all I'd been through with him, he was still able to make me think that only one more favor from me would be the little boost he needed to get back on his feet. When I told him I barely had enough money to get myself by, he had the answer. "I talked to a guy at a restaurant on Wilshire Boulevard. I told him about you. He said he'd take your application. Let's go see him this weekend."

On Saturday afternoon, I went by Nibblers Restaurant in Beverly Hills and applied for a position as a short-order chef. The manager offered me the night shift, from 6 to 11 every evening. I took it.

For about a month, it seemed that I could handle the job. Having a little extra cash in my pocket made it seem worth the trouble. I hardly saw my roommate, and we rarely got a chance to talk. I didn't know how his job might be going. I kept telling myself that there was no one else who could help him. *One more favor,* I thought, *and he'll be back on his feet.* The favor would cost me.

One night in the middle of October, I left Nibblers about midnight and took the No. 12 bus west on Wilshire Boulevard. Where the bus turned south and intersected Pico, I had to get off and walk one block to pick up the No. 44, which would take me all the way to Santa Monica. Just as I got off the first bus, I saw the second—the last bus of the evening—at the bus stop at the end of the block, just shutting its doors. I was about five miles from my apartment, so I didn't want to miss the ride. I would have yelled to the driver to wait, but this was Compton, a very rough neighborhood, and I didn't want to attract attention.

The bus started moving. I figured I could sprint up beside it and hail it before it got up to speed. As I crossed the intersection, running as fast as I could, my foot hit the curb at the wrong angle, and I felt something tear apart behind my right ankle. I could actually hear the rip, as if someone standing behind me had snapped a stalk of celery. I hobbled to a stop. For about 60 seconds, I just stood still, breathing hard, scared by the noise and hoping it didn't mean what I feared. Then the blood rushed back into my ankle, the pain hit, and I screamed, no longer worried about the danger.

I sat down on the curb and grabbed my ankle. It hurt all the way up to my hip. I thought I might not be able to get up, but I knew I had to get out of that neighborhood and get home. I stood, collected myself, and started hopping. Four hours later, I reached the apartment. Dad was snoring. I fell on my bed and clenched my teeth. The throbbing in my ankle was violent, but eventually fatigue overcame me and forced me to sleep.

I skipped classes the next day, sitting at home with my foot in a pale of ice water. My hope was that by three that afternoon, when I was supposed to report to the gym, I could take the swelling down enough so that the team trainer wouldn't notice it. I didn't dare tell my coach about my injury. He was a canny, suspicious man, and I was afraid he'd see through any explanation I could manufacture. He might even guess that I had a night job. If he found that out, he'd kick me off the team.

I got there by three o' clock for the most miserable afternoon I'd ever spent in a gymnasium. I ran around for two hours trying to keep my weight off my right toes. Bad landings on my right foot were instantly punished with shooting pains up the back of my leg into my buttock. My performance was terrible. The coach never asked if something was the matter. He just became more and more irritated at my failure to execute the plays with the timing he wanted to see.

The ankle stayed bad all week, and so did my play. The coach got abusive. Finally, during a time-out in the game against El Camino College, he confronted me. "What the hell is wrong with you, Du Pre?" he shouted.

"I hurt my foot, coach."

"Sit down, goddamnit!"

It turned out I'd torn my Achilles tendon. I stayed on the bench for about two weeks. My tendon healed enough for me to manage a careful run, but I had lost my starting position for the rest of the season. I was no longer the coach's fair-haired boy. From then on, if he wasn't ignoring me, he was shouting profanities at me. He kept me on the bench much of the rest of the season. There would be no phone calls from the coaches at UCLA or anyplace else.

It was worse at home. One day I picked up the phone and got no dial tone. I went to a pay phone and called Pacific Bell. The woman in the business office told me I had an outstanding bill of $878. I went to her office, and she showed it to me, a long list of calls to South Carolina—Walhalla and Greenville and Columbia—and some to Atlanta and Miami and New Orleans. All were places where my father knew people. When the bills had come in, he'd thrown them away so I wouldn't find out. I told the woman what had happened. She looked at me pityingly and said, "I'll process this bill as 'unpayable,' but you have lost your phone privileges."

My father wasn't around when I got home that night or when I got up the next morning. He must have realized, when the phone went dead, that it was time to make himself scarce. By the time I saw him again, I was too dispirited to dredge it all up and listen to his evasions.

Two weeks later, I came home from work and found the apartment door locked. I opened the knob with my key, but my father had shut the clamp, a locking device that slid into place like a deadbolt. I knocked. No answer. I tried for a while to push the door open, then pounded on it. One of the neighbors came out and threatened to call the cops if I kept on pounding, so I tapped for a while, then gave up. It was 1:30 in the morning. Exhausted, I lay down on the grassy plot near the apartment to wait until my father appeared. I went right to sleep. Two hours later, I woke up to the sound of the door opening. Dad came out with a woman in a short, tight red dress. She looked like a prostitute. He'd had a hooker in the apartment. They didn't see me. They went off together, probably to find a drink. I asked myself what he'd used to pay her, and I froze. I'd left my stash in my dresser drawer, about $500, money I'd saved from my job. I ran into the apartment and counted it. A hundred was gone.

The next day, he came back and I confronted him. He told me the woman was none of my business. I asked about the hundred dollars. He blew up in my face. He asked if I was accusing him of stealing and called me an ungrateful little bastard. It turned into a fight. He got in my face and started pushing me, so I pushed him back. He took a swing and hit me in the chest. I grabbed him and put him in a headlock. He cursed and hollered, but I kept him in the headlock until his body went limp and I was sure he was giving up. And that was the end of it.

After that, my relationship with my father was one of endurance. Between classes and practice and study and work, it was easy to avoid him. When we did see each other, we rarely spoke. Neither of us wanted another fistfight. He was sullen but unrepentant, and I was disgusted with him.

The months passed, and incredibly, because I was so busy and my schedule so tight, I guess, I never got around to opening a bank account and putting my money into it. The next thing I knew, the rest of my stash had disappeared. Dad had taken it and spent it—on booze, no doubt, and hookers. I was left with nothing to pay the bills, and after a little while, the electric company turned off our lights. After I paid the rent, I didn't have a dime to buy groceries. For the five days until I got my next paycheck, we lived on yeast biscuits and water and whatever I could sneak out of Nibblers.

By this point, my father had become a heavy burden. This was my lowest point. He couldn't make anything happen for himself, and he had an uncanny ability to ruin things for me. Through it all, he continued to play on my guilt and my sympathies, insisting that if it hadn't been for me, he would have been destitute. I could have thrown him out a hundred times, but I knew that the pangs of guilt would punish me for abandoning my father and, besides, I couldn't get rid of him anyway.

Looking back, I can't imagine how I let the situation go on for as long as it did. But strangely, I don't regret it. I had watched my father give of himself to so many people who were helpless and who had no way of rewarding him. Now, he had become one of those people, and he had turned to me for help. I knew he was using me, but I couldn't let him down. I felt I wouldn't be able to live with myself if I'd turned my back on him.

I had a poor year in basketball, but all those weeks on the bench, along with daily therapy, had allowed my injury to heal. I decided to go out for the track team because I didn't want the year to be a complete waste of time. Much to my surprise, I did pretty well. I took second place in the Southern California relays in the triple jump, breaking the school record, and took third in the long jump. Maybe I could do something with those credentials. It wasn't much to go on, but at a time like this, you'll follow any glimmer of hope. My ambitions, though, were dulled by a sense of exhaustion. This school year, carrying a full load of classes and a part-time night job and a 245-pound deadbeat on my back, had worn me down. More than anything, I just wanted it to be over with. I had reached the lowest point of my life. I had failed in trying to help my father, and in the process, I had let him drag me down. I realized I couldn't do any more for him. I had to get away from him.

In April, as school was coming to an end, I realized I had no plan, no place to go. For the first time in my life, I didn't know where I was going next. It was time to break out of my father's world and reach into my mother's.

"I need a place to crash," I told her on the phone, "just for a bit. Could I use that guest room of yours a little while?"

"That would be fine," she said.

"Bill won't mind?" I asked.

"Bill won't mind," she replied, not quite convincingly.

She and Bill had bought a small house in Mira Mesa, a quagmire of tract housing outside San Diego. Living with Bill would be demeaning and frustrating, I knew, but at least I'd be free of my father's suffocating influence.

Mom picked me up after my last exam. She greeted me with a big, warm smile; she hadn't smiled that way in years. She had no idea what I'd been going through. I jumped in the car and we drove one block down Pico Boulevard, turned left, and pulled up in front of my apartment building. She stayed in the car while I ran inside to collect my bags.

Dad wasn't home. I left about half my clothes, the stuff I knew he could wear, and all of my cash, about $150, in the dresser drawer. I didn't leave a note. He had exhausted my desire to say anything to him, even good-bye. I walked out that door and slammed it behind me.

"How do you think you did on your finals?" Mom asked as the Pinto sputtered along Interstate 405 toward San Diego.

"Fine, I guess," I said, preoccupied with matters much graver than my test scores. I was profoundly disappointed that I hadn't pulled my father back up on his feet. I knew he'd be kicked out of the apartment within a few weeks. Beyond that, I had no idea what might become of him. I realized I didn't much care. I couldn't. I was desperately afraid for my own sanity.

❧ ❧ ❧

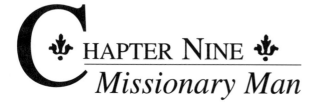

CHAPTER NINE ❧
Missionary Man

om spoke too quickly when she assured me that her new husband wouldn't mind if I stayed with them awhile. He minded very much. She had to work hard to convince him to let me occupy their empty bedroom. He finally gave in, stipulating, of course, that I pay rent. I didn't mind paying rent, except that it upset my mother, and I resented her husband's ignorant attempt to teach me some sort of lesson. He didn't know that I'd just completed two years of college with a B grade average while supporting my father. Mom wouldn't speak of her first husband around Bill because she didn't want to hear how stupid she'd been for staying with a loser like that in the first place. I didn't say anything about my father around my stepfather because Bill might have said something critical, and then I would have said something about what a shame it was that my mother had married two losers in a row.

Mom had a scheme to get around him so I could save my money for my next year of college. She planned to take my monthly payments and keep them in her purse, then slip the money back to me when Bill wasn't looking. She dearly wanted to help me move in the right direction. I'd never told her of my troubles with Dad, but she understood better than anyone what I'd just endured. She was clearly trying to make up for what she hadn't done, or hadn't been able to do, for my brothers and me.

I got a job in a San Diego paint factory hauling cans of paint from the conveyor belt to the labeling machine, then stacking them on the pallets. The air was thick with chemical vapors. I'd take a deep breath before entering, and, once inside, hold it as long as I could. The fumes gave me savage headaches. I knew that working in that factory was bad for my lungs. More than that, it was bad for my morale. Every day in the factory was one more day not pursuing my dream of getting a college education, launching a career, and making something of myself.

During lunch breaks, I listened as the other workers talked about their lives, particularly Gabe, a 50-year-old man who was a grim example of what a toxic job could do to a human being. Gabe was esteemed because he had lasted on the paint line for 18 years. He looked it. The skin on his face was so tight that his lips wouldn't close. It made him seem to be smiling all the time, like a skeleton. He told stories about the great paint spill of 1976 and the chemical fire that forced everybody out of the plant for two days. He had a hacking cough that seized him every few minutes. Gabe frightened me—not because I thought he could harm me, but because I thought I might put myself on a course to become like him. I didn't want to work on a factory line my entire adult life. These people worked long hard hours for very little money. The thought that I could become one of them panicked me.

I had nothing on my agenda but continuing with college, but my mother, in conspiracy with T.J. and Maryann Jensen, had another plan for me.

In the Mormon church, young people often take two years and go on a mission, living among non-Mormons, teaching the faith, and doing good works. Marq had volunteered and was sent to Toronto. The letters he'd sent home convinced my mother that the experience would be the best way of turning me into a man. After several weeks of tiptoeing around the subject, she got up the nerve to say something at breakfast one morning. Bill was out playing his daily round of golf, and I was about to leave for work.

"Jon," she asked timidly, "have you thought of going on a mission?" It stopped me cold. It was the first time in years that she'd attempted to guide me or involve herself in my affairs. The last time, in fact, was when I was 15 and she persuaded me to be baptized. I did that for her, mostly, and afterward had drifted into inactivity as a church member. Now here she was, urging me to drop out of school and devote two years to missionary service.

I'd worked so hard to get through the first two years of college that I might have resented her suggestion. Instead, I was touched by her sincerity and moved by her belief that this could be a good thing for her son. I promised her I'd speak with the local bishop. I also began accompanying her to Sunday services again.

❧❧❧

While I'd been off at school, Marq had been in Canada looking for converts—and looking for himself as well. When his mission was over in the spring of 1978, he flew home. As was their custom, T.J. and Maryann made a party of the occasion. They organized about 20 of us from the neighborhood, piled us into their big, brown Ford van, and led the caravan to the San Diego airport. Squeezed into the back of that van, I remembered the good times it had carried us to during those years in Encinitas, trips that made that period bearable—church picnics, summer softball tournaments, and drives to the beach. This welcoming party for Marq reunited me with friends I hadn't seen since that time—Laura and Randy and Steve and Richard—all of whom had helped me adjust to a strange new place. Bouncing along in the van, I felt happy again, for the first time since my blissful days at Anderson College.

We all gathered at gate C-4 in the Delta terminal at Lindbergh field. Kitty and Laura unfurled the ten-foot-long paper banner they'd made for the occasion: *Welcome Home, Marq!* Deplaning passengers looked at us with puzzlement, trying to figure out who the celebrity was on their flight. Then, greeted by cheers and applause, our conquering hero stepped through the portal, a smile of surprise and gratitude on his thin, handsome face. The celebration moved up I-5 to party central, the Jensens' house. Marq opened gifts and told stories of his tour of Toronto and other parts of Eastern Canada. Later, when the clamor had ebbed and most of the kids had gone home and Marq and I were standing around in the backyard shooting hoops on the Jensen's sagging basketball standard, he turned and looked me square in the face. "It's totally worth it, man," he said. "Go on a mission. You won't regret it."

I watched him carefully for months, studying the way he managed himself, marveling at the change in him. He seemed to stand a little taller than I'd remembered and to speak more clearly and with more confidence. He now could rise above the petty concerns that used to throw him off and make him angry and sullen.

And he made good decisions. Instead of going back to the house Mom shared with her new husband, he went to live with Grandma and Grandpa Peek. It was a smart move. The former police chief and his wife did more to teach and encourage him than anyone else ever had. Grandma Marie kept him well fed and made sure he cleaned up after himself and showed respect for his hosts and their home. Grandpa Marquis, less strict and more patient in his old age, found ways of giving him advice—on everything from car maintenance to career planning—that didn't make Marq feel as though he was being put down. It was during this time immediately after his mission, when he lived with his grandparents, that Marq was at his best. He was employed, organized, and filled with confidence and optimism.

The bishop of our congregation, Gerald Haddock, was a fireplug of a man. Just open one of his valves and he'd blow you away with his enthusiasm. "Okay,

Jon," he said as though this was the biggest event of his year. "How long would it take you to get yourself ready?" It was clear he wouldn't take no for an answer.

I didn't mind. I still wanted college, but I had to admit that there were no college coaches knocking on my door, and that my prospects for raising enough money to pay tuition for the fall semester at any local state university weren't glittering. I wanted to please my mother, and I also wanted to get out of that paint factory and into something meaningful. Most of all, I wanted to follow in my big brother's footsteps and turn out as good as he appeared to be. And so as we sat in the living room of the Haddocks' modest Encinitas home, talking about what I might want my mission to be, I knew that my mind was already half made up.

Bishop Haddock really believed in what he was pitching. "You go out a boy," he said, "and you come back a man." He spoke fondly of his two years in what he called the Eastern States Mission—Virginia to New York and west to Ohio. I listened at first, but then only pretended to. Sounds coming from the kitchen pulled away my attention. I heard the tinkle of the Haddock children's forks and spoons as they filled themselves with Mrs. Haddock's good, warm food—barbecued chicken, from the smell of it.

"Now rinse your plates," I heard her say gently, "and put them in the dishwasher."

"Me first!" said one of them, jostling for a place at the sink.

"No, me!"

The faucet was opened full throttle. "No splashing," I heard the eldest girl say. "Be careful. You'll chip Mommy's dish."

The dishwasher door slammed shut as the last child, probably the smallest, dropped in her dish and, carefree, ran off to play with the others. The commotion moved outside as the three children scurried into the backyard to play in the twilight.

The noises of the daily routine in the Haddock household seemed almost musical to me. They were the sounds of love and cooperation, sounds I hadn't heard since we lived in our little house in Mauldin, when I was five years old and my family was perfect. I yearned to once again be a part of something that made sounds like those. If doing missionary service was the key to an approach to life that might bring me that kind of family, then it was well worth the sacrifice. Besides, compared to what I'd been going through, two years of missionary work in a foreign country sounded like a vacation at Club Med. I told Bishop Haddock I was ready to go.

At my mother's suggestion, I moved out of Bill's house and in with the Jensens. T.J. and Maryann had turned their home into a sort of halfway house for young people who were getting it together to go on their missions, and they'd done so for Marq. Mainly, I had to earn some money; Mormon missionaries must be self-sustaining. Bishop Haddock talked his brother Rick into hiring me on as a laborer in his construction firm, and T.J. and Maryann let me share a room with one of their sons. I paid no rent, but after seeing me eat, Maryann asked if I wouldn't mind kicking in a few dollars a week for the extra milk she would have to stock in her refrigerator.

The Jensen family practically adopted me. Laura was the sister I'd never had, and Steve, two years my junior, became my younger brother, always begging me for tales of my athletic exploits. He never seemed to mind that my scoring average grew almost every time I talked basketball. When he wasn't at school and I wasn't at work, we did everything together. He shadowed me the same way I had once attached myself to Marq. There was always something going on in the Jensen home, always something fun. The parents made it a place where the kids wanted to be, and a place where their kids' friends wanted to be. My eight months with this surrogate family were blissful. Once again, someone had stepped in and provided leadership that I needed at a critical time.

The letter from church headquarters in Salt Lake City came on April 5, 1979. "You are called to labor in the Italy, Rome mission," it announced. I'd be serving overseas. That excited me, as I'd never left the country before. I sensed that I was about to be lifted out of a little life and shown something larger.

T.J. and Maryann began scrambling to help me prepare for my mission. They knew what I'd need, and they saw to every detail. In the course of this preparation, I was treated to one of the strangest experiences I'd ever had.

Bright and early on a Saturday morning, T.J. yanked me out of bed, rushed me through breakfast, and pushed me into the passenger seat of his black Toyota Celica. He did all this with a sort of wild glee, as if something hilarious was about to happen and he could hardly wait.

Soon we were driving down I-5 toward San Diego, me groggy, and T.J. grinning. I had no idea what he was up to. He was an outrageous tease and practical joker, and I assumed that this was just another of his pranks. But at 8:00 on a Saturday morning?

Halfway down the freeway, T.J. made that noise he often made when he was teasing. He giggled.

I shot him a look. His grin seemed about to crack his round face in half. A moment later, he giggled again, longer and louder. He was beaming with mischief. "Oh, boy," he said, shaking his head, slamming his hand on the steering wheel. "Oh boy oh boy oh boy!"

"What's with you, Teej?" I asked, suspiciously. The giggles became guf-faws. He looked like the Pillsbury Doughboy, his cheeks puffing as he pre-tended to stifle his merriment.

"C'mon, T.J.!" I said. "Tell me!" But he wouldn't tell.

"T.J.!" I yelled. "If you don't tell me, I'm out of this car at the first traf-fic light."

He prolonged the torture a while longer, then spoke. "Hey, don't get me wrong," he said. "I'm ordinarily not the kind of guy who would want to see another guy in his underwear . . . but I can't wait to check you out in those *garments!*"

So that was it. This was the day I'd get my garments.

Early in my time as a member of The Church of Jesus Christ of Latter-day Saints, I'd learned that when I became what was called an elder, I would be, in effect, a member of the Mormon clergy. The clergy in other denomina-tions wore special clothing—white collars and robes and capes and sashes—and the Mormon clergy wore special clothing, too, not *outside* their street clothes but *under* them. Underwear. The "garments."

With my assignment to work as a missionary, I'd advanced in the Mormon priesthood, and I was now expected to put on the garments. I had known this going in. It had been explained to me. The time would come. Now it had arrived.

"All right," I said to T.J. "What's the deal with this underwear? Really, man, am I going to regret this?" I tried to seem cheerful, but I was anxious. I was half enjoying T.J.'s amusement at my expense, but I also worried that I might be getting myself into some weird religious practice that would turn me off and alienate me from this great church I'd found.

T.J. sensed my concern and turned serious. "Hey, don't sweat it, Jon," he said. "You wouldn't be normal if you didn't have this fear. Anything new is going to feel strange at first, but once you put them on and feel how much more comfortable they are than those bun-huggers you've been wearing, you'll won-der how you ever got along without them."

He glanced over to see how I was reacting. "And then," he went on, "once you begin to understand their purpose, you'll appreciate the protection they afford you."

"Protection?" I cut in. "Protection from what? Are they fireproof or some-thing?"

"No, boy. Protection from the world—a constant reminder of who you are now."

"So who am I?"

"You're a young guy who has done the courageous thing and chosen to play it straight, to stay out of trouble, to do something good with yourself."

He was right. I'd made that choice. "But what," I asked, "has this under-wear got to do with all that?"

"Let's put it this way," T.J. said. "You find yourself in the back of a car with a girl, and things are getting hot and heavy, right? Okay, just try peeling your clothes off and see if she doesn't fall out of the car laughing at you when she catches a glimpse of those garments. Brother, you ain't goin' nowhere with her. There's your protection!"

T.J. had a knack for talking to young people on their level. He'd give you the kind of advice you could understand and would always remember.

We were headed for a store in San Diego that was to the young Mormon missionary what L.L. Bean was to the outdoorsman, a one-stop supply center where I could buy everything I'd need—two dark-colored suits; two pairs of dress shoes; and six crisp, white shirts and a half-dozen neckties—and the gar-ments. The salesman gave me a set of garments in my size and directed me to the dressing room. T.J. stood outside the dressing-room door—like a prison guard, it occurred to me, ready to grab me if I bolted. I locked the door, pulled down my Levis, and dropped my skivvies.

I picked up the garments and looked at them. They were made of stretchy cotton. The top part was like an ordinary T-shirt but a little more sheer and tight-fitting. No big problem there, but the bottom was like a cross-section of long winter underwear, extending down to my kneecaps. I took a deep breath. A man's self-image has some connection to the way he binds his privates. For 20 years I'd been wrapping mine in briefs and jock straps. This was something else entirely.

"It's awfully quiet in there," said T.J., his voice coming through the locked door.

I tugged on the garments, then stood before the full-length mirror and stud-ied myself. I scarcely recognized the guy in the mirror. I didn't know whether to laugh or cry.

"T.J.," I called out, "are you sure there's no way I can go on my mission without the underwear?"

As I knew he would, he burst into laughter. Then he reassured me one more time. "Listen, Jon," he said. "I hear those Italian women are gorgeous and dan-gerous. If I were you, I wouldn't *want* to go without the garments."

I was to learn later that whatever dampening effect the garments may have on the ardor of dangerous foreign women, they don't spoil things for Mormon couples. The libido adjusts. It's all in the eye of the beholder. If a Mormon newlywed is crazy about his bride, pretty soon her garments start looking like something out of Victoria's Secret.

❧❧❧

On June 3, 1979, weird underwear, nervous stomach cramps, and all, I landed in Rome to begin my mission. I spent the first couple of months near the mission headquarters, just long enough to get over my jet lag and go through two months of intensive language training. Then I was sent south to Naples to begin my missionary service in earnest. Napoli, or "Nah-pu-la" as the natives called it in their guttural dialect, was the oldest city in this ancient land, older than Milan or Florence or even Rome. Before there was a Roman empire, Egyptians and Africans were sailing in and out of the Neapolitan port. Walking the crowded, narrow, winding streets, it was difficult to imagine that some of the cobblestones under my feet dated back to the 15th century. I was transported to another era.

Nothing looked or sounded or smelled familiar. The people seemed to sing when they spoke their rhythmic language. Everyone perspired through their clothes in the dank Mediterranean heat, making them seem crudely sensual, and at the same time, repulsive. Before long, I let myself go and allowed this strange culture to overwhelm my senses. Only then did I begin to see the Italians for who they were, amazingly positive people, indefatigably compassionate.

It was only a few months later when I was sitting in an Italian family's parlor telling them about our church that the earth began to move. The grandmother rose from her chair and screamed, "Terremoto!" That word wasn't part of my vocabulary, but I knew what it meant. There was a low rumble, like somebody beating bass drums in hell. The sound grew so loud that we couldn't hear ourselves screaming. Then, as if we were all sitting on an inflatable raft, the tile floor rippled like a wave from one side of the room to the other. As the wave passed under us, I watched my partner rise and drop, then he watched me do the same.

We jumped up and scrambled out the door as rapidly as we could. The centuries-old limestone block building had stopped swaying by the time we reached the street. Hundreds of people stood around anxiously talking to each other, trying to calm the crying old ladies, afraid to go back inside, with no idea what to do next. That earthquake, which had come from beneath Mount Vesuvius, the very volcano that had spewed its guts and entombed the city of Pompeii centuries earlier, had forced more than a million people out of their homes that night. I spent the next six months helping to deliver provisions and clothing and temporary shelter to people who needed it. While earnestly engaged, I began to see myself in a whole different light.

On the seventh day of each week, tired of walking the streets, I wrote in my journal or wrote letters to Marq, Mom, or the Jensens, usually about how the veil of ignorance was slowly but surely being lifted from the nation of Italy— as if my presence could make any difference in a culture 4,000 years old. Reading those letters now, I am chagrined by their naiveté and indoctrinated language, but I'm delighted by their absence of fear and anger. I can see my life changing in those letters. Nowhere in anything I wrote was there a trace of self-awareness. I forgot about my interests and concerns during those two years in Italy.

I involved myself completely in the lives of others, Italians who struggled merrily every day to eke out an existence. Their children seemed oblivious to the fact that they were poor. On the streets of Naples, *everyone* was poor. Most Neapolitans lived in apartments that would have made the Encinitas duplex seem luxurious. It was common for three generations of an Italian family to share one small living space. They were poor, but only in terms of money. No one ever went hungry, including the "Americani." Many were the late evenings that someone would shout an invitation to me and my missionary companions to come inside and sit and ". . . mangiare. Forza! Dai! Su!" We would eat until midnight or until we couldn't stuff another ricotta-filled cannoli into our bellies, whichever came first. Sometimes, we would even get the chance to say a few words about our religion and how it makes families and nations stronger. The Neapolitans marveled at my fluency, which was often better than theirs. I usually answered their compliments by saying something like, "That's what happens when you're in the service of God."

My mother was my most faithful correspondent. I received a letter from her every week, like the turning of a calendar page. Her messages were always upbeat and encouraging, never a mention of troubles with her selfish, simple-minded husband. But then I received a letter more gleeful than all the rest. "Your brother is getting married!" Mom wrote. "He has met a wonderful girl who is also new to the church. The two of them make the most handsome couple I've ever seen." And then, "At long last, your brother seems to have found his way in life. He's a man, a gorgeous, good man."

My mother seemed happier about Marq's engagement than she had about her own wedding a couple years earlier, certainly happier than she'd been in years. The enthusiasm that bubbled right off the pages of that letter made me cry tears of joy—joy for my mother's pleasure and appreciation that Marq had made Mom proud. It was about a week later that I received another letter, this one from his fiancée, Karen. "I'm just writing to tell you that I feel blessed to have met such a wonderful man as your brother, Marq. I've heard so much about you. I look forward to meeting you and especially to being a part of your family." This woman practically dripped off the pages of her letter. Little did she know that she was the best thing to happen to our family since Daryl was born. I couldn't wait to meet her, and, more intensely, I looked forward to meeting someone *like* her who would fall in love with me the way she had fallen in love with my brother.

I returned from Italy with a broadened mind, fluency in a language, and an even greater desire to go to college. Once again, I took inventory of my assets and decided that if I were to have any chance of getting there, I'd have to do it with my legs. Many of the other missionaries in Italy spoke glowingly of "BYU." That was Brigham Young University, the church-sponsored college in Utah. I didn't know much about it, except that the school fielded a competitive football team, a sometimes noteworthy basketball team, and a powerhouse track-and-field squad.

I wrote a letter to a man named Clarence Robison, the track-and-field coach at BYU. My hope was that the church-sponsored university might be a little more sympathetic to an aspiring student who had just donated two of his college years to missionary service. Besides, I'd heard wonderful things about this man. Of course, he'd never heard of me, so I talked up my talents as an athlete, making a big deal of my triple-jump record at Santa Monica Junior College and my two silver medals at the Southern California Conference Relays. I mailed the letter and worried, praying that once again I could parlay my mediocre athletic talents into a college education. The odds seemed long. This wasn't Anderson Junior College or Santa Monica; this was BYU, one of the best universities in the west. As the days passed, I made inquiries at San Diego State, Cal State Northridge, Fullerton State, and UC Irvine, just in case my letter to BYU had been an overly optimistic waste of paper and ink.

The coach was gracious enough to send a short response saying he'd be pleased to meet me if I ever found myself on campus. That was all the excuse I needed. I took it as an invitation to audition. I tried to suppress the knowledge that, after two years away from athletics, I probably couldn't do much. I phoned him and said I'd be driving to Provo during the Christmas break with my friend Denise (who was also traveling to that area), and would he suggest any drills I might add to my workout regimen, falsely suggesting that I had one. I called Coach Robison almost every other week for the next five months to report on my progress. And I called Marq, who was living in Provo with his new wife, Karen, and arranged for a place to sleep.

I was at the wheel that evening when Denise's Mustang reached Nefi, a tiny Utah town perched where I-15 rises to a high point. I could see 20 miles ahead, and there, up on a plateau at the western foot of the Wasatch Range on the westernmost face of the Rocky Mountains, was the campus of Brigham

Young University. It stood alone in the middle of the high desert. I could see its lights sparkling in the dark, a sort of beacon. "There it is!" I exclaimed to Denise, but she was asleep. I pulled over. I wanted to get out and take a long look. The air was thin and dry and clean.

Coach Clarence Robison was a tall man, about 6'5", his hair white and flowing. Lines handsomely creased his face, making him seem both wise and warm. He still walked with the gait of an athlete, long smooth strides carrying him a great distance with each step.

I arrived for my appointment early. On the wall outside his office was the record board, which bore the names of the school's most decorated track-and-field athletes. Ralph Mann—110-meter high hurdles—world record. Doug Padilla—two NCAA championships. Ed Eyestone—10,000-meter champion and three-time Olympian. Henry Marsh—steeplechase champion and four-time Olympian. Pertii Pousi, a name I had never seen or heard, topped the list of long jumpers and triple jumpers, my events. My heart sank. His records were three feet and five feet beyond my best long jump and triple-jump marks. I suddenly felt terribly foolish, standing there waiting for an interview with the man who had coached all these world-class athletes.

The long jump and the triple jump are competitions that separate the best from the rest by fractions of an inch. Athletes work for years to add mere inches to their jumps. The performances on the record board made my best efforts look like something from the playground at Centerville Elementary School.

"You must be Jon." Coach Robison's bass voice drowned out the noise in the fieldhouse. I spun and saw him, standing by the office door, smiling, holding out his hand.

"That's me," I said, hoping he hadn't noticed my mouth wide open as I'd read the record board. His shake was gentle but enthusiastic.

"Let's sit down and chat," he said, motioning me inside.

Photographs of past great athletes adorned the walls. He stopped to let me gaze. "You coached Ralph Mann?" I asked.

"Oh, I don't know about that," he said with a smile. "Ralph didn't need much coaching." He looked up at the picture on the wall. "Hard worker. I had to run him out of the fieldhouse many a night. He's married now, with three children. Lives in Florida."

The coach's response seemed odd; he'd said nothing of Mann's world-record sprint. "And Henry Marsh?" I asked.

"He's an attorney in Salt Lake City. Well respected. He's married. Four children." Nothing about Marsh's bronze medal at the Summer Games in Seoul. I noticed that the NCAA championship plaque wasn't in a place where it was immediately visible from the entrance, but was at the back of the office.

Notwithstanding the warm welcome, I sensed that I shouldn't waste this man's time. I started right in on the speech I'd silently rehearsed a hundred times during the drive from San Diego. "My best marks at Santa Monica College were nothing," I blurted out, apologizing for how poorly they compared to the records I'd read on the board outside the office. "I competed in track and field as a way to stay in shape for basketball. I was virtually uncoached as a jumper at Santa Monica College. I'm sure that as I learn proper technique, I have the ability to improve on my best marks."

It was overkill. Robison had decided weeks earlier that he liked me. He could see I'd followed his workout regimen, and there's not a coach in the world who doesn't appreciate an athlete who comes to camp well conditioned. Although I tried to speak without getting emotional, my cheeks were flushed, and my eyes shone with tears. He could see I was ready to step onto the runway right then and snap off a 25-footer in jeans and T-shirt if he'd asked for a demonstration. Besides, his recruiting budget was nothing close to what the school gave the football and basketball coaches. He liked the idea of spending the price of a postage stamp to recruit a long-legged athlete who was willing to work as hard as I. And as it happened, he'd been in the process of trying to fill out his roster with a few good jumpers.

After questioning me about my trip to Italy, my academic interests, my career goals, and my study habits, the wise old man smiled and leaned back in his big leather chair. His expression said that I didn't have to try to sell myself like a used car. "I propose this, Jon. Let's meet back here tomorrow morning. Come dressed out. We'll go through a little workout and talk some more."

The muscles in my legs twitched with a rush of adrenaline. I tried to appear composed. "Sure," I said. "I'll be here."

I lay awake all night on Marq and Karen's living room floor, wondering what the coach might ask me to do the next day. Would I run a few miles for him? I could do that. Would he ask me to sprint the runway and hit the board a few times? That made me nervous. I hadn't long-jumped or triple-jumped in three years. I decided that whatever the next day might bring, I would do it, flat-out.

It was a relief to get up the next morning. I put on my sweats for a run, careful to save my best shorts and T-shirt for my all-important workout later that day. The fog on the floor of the Utah Valley was heavy and still as I jogged around the neighborhood, about two miles. I watched the ground carefully, looking for rocks and sticks and ice patches and anything else that might cause me to trip or slip and risk pulling a muscle. My demons ran along with me. *Don't snap another tendon.* I remembered the night I chased a bus through Compton and ended my college basketball career. Maybe more important on this day, though, was my certainty that my father wouldn't show up for this one.

Karen kindly offered me the use of her car. I drove to the giant, dome-roofed fieldhouse, looking at the fresh-faced students along the sidewalks and wondering if I'd ever take my place among them. By the time I arrived at Coach Robison's office, I was covered with a thin layer of nervous sweat.

He was busy taking phone calls and giving instructions to his assistants and trying to organize something that was obviously more important than my visit. I waited for him to look my way, and when he did, I waved at him, motioning that I'd stand outside. He hardly seemed to notice. It was nothing like the enthusiasm he'd shown the day before. I couldn't help but wonder as I walked around the track: Had he changed his mind during the night? Had he reevaluated my performances at Santa Monica and decided they didn't measure up? Had he called somebody and heard negative reviews?

Finally he strode out. "Sorry to keep you waiting, Jon," he said.

"No problem."

"Let's go over to the field, and I'll explain what I want to do today."

We walked to the south end of the big steel building, where it opened up to a practice field 50 yards long and wide, covered by green synthetic turf. Coach Robison calmly described a series of exercises he wanted me to perform for him—"just to get you limbered up for the workout." The limbering up part itself sounded like more strenuous labor than I could get through in one day.

The stretches felt as if they'd rip my hamstrings from their posts. The exercises discovered muscles I didn't know I had. Then we prepared for the workout. It was to start with a drill he called pop-ups. I helped him line up 12 hurdles in a row, about three feet from each other. All were hitched up to their highest setting, at about my waist. "Go ahead and pop over these," he said casually. "High knees will keep your toes clear as you pass over them."

It must have been the adrenaline generated by fear of tripping over one of those hurdles. I amazed myself by clearing them all, five times through without a crash.

Then came the box drill. We lined up five white wood boxes that looked like pyramids with the tops cut off, from the shortest, about knee high, to the tallest, at about the level of my hips, about ten feet apart. "This is a good bounding exercise," he said. "The key here is to maintain your speed through the drill." He directed me back about 20 yards and instructed me to hit the first box in a sprint.

I bounced off the top of the first box, stepped hard from the floor to raise myself to the second box, jarred myself as I stomped the floor to rise to the third box, gritted my teeth as I lunged to make the fourth box, and grunted as

I reached with all my might for the fifth box. I slapped my foot on it and pushed myself over it, trying to land as softly as I could and slow to a stop. I was utterly astounded that I hadn't crumpled to the floor and skidded face-first into one of those boxes.

Coach Robison seemed unimpressed. "Good," he said, still calm. "Let's do four more of these, and we'll move on." I had to go inside myself, to a place I'd never been, to find the concentration I needed to clear those boxes four more times. The workout lasted about an hour and a half. All the while, I tried to focus on breathing deeply so I wouldn't appear overtaxed, and on seeming light and graceful, like a dancer. I listened for my mother's shrill voice in my mind, instructing me to keep my chin high, stomach tight, "Relax. Relax! Smile!" I almost wished that I had stayed in her class and become a better dancer. Almost.

Coach Robison slapped me on the back to signal the end of the workout. "How do you feel?" he asked with a wry smile.

"That was a little different from anything I've done," I told him with a relieved laugh, unwilling to admit that my legs felt like sponge rubber.

"Well, you seemed to get the hang of it. Most jumpers have to sidestep the last box on the first few run-throughs." That was encouraging. "You look strong," he went on, "but you're a little heavy for a jumper."

Heavy? Hell, I was 6'4" and all of 180 pounds. I wondered how I could be any skinnier. As a junior college basketball player, I was a stringbean— Humpback Jack from Across the Track. Compared to the world-class athletes Robison had coached, I was soft.

"Track-and-field athletes don't get training table," he said, "which is fine by me. It just fattens people up and slows them down." It sounded as though he might be saying that I was on his team, but I couldn't tell.

Back in his office, he ended the suspense. "I think you can help this team," he said. Then he solemnly added: "And it's pretty clear you wouldn't do any-thing that would bring disfavor or embarrassment to this university." I got the impression that he thought the second part was more important than the first. "Our indoor season begins in late January. Let's figure out what we need to do to get you enrolled in the winter semester." He never mentioned scholar-ship money, and I wouldn't have dared ask about it. He seemed to know I was flat broke with no means of support.

As we parted company, my heart was doing triple jumps inside my chest. I got about a block away from campus to a side street where I thought no one would see me and screamed at the top of my lungs. "Thank you! Thank you! Thank you!" I knew this stroke of good fortune would change the course of my life. I got in the car and drove until the tears in my eyes blinded me and I had to pull over.

✤✤✤

The university accepted few of my academic credits, insisting I drop back and become a second-semester freshman after two full years of junior college. I didn't mind. I was in. That's all that mattered. Coach Robison paid my tuition out of his scholarship allotment, and I took care of everything else. I found a job as an Italian-language instructor. Twenty hours a week at $4.40 an hour would be enough to buy groceries after my paint factory money ran out. Oatmeal and juice in the morning, macaroni and cheese at night—enough to get by on, and I wouldn't be drinking powdered milk. Never again.

It wasn't just my fear of going back to the paint factory or some other lousy job. I loved this place and the people in it. The teachers, the students—all of them seemed to be up to worthwhile, fascinating things. I wanted to be one of them, and was afraid I never could. I hardly spoke to anyone; I didn't dare, for fear they'd realize I didn't belong there. With little money and no car, I had no social life. I couldn't think of asking a girl out on a date. Where would I take her? How would I pay for anything once we got there? Besides, I didn't want anyone to ask me questions. The first question was always, "So, what year are you in school?" followed by the second, "What's your major?" I didn't want anyone to know that I was a 23-year-old freshman who hadn't declared a major.

Also, I didn't want anyone to know who I was or where I came from or, especially, what my family background was. I was trying to create a new identity for myself. I was trying to build a new life. How could I explain that to a date in a casual conversation? No. I would just lie low and work hard.

✤✤✤

CHAPTER TEN ❦
Good-bye, Huckleberry Finn

I had another reason to go to Utah—to visit my older brother. I'd hardly seen him in the nearly five years I'd been away from home since my high school graduation. Marq and his wife, Karen, lived in a one-bedroom apartment on the second floor of a tidy little complex on Provo's south side.

By most standards, the cloister of modular apartments would have been considered lower-class. But this was Provo. Young Mormon couples migrated here from all over the country to attend the university and start their families. In that culture, little time was lost in getting pregnant. The assumption was that as long as young people worked hard and remained faithful to the simple principles of good living that they'd been taught, they'd be able to provide for themselves and their children. Marq and Karen soon had a baby. Life was good. As always, I aspired to follow in his footsteps.

When I arrived to stay at their apartment, Karen opened the door and greeted me with a smile. It was as if I was meeting someone I'd always known. Marq had done well for himself. She had a warm, bright expression. From her Italian ancestors, she had inherited olive skin, dark hair, and brown eyes. She was about 5'5", and in many ways she resembled my mother.

Karen looked tired, as would any new mother and housewife who worked a daily shift waiting tables. But she seemed to be holding it together quite well. She had bounced back from her pregnancy in good form. I could tell that my brother's wife was a strong woman. She would need to be.

The wispy-haired blond crawling around on the floor was my nephew, Anthony, their first-born. Marq was sprawled out on the couch, hands behind his head, a big smile on his face. He nodded in the direction of Karen, and I flashed ten fingers, to mean, "You scored, bro." He nodded toward the toddler on the floor and poked a thumb into his own chest, as if to say, "I made that, and ain't he handsome." Marq, the family man. The transformation was astounding.

He hoisted himself up to give me a hug, the prelude to our customary wrestling match. We strained to throw each other on the floor, laughing and growling as we grappled. "Don't step on the baby, boys," Karen said, smiling.

Although Karen was only a semester away from graduating from BYU and earning her teaching credential, they'd decided to put Marq's education first. Karen would work and care for Anthony; Marq, when he wasn't working in the warehouse of a nearby vitamin company, would tend to his studies. He was to earn a degree in physical education, then teach and coach.

"We have it all planned out," he told me.

"And once the kids are in school, I can finish my degree," Karen chimed in from the kitchen.

"We'll both be teaching," Marq said, "so we'll always be close to our children, even when we're working."

"Children?" I interrupted. "As in more than one?"

They smiled. "We think we'd like three," Marq said proudly.

"I'd have as many as five," Karen added.

What impressed me most was that they had obviously talked about these things. They had sat down together on a number of occasions and discussed what they wanted to do with their lives. They had a strategy for earning their living. They had a plan for how big they wanted their family to be. They were communicating with each other. They were cooperating. Marq seemed to be doing everything right. It was such a relief; he seemed to have come through his childhood intact. He had listened to people like T.J., and it seemed to be working for him.

One autumn afternoon, I dropped by the apartment (by this time I had found my own place). Marq wasn't there, and the baby was napping. I could tell that Karen wanted to talk. She poured me a glass of milk and set out a dish of cookies, and we sat at the kitchen table.

"One day this fall," she began, "Marq came home wearing gym trunks, a T-shirt, and basketball sneakers. He was soaking wet with sweat. Now, that didn't make sense; the timing didn't fit. He was supposed to have been in class for four hours. I didn't say anything, but when it happened again the next week, I began to wonder if he'd been in class at all.

"And then I began to wonder if he was doing any studying. I'd never see him open a textbook at home, but I assumed it was because he was doing all his homework at the library. Now I wasn't so sure."

She was afraid of how Marq might react if she questioned him. She was even more afraid of what his answers might be. But she finally worked up the nerve to ask: Where had he been?

Marq had never been one to hedge. "He just shrugged," Karen told me, "and he said, 'At the PE building.' He was at the gym playing basketball instead of attending class! And then he dropped the bomb. He said, 'I haven't been to class yet. I'm starting to think this college thing isn't for me.'"

Karen was devastated. Just like the old days back at the Anderson YMCA, Marq was enjoying eight-hour basketball marathons. This time, though, they came with a price. His irresponsibility didn't just disappoint his young wife; it betrayed her. She had made such a sacrifice to get him started, putting off her own career and dreams, working as a waitress. Marq had squandered that sacrifice.

Karen had discovered the enigmatic side of my brother's personality. She had witnessed what those of us who knew him best had come to accept as "Marq's way." Whenever he did something that seemed to defy logic, that seemed to contradict what would have been rational and defeat everything he was working for, we'd just say, "That's Marq's way." Whenever he found himself on the brink of success, something in him would explode and destroy it. I was always reminded of the way he would thrill crowds with his impassioned play on the basketball court, diving for loose balls and grabbing rebounds from much larger opponents . . . only to dribble the ball off his foot or throw it out of bounds. Marq had lived his life as if he were at war with himself. His way of doing things gradually came into view for me, and shockingly resembled "the pattern," the way our father self-destructed. I'd never thought to warn his trusting new bride about "the pattern." Why should I? My brother had fought back from a huge deficit. Who was I to think he couldn't shake his demons and start fresh? Who was I to jinx his best chance at happiness?

"I'm shaken," Karen told me that afternoon. "Really shaken. I don't know how I can trust him after this." As much as I might have empathized with my sister in-law's shock and disappointment, I couldn't condone what she had just done. She had ratted on my brother, and by so doing, she had lost an ally in me. I was sure Marq couldn't trust her either. By confiding in me, someone she barely knew, she had betrayed her husband. Surely she couldn't have thought she would find solace and support in me. No. Her motive was clear—to expose Marq's unforgivable act of irresponsibility. Perhaps she thought she could teach him a lesson by embarrassing him in front of the rest of the family. I could only imagine what she'd told her parents, a doting couple who had objected to the marriage in the first place. My sister-in-law had gravely misjudged me. I would not take her side, if that's what she wanted. I decided then and there that I would stay out of the business of my brother's marriage. I didn't utter a word about his missteps. I wouldn't have to.

With his own punishing brand of self-deprecation, Marq admitted he'd thrown away a golden opportunity. I'd seen him put himself down for other transgressions—the shoplifting conviction and subsequent prison stint; the bad grades; the fistfights; all the way back to Mauldin, and the broken bottles in the neighbor's garage. He beat himself up, as if berating himself in front of others would somehow redeem him.

"I'm an idiot . . . an idiot and a loser," he kept saying over and over again, fists clenched.

Karen conceded she'd put too much pressure on him, but I could tell she took no blame. The couple decided not to talk about it. But she never forgot. And she never let her wayward husband forget about it either. Whether intentional or not, Karen had a catty way of reminding Marq of his inadequacies. "Marq, the baby needs a new diaper, if you can change him without making a mess." "Marq, could you set the table for dinner, without dropping another dish?" "Marq, could you take the garbage out, without getting lost?" Her sappy-sweet voice tinged with sarcasm. It ate away at Marq's vulnerable self-esteem. Karen also had a quick tongue and an instinct for how to belittle and insult her husband when she wanted to win an argument. With just a few words, she could lay open Marq's insecurities and expose his resentment of women.

"One night I had just gotten the baby to sleep," she confided to me during the winter. "It had taken about an hour of rocking. Marq was lying in bed watching some comedy show on TV. Right when I lay Anthony in his crib next to the bed, Marq burst out in laughter and woke the baby. I was furious. I just said over and over again, 'I can't believe you're that stupid.'"

I was 12 years old the last time I'd used that word in reference to my brother. On that occasion, the next thing I knew I saw a croquet mallet coming at my nose. But Karen didn't know; no one had told her never—NEVER—to call Marq stupid.

"You shut your mouth!" he roared, as he put his fist through the bedroom wall over the bed, as though he were punching a hole in a sheet of paper. The entire dynamic of their relationship changed that day. Karen could never again be at ease around her combustible husband, and he could never again trust himself around her.

Propelled by nothing more than the inertia of their great expectations, the couple went on. Two years after the birth of Anthony, their second child, Ryan, was born, a handsome boy with jet-black hair. The euphoria that accompanies a newborn baby only lasted a few days. Then things got back to normal. Their invitations to me to come over for dinner became rare, then stopped, and I seldom visited. I could tell by Marq's silence when I called to chat that something was eating at him. He was getting frustrated, feeling the stress of disapproval, and I knew how poorly Marq handled disapproval, especially from women. When he spoke at all, he talked about what an idiot his boss was. He had little to say about Karen and the kids and treated my inquiries about them as invasive. I was offended by the way he shut me out. Eventually, I stopped calling. He seemed to want it that way. We lived a few miles apart, but we seldom spoke. Our reunion was over.

Just as my older brother was losing his way, I was finding mine. My first step was an accidental one, seemingly in the wrong direction. Enrolled in classes at Brigham Young, I took my seat in room F-243 in the basement of the Harris Fine Arts Building for a class called "Communications 316." No sooner had it started than I realized I'd made a mistake. I'd thought it was a regular writing class, one that would lead to a spot on the school newspaper and let me assemble the beginnings of a writer's portfolio. Instead, I had accidentally fallen into a broadcast writing class. I would have walked out that first day were it not for the man standing at the front of the room explaining the syllabus.

Lynn Packer was a veteran investigative reporter for the CBS television affiliate in Salt Lake City. Packer was the one they sent to cover stories that no one else had the stomach for. People who had something to hide called their lawyers when they saw him coming. And for good reason. When Packer reported a story, he took no prisoners. His demeanor suited his approach to journalism. Angular and serious, he seemed to sneer at us through squinted eyes and clenched teeth. He looked and talked like a Clint Eastwood character.

It was his fervor that struck me that first day and kept me from transferring. He spoke passionately, although in monotone, about a television reporter's power to tell compelling stories through the use of pictures and sound and tightly written declarative sentences. Packer detested mediocrity and systematically blasted it in his class sessions. I liked his style and vowed never to be among those unfortunate students who found themselves at the wrong end of one of his scathing critiques. The more he talked about his class being the toughest any of us would ever take and how we ought to drop out if we weren't committed to journalism, the more determined I became to stay right there in my seat. I began to feel that being a reporter was what I wanted to do for a living, and that this man could give me a jump-start.

At the end of the first session, Packer handed out our first assignment: Find a newsworthy happening somewhere on campus and, with the assistance of one of the novice camera operators from the corresponding technical class, assemble a cohesive report on a videotape cassette. He explained in detail what kind of quality he expected and offered very few specific instructions on how to achieve it. Then he walked out of the room, leaving most of the 20 students in our class moaning.

I had a hunch he was testing us—to see who would come back with something, anything; who would come back with excuses; and who wouldn't come back at all. Eleven years into my career, I still refer to it as "Packer's Axiom," the most useful lesson I've ever learned on television news reporting: Bring home a story. Beat your deadline. No excuses.

I went right to work on it. I learned that the governor would be appearing on campus that evening to give a speech. I scoured all the newspapers I could get my hands on in the library. I even went to the microfiche and read old articles that referenced him. As he entered Harmon Hall, there I stood, microphone in hand, blocking his path. He was gracious as I stammered through a series of clumsy questions I'd gleaned from all the newspaper articles. The governor was congenial and responsive. He spoke intently and with conviction, but I didn't understand a word he said. His impatient aides gave us all of three minutes before they whisked him into the auditorium.

I spent half the night studying the videotape and piecing it together into something that might make sense and would run exactly 90 seconds. Two days later, I was back in class, handing my cassette to Packer. My breath quickened as I watched him plug it into the player to show it to the entire class. When it ended, he appraised it, using words such as "enterprise," "timeliness," "immediacy," and "clarity." I wanted to cheer. The assignment had cost me an evening's study and a night's sleep, neither of which I could afford, but it seemed well worth the loss. I'd found what I wanted to do for a living.

Packer became my new mentor, like Casey, Gentry, and Jensen before him. He taught me how to become a television newsman and helped me lay the foundation for my career. It was only recently that I learned that he had singled me out for special attention—and not because he saw talent or intelligence.

"The day you walked in, I said to myself, this kid came from the streets," he told me. "I thought, hey, if he goes after a story the way he goes after a class assignment, then BYU just might have a first-team all-America journalism student."

Packer's class was one pole of my life, and the long-jump runway was the other, the place where I offered up my daily prayer that I could stretch myself further than I knew I could go. The only other jumper who had made the traveling squad, a freshman named Steve, had better legs than I did, but a lousy work ethic. His immaturity caused him to be overly impressed with himself, as though he fancied he was some sort of local celebrity by virtue of his scholarship-athlete status. He often missed workouts and loafed when he did show up. His laziness eventually caught up with him. Strained leg muscles sidelined him

The earliest existing photo of my father—summer, 1937, Walhalla, South Carolina; Bobby (right, age 8) "boxing" with uncle Jimmy.

Bobby (age 13), looking more serious than a young boy should.

A Paul Newmanesque Ensign Bobby Du Pre, circa 1946, with Navy buddy in Charleston, South Carolina.

A skinny new sailor— Bobby at a naval base; I don't know where.

The Du Pre children, circa 1945. Clockwise from lower left: Bobby (age 16), always the serious-looking chap (squatting, wearing shirt and tie); Ann (age 23); Frank (age 21, visiting the family during leave from the Army); Betty (age 18); Jimmy (age 12).

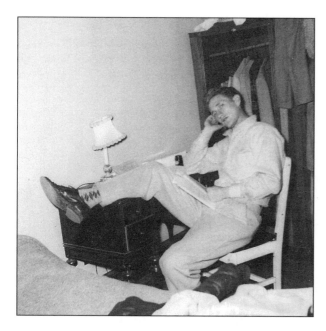

Bobby in law school, circa 1952, hitting the books at the University of South Carolina.

Postmaster Mason—Grandpa Mason Du Pre with his dog, cigarette, and two youngest boys: Bobby (age 21), and Jimmy (age 17). I can only guess why it was common practice for young men to squat when they posed for pictures.

Robert Owen Du Pre, law school graduate, September 12, 1953, University of South Carolina.

Papa Mason's golden boy—Bobby as a handsome young lawyer.

FBI Special Agent Robert Du Pre, 1953, Los Angeles, California.

Grandma Marie—Marie Peek, mother of three (one deceased at the age of six months); restaurant owner/operator; pastry chef; floral designer.

Grandpa Marquis Peek, chief of police, Montebello, California; combat veteran, WWI and WWII; guard, Illinois State Prison in Joliet.

Mason and Sally Du Pre's 50th wedding anniversary, December 24, 1969.

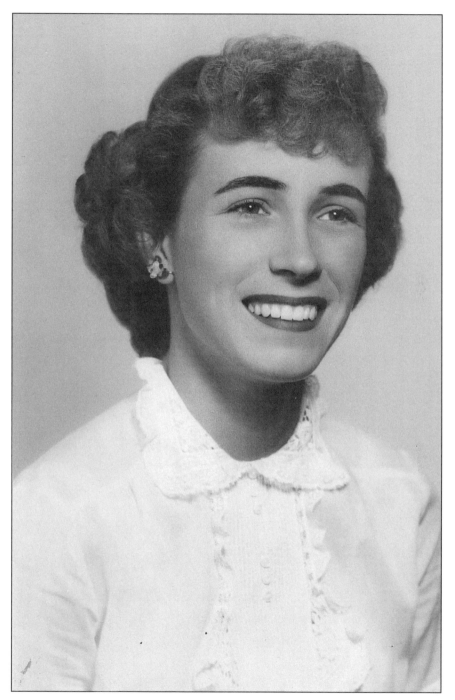

My mom, Marquise Ann Peek (age 18), the drum majorette—spring, 1953,
Montebello High School, Montebello, California.

Their wedding day was my parents' happiest day.

Marquise and Bobby's wedding, September 22, 1957, Westwood, California.

Setting out to see the world after the wedding.

My birth makes news—*Greenville* (SC) *News,* November 6, 1958.

Thurmond Office Worker Adds To Family Circle

Greenville News Bureau
132 Third St., S. E.
By Leased Wire

WASHINGTON—Mr. and Mrs. Robert DuPre, formerly of Walhalla, announce the birth of their second son, John Mason, weighing nine pounds, six ounces.

Mr. DuPre, son of Walhalla's Postmaster Mason DuPre, is a member of the Washington staff of Senator Strom Thurmond (D-SC). Mrs. DuPre is the former Marque Peek. Their older son is named Marque.

John Mason arrived at Columbia Hospital here Thursday, and provided the biggest news in the Thurmond office that day.

My big brother Marq and me (at left).

My dad; Marq (age 7 in background); me (at left, age 5); and Daryl (age 3).

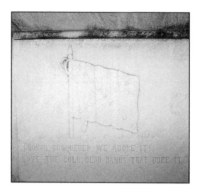

(below right)
A warning to the idealistic lawyer who challenged local tradition—Civil War veterans' memorial, Anderson, South Carolina. The inscription below the confederate flag reads: "Though conquered, we adore it! Love the cold, dead hands that bore it!"

(above left) Law offices of Robert O. Du Pre, circa 1965, 132 East Benson St., Anderson, South Carolina.

Anderson County Courthouse—public defender Du Pre fought many battles here and made many enemies.

Gap-toothed and shy—here I am at age 7, hoping to blend in and be unnoticed.

Our daily reward—Dickson's Ice Cream Shop, where my brothers and I spent our quarters after watching our father show off in the courtroom.

At age 9, I have a chipped tooth and a broken nose.

"Mr. Clutch" and me—summer, 1969, Duke University basketball camp, Durham, North Carolina. I posed for a photo with NBA Hall of Fame guard Jerry West. This was the day I decided I wanted to be a pro basketball player.

Baptism day, winter, 1968, Grace Episcopal Church, Anderson, South Carolina. From left: Marq (age 12), Grandma Sally, Grandpa Mason, Daryl (age 7), Mom, Dad, me (age 10), and Eunice Pracht, our godmother.

Dad and "Sweetheart Boy,"circa 1971. Dad with Daryl (age 10).

Marquise Du Pre, dance instructor, July 1971. Mom performs for the audience at the "Marquise Du Pre School of Dance" annual recital.

(top)
My "field of dreams"—the baseball and football fields at the YMCA, Anderson, South Carolina.

(above left)
My sanctuary—the gymnasium at the YMCA in Anderson.

(center)
Dinner at the vending machines at the YMCA.

The "warm wall" between the furnace and the east entrance to the YMCA, where my brothers and I waited for our ride home.

Lake Hartwell in Anderson, where the dream house would be built.

The hoop on the driveway of the dream house near Anderson, where my older brother and I learned to play basketball.

The "dream house" outside Anderson.

Miss Casey's class, second floor facing left, North Anderson Elementary School, where my teacher told me the tales of Narnia, and taught me I didn't have to be ashamed.

Skinny, but slow, here
I am at age 17.

The end of innocence
—Daryl at age 13.

At my high school graduation, third from right (age 17), San Dieguito High School, Encinitas, California.

Me, the budding broadcaster (age 24) in the KBYU-TV studios, Brigham Young University.

My first publicity photo (age 25), KTVX-TV, Salt Lake City.

The day I married up—way up—August 7, 1986, Salt Lake City.

I'm a Dad! With my kids (from left) daughter Jessie (age 12 months); and son Kasey (age 4), March 1994, Hingham, Massachusetts. (Jessie's not grumpy—she's just squinting into the sun.)

March 1994, San Diego, California— my second glimpse of my father in 20 years.

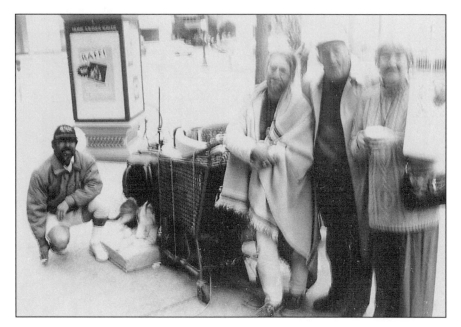

A blurry photo of the street lawyer and his clients, March 1994 in San Diego.

March 1994, Pickwick Hotel, San Diego. My father attempts to cajole Jerry into letting us sleep in his room. It worked.

6-2-95

Dearest Jon & Gina:
I have just saw
your announcement of
the birth of "Jonny". 8'13g
Congratulations to you both
and also take this occasion
to tell Jon how very
much I enjoyed his
visit to San Diego. If
any dream I have is
stronger than having
all of you "boys" together
at one time, I can not
imagine such a dream.
I'm still at Jimmie's. I
left Tucson about the
20th and have been
enjoying seeing Jimmie
and his family.
Let's not wait so long
till we get together. Dad
will be 68 in Sept. — so,
I won't be sitting any

Letter from my father, June 2, 1995.

guarantees that these
gorgeous, shapley
but wrinkled legs will
keep holding out for
many 3000 mile walks.
You both enjoy and
give all my love to
the other two.

Love,
Dad!

Grandpa Bob meets Jessie, September 22, 1995, Mesa, Arizona.

Grandpa Bob meets Jonny on that same date.

My father with my children,
September 22, 1995,
Mesa, Arizona.

September 23, 1995, Mesa,
Arizona. Dad pauses for a
picture before he hits the
road again.

May 16, 1996
702 So. 6th ave.
Tucson, az. 85701

Dear Jon,

Good to see you, and thanks so much for coming through and bailing me out again. I bought food with your gift, but have had to give up smoking again. The motor home deal is great, with the exception that I have to ~~boot~~ buy the gas bottles for the stove at $5.00 each and the water line on the pump inside is so old I have to use a hose. We have a common bath house up the street for showers and a potty.

Jon, I am a drag sometimes and know it. I wish I could get out of this pit, but it is always just out of reach. This morning I have a little bit to eat, but I'll run out in a few days. If I can make it till the 31st I won't owe anyone, and I'll have plenty to pay the rent and stock up with food for June. The rent is $300.00 I make $688.00 on Social Security and VA Disability. My skills are no ~~so~~ longer marketable here. Everyone I try to hustle for some paralegal work is one step ahead of the process server.

If there is any way you can spare a few bucks, daddy will be so grateful. I'm trying to stay happy, avoid bitterness, and treat everyone right. Maybe you will be the answer to my prayers again. Give my love to Gena and the kids, Love, Dad

Letter from Dad, May 16, 1996.

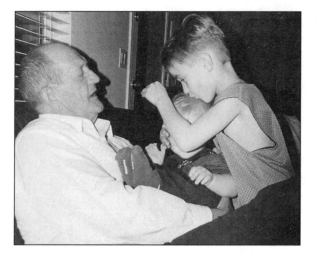

Dad revisits Kasey.

My family posing for our annual holiday greeting card photo, December 1999, Point Dume Beach, Malibu, California. Daryl took the picture.

halfway through the season. By stark contrast, I felt luckier than ever to be in college. And the runway was all mine.

I wasn't much, but I was the only competitive long- and triple-jumper we had. Our distance runners and weight men would win the titles; it was up to me to protect as many points as I could in my two field events. I actually won a few during my first two seasons, but my marks were mediocre at best. If there was anything close to a high point, it came at the 1984 Western Athletic Conference Championships in El Paso, Texas. The university was favored to win the title, again, on their home track. They were loaded with world-class runners from countries such as Ethiopia, Tanzania, and Namibia.

I was midair in the last of my preliminary rounds of jumps when I felt a fierce pain in my right buttock. Somehow I managed to ignore the stabbing sensation and stretch the leap past the point where I thought my legs would snap free at the hip. The demons had reached out and grabbed my leg and had torn my hamstring to shreds. I wasn't sure why I instinctively covered the searing pain in my right hamstring and buttock with a blank facial expression as I carefully walked back to the jumpers' staging area. Maybe it was the ever-present belief that someone was watching, ready to blow an imaginary whistle and announce to the crowd that the BYU jumper named Du Pre was a fake, just a mediocre basketball player who was conning his way through college on a track-and-field scholarship. Faked or real, my desperate jump was good enough to take third place in the competition. I knew, though, that I'd had it. Later I learned I'd torn the tendons in the back of my right leg from my pelvic bone. I'd never jump again. All the effort wouldn't have been worth much, except for something that happened as I limped back to my spot on the grass, just as I was about to give in and let my spirits dive.

"Way to go, Jon!" It was Coach Robison's deep voice booming down from the stadium bleachers. The sound surprised me. I had never heard the man shout before. I didn't think he was capable of raising his voice. Knowing exactly where he was sitting, I looked in his direction. He was easy to spot, standing, his head of white hair above the rest of the crowd. I waved, appreciatively, so as to acknowledge his cheer but not seem as though I was celebrating a third-place finish. He waved back, unabashed. I turned away. I didn't want him or anybody to notice the tears that welled in my eyes. I grabbed a towel from my duffel and dabbed them dry, pretending to wipe away sweat that wasn't there. For an instant, I was back in Anderson, snaring another of those perfectly spiraling passes and feeling the long-forgotten thrill that my father's "Way to go, Jonny boy!" caused to swell within my chest. But the thought only lasted an instant.

I was now further from my father, and for that matter the rest of my family, than I'd ever been. I hardly gave any of them a thought anymore, even though everything I did was motivated by the memory of them. Even Marq—the Huckleberry Finn of my childhood, who lived a few miles from my little apartment and whose renewed companionship I had so relished when I'd arrived in Provo—hardly occupied my thoughts at all. I was emotionally detaching from my past and reaching out to a future that was beginning to come into focus. I was my own person with goals of my own and accomplishments owed to no one but myself. I paid no mind to the fact that my every action was probably fueled by a still intense desire to please my father, and enabled by the strength of resolve developed from the disappointment he had caused. Going to college, this time with independent purpose, filled me with a sense of liberation. As such, I wanted nothing to do with Marq's phone call.

He rang me late one night in the fall of 1983. It was a surprise; his calls had become rarer than mine.

"What's happening, Jon?" he said.

"Hey, not much, man. What's happening with you?"

"Nothing," he said. "You're the college guy. You should have all the exciting stories." I heard his undertone—resentful, bitter.

"Homework," I said with my own undertone. "Excited?"

He paused, then got to the real reason he'd called. "Pops phoned me."

I had to think for a moment. Pops? My father. I was startled. The mention of him made me realize I had hardly thought of him in the five years since I'd left him in that Santa Monica apartment. Chagrined, I tried to sound interested.

"How's old Dad doing?"

Another short pause. "You really want to know?"

I didn't know when that part of Marq's personality had changed. Until he was in his late teens, he said what was on his mind. Now he spoke in riddles and remarks that were heavily laden with meaning only he could have discerned—hazy, roundabout stories, only hinting what he might be getting at, making you guess. It annoyed the hell out of me. And now that I could stand toe-to-toe with him, I didn't feel the need to tolerate his game of psychological checkers. "What do you mean, do I really want to know? I asked you, didn't I? So how is he?"

Another pause. "Well, he's surviving, barely. But you'd probably know better than me that he's not doing great."

I wondered why he'd said it that way. My guess was that Dad had bad-mouthed me to Marq, had told him something about how I'd left him stranded in Santa Monica, causing him to lose his car and his job. I could practically hear the old man ranting. I wasn't about to try to justify my actions of five years earlier. I'd gone beyond generosity and barely survived. If Marq preferred to believe Dad's version of what went down, screw the both of them.

"What the hell would I know? Say man, if you're trying to tell me something, then spit it out. Something about Pops? What's up with him? Where is the old bastard?" I didn't feel the need to be polite and monitor my language, either.

"I don't know," Marq said, with no tone at all.

"What do you mean you don't know. Didn't he—"

"I mean I don't know where he lives!" Marq shouted. Finally, I could hear why he'd called. He'd been terribly upset by Dad's phone call. I couldn't remember a time since 1975, the year Dad left, that Marq hadn't been disturbed by having contact with his father. "You know," he said in a curious, almost disbelieving tone, "I think he's living as a homeless person."

"What makes you think that?" I asked.

"I don't know," Marq said. "After I hung up, I realized that he had never really answered me when I asked where he lived. He just told me that he was on the road a lot. Then he changed the subject and rambled on about conning some VA hospital shrink into signing him up for disability benefits . . . said he cashed his first check at the pawn shop . . . free money . . . said he had to kick some dude's ass when the guy tried to pick his pocket and steal his disability payment."

My thoughts raced. Pity? Empathy? Neither. What overtook me in that moment was a sense of profound relief that my father hadn't taken me all the way down with him. I'd done everything I could muster up for him. The news that he might be homeless didn't surprise me. I'd seen him leaning into dereliction during the last months of my miserable attempt to salvage him in Santa Monica. *I've had enough,* I thought. *I gave at the office.* As hard-hearted as that may have sounded to Marq or anybody else, I've never felt the need to justify my attitude to myself. I've had good friends ask me, "How could you let him go homeless? How could you not take him in or something?" But you had to understand my old man. You had to know my family's history. He was hell-bent for this.

I had contemplated this possibility years ago. When I'd left Santa Monica, I'd wondered what might have become of my father. It was hard to imagine that he could have sunk any lower than the place I'd left him. But without me to pull him up . . . I didn't want to think about it. I pushed back my brother's announcement that our father was now homeless. I was allowing no room in my heart for such things. My plan for my life was all that mattered.

"So what are you telling me, Marq? Am I supposed to go looking for him? Huh? Am I supposed to go save him again?" He didn't answer. "Hey man," I said. "been there, done that. No thanks. Not me. Not again."

Another stretch of silence. Finally he spoke. "I was just going to say that you and I might want to remember him in our prayers tonight." Marq's voice started to crack. "It sounded like he could use a good word."

I didn't know what to say to that. A long pause. "Hey," he said, "I didn't mean to darken your day."

"No, you didn't," I said. "I'm sorry. You're right. Of course I'll say a prayer. Thanks for passing along the news." Then, suddenly attempting to sound upbeat, he said, "Okay, well, you keep up the good work, Jon boy. Make us all proud." Again, I couldn't tell whether Marq really meant what he said or whether he was implying something else. Something like, "You're the only one of us who isn't a dismal failure, Jon boy."

I'd never thought of my brothers in that way. To the contrary, they were two of the most resilient young men I'd ever known. Marq's undying devotion to our father was beyond my limited emotional expanse. He had gotten married and had brought two children into the world, an act of faith greater than mine. Daryl's imaginative, sometimes ingenious way of staying afloat through his teenage years when there was no adult to throw him a life jacket was a marvel to me. When I was away in Italy, Daryl kept my mother company, keeping out of her new husband's way and staying out of trouble so he would never be a hardship to Mom. He learned to play the saxophone and marched in the Mira Mesa High School band. And he never, ever said a harsh word against anyone, even though he had every right to blast us all for leaving him behind. His patience and kindness were an example to me, especially after I learned, years later, what he'd gone through after leaving Mom's house.

❧❧❧

My brothers had shared my disappointments and setbacks. For all I knew, they'd had it worse than I had. My brothers weren't failures. I lay awake for hours that night, staring at the ceiling.

A few months later, I called Marq but got Karen on the phone. Her voice, once cheerful, had dulled since I'd met her. After an exchange of pleasantries, she carefully told me the news. "Marq and I have decided to move," she said. "We're going back to San Diego."

She tried to explain the reasons behind the decision, speaking as if from a script. "Marq's job just didn't look like it was working out. The opportunities for advancement in the company didn't materialize. His boss had a personal grudge against him. We think we might be able to find better opportunities in San Diego, where we know more people. Several people down there have told Marq they would love for him to work in their company."

She sighed, her feigned enthusiasm scarcely veiling a tone of defeat. She explained that they had decided to move in with her parents until Marq found work and they could get into a place of their own. "My folks have fixed up the garage into a little apartment," she said. "It's only for a little while."

We chatted, trying to sound pleasant, both of us pretending we didn't know that this move marked the beginning of the end of their marriage.

I was sick to my stomach when I hung up the phone. It frightened me to think what might be in store for my brother and his family. I looked around my apartment and felt completely alone. Even though I hadn't seen much of them during my first year in Provo, I had taken some comfort in knowing they were nearby.

I felt that buzzing sensation in the back of my head again, the way it had buzzed when Dad left. I felt I could hardly bear this kind of disappointment again. And then a specter of fear rushed over me: Could this be my inevitable fate as well? Were we Du Pres all marked for failure? Was I rotten, too, because I was also the fruit of this broken branch of the Du Pre family?

I was on my own from that moment. My big brother, my Huckleberry Finn, was lost. I couldn't follow him anymore.

❦❦❦

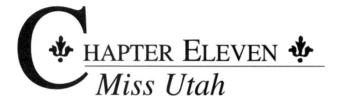

CHAPTER ELEVEN
Miss Utah

I can't really say she walked into the room. It was more like a bounce. I was sitting at the assignment desk of BYU's student television station one afternoon, poring over my erasable-ink-covered plastic desk calendar and trying to shut out the din of the police and fire radio scanners and the ringing telephones, when a young woman, a student, came in. She moved with a confidence that suggested she'd been on staff for months, but I knew I'd never seen her. She walked straight to my desk and introduced herself.

"I'm Gina Larsen," she said in a controlled, rich, pleasant voice that I immediately knew would sound good on the air. "I'm a reporter in the Communications 316 class. I'll be stopping by for story assignments every day at one o'clock." She seemed pleasant and intelligent. But those were attributes I had to concentrate on to notice. She was drop-dead gorgeous—a blue-eyed blonde with a stirring figure, the very type of aspiring TV reporter who would rely on her looks rather than her intelligence or her work ethic to get by.

But this one meant business. I knew nothing about her goals and aspirations, but I could tell she was busy reaching them. Gina Larsen never missed a deadline and never showed up late for work. In fact, she quickly got to the point where she didn't need me to spoon-feed story assignments to her; she came to work with ideas of her own. That eliminated the one excuse I'd had to talk to her, so I looked around for another.

As assignments manager, I decided which photographer would work with each reporter. It suddenly came to me: Why would I want to send some other guy out with Gina when I could go myself? I kicked myself that it had taken me four weeks to figure it out. From then on, Gina never covered a story without me hovering nearby, shooting the pictures and recording the sound. It gave me the perfect excuse to look at her all I wanted, if only through the viewfinder of my camera. It also put me in a position to observe her at work. Her on-the-job performance was perhaps even more impressive than her physical beauty. She held up under deadline pressure. She worked long hours without complaining or wilting under the fatigue. All the while, she was persistently pleasant, and her smile was quick. I found myself watching the clock every day at around 12:45. I wanted to look busy and important when Gina entered. I wouldn't find out until years later that she had looked for excuses to come down to the newsroom just to see if I was behind my desk.

I didn't ask her out on a date. Maybe I was scared, I don't know. Maybe it was more a sense that I didn't want anything to get in the way of this genuinely healthy relationship, one unlike any I'd ever had with a woman before. I'd dated plenty of girls by that time and had found the whole process redundant. I was 25, and most of the girls on campus were too young for me. When there was some attraction between my date and me, we'd end up necking and petting in the cramped bucket seats of my beaten old car . . . pleasurable, momentarily, but empty.

I think the receptionist from the Beverly Hills law office had done more than scare the hell out of me when she opened her blouse and invited me to enjoy her perfect breasts. I think she forced me to make an intuitive decision that would dictate the terms of my relationships with women—to avoid those based on physical attraction. I was also affected by the shame I felt when my father took me along on his visits to Miss Tilly. I didn't want to feel dirty again. I couldn't bear the thought that my physical attraction for Gina might make me do something that would offend her and taint our relationship. So for almost a year, I didn't do anything at all. I just let our working friendship continue. Until the party.

One of the kids in the broadcasting program lived in an apartment complex with a clubhouse that had a barbecue and big-screen TV. He invited a group of us to grill burgers and play volleyball and watch videos. Gina was there, but she'd come on her own.

I was sitting on the couch in the TV room. The phone on the table at the end of the couch rang. It was right next to my elbow, so I picked it up.

"Is Gina Larsen there?" a girl's voice asked.

"Sure," I said. "Let me get her."

Gina was in the next room, standing around talking to some of her friends. I walked over and told her she had a call. She picked up the extension phone on the wall and turned her back to the noise.

I walked back into the dark TV room and sat down in my old place on the couch. I noticed the phone was off the hook, and I started to hang it up. But something made me cover the mouthpiece and listen in.

"How's the party?" the girl asked.

"It's okay, I guess," Gina said.

"What's the matter? Isn't Jon there?"

"Yeah, he's here. He's just watching TV."

"Haven't you been out with him yet?"

"No," Gina said with a sigh. "And I'm getting sick of waiting for him to ask me."

I slowly, carefully, depressed the button on the phone and quietly hung up the receiver. I sat there in the dark for a minute, thrilled. It didn't take me long to finally make my interest known.

❧❧❧

The driveway to Gina's parents' house wound through 15 acres of fruit orchards—trees laden with apples, peaches, pears, cherries, and apricots. The house was one-story, brick, L-shaped, with big picture windows looking up to the granite face of the Wasatch Front, and down to the valley and Utah Lake. "Hmm, quite a spread," I mumbled to myself.

As I brought my rusty old Pinto to a halt, I noticed a heavyset man wearing overalls, plaid shirt, and work boots. He was stooping in the dark, moist soil of the flowerbed that ran along the front walk. *Hired help,* I thought. No wonder their landscaping was so impressive. It was just as I'd suspected: Gina's folks were loaded. She seemed like the kind of girl who came from money—classy, proper, always well dressed, a brand new car.

"Hi," I said to the man in the dirt, a friendly smile on my face. "You the gardener?" I wanted to seem polite, just in case Gina's parents might be spying on me through a window.

He scowled as he rose to his feet, removed his straw hat from his bald head, and looked me over. For one brief second I thought he might be about to punch me. He was a stout man—big around the belly and across the shoulders; with large, heavy hands hanging from the ends of arms that were as thick as my thighs. And he had no neck. This man was a bear.

"Boy," he growled, "I own the ground you're walkin' on."

I'd done it. I'd insulted Gina's father. This burly 57-year-old had poured the open hearth at the U.S. Steel plant in Orem for 38 years. It was one of the most demanding and best-paid jobs in the plant, and Lorrin Larsen had been able to build a small fortune and a large, beautiful homestead for his family. I'd mistaken him for the gardener. He could have swatted me to the ground with one of his leathery paws. But worse, he could have blocked my attempt to court his daughter.

"Great place you have here," I said.

"Yeah, right," he said. "I guess you're here to see Gina." He looked me over again. I imagined what he was thinking: *Skinny kid. What's my daughter wasting an evening with him for?*

"Lorrin Larsen," he said as he extended his huge, leathery paw. It was like shaking hands with a man wearing boxing gloves.

"Jon," I said, sighing in relief.

"I know. I'll go get her."

Mercifully, Gina didn't make me wait. She came bounding out the front door before I even had a chance to ring the doorbell. Her mother, a tall and distinguished-looking woman, had come around the corner of the house; she smiled and waved. I smiled and waved back. Gina bounced right over to my car. The brown Pinto had been nothing to look at even in its better days. Now, it was splotched with Bondo hole-filler; Bondo was practically all that held it together. The car was a metaphor for my life—held together with whatever I could find but still running hard, and getting somewhere. Without blinking, my beautiful date climbed right in.

The plan was to go to a fraternity picnic in a park near the mouth of Provo Canyon. We didn't stay long. We both knew that we wanted to be alone together. I suggested we drive farther up the canyon and explore South Fork. "I've always wanted to see it," I said. My meaning was clear; I might just as well have said, "I've wanted to hold you and kiss you since the first time I saw you."

I parked at the end of the narrow, curving paved road, at the top of South Fork Canyon. We got out and leaned on the hood, both of us trying to seem nonchalant. In the darkness of that remote canyon, there was nothing to look at but each other or the sky, so we both looked up. Against the perfect black- ness, stars I was sure I'd never seen before shone like crystals. Lying back on the warm hood of the Pinto, I felt as if I was suspended in space, swimming in the blackness, tickled by the twinkling lights. This was the most liberating feeling I'd ever known, better than the night of dancing at "The Whip" with the great friends of my freshman year of college. For the first time since I was a child, I could allow myself to experience pure joy, unencumbered by pre- occupation and doubt. In a rare act of self-indulgence, I allowed myself to enjoy the moment, and I felt as though I deserved it.

"I can't believe I'm actually here," I said, thinking not only of how sur- prised I was to be on a date with Gina, but also of all I had gone through to get to this place and this moment.

"It's about time," Gina said.

I turned to look at her leaning against my Pinto. Even in the dark, her blue eyes glowed, and her smile was bright. I don't know exactly where our kiss began or where it ended. It was as though we were continuing something we had started long before. A feeling of total comfort overwhelmed me. All distractions ebbed, and my thoughts focused on the moment and how content I was to be there. I gently pulled her arms toward me, and she willingly responded, wrapping them around my neck and kissing me more. We rolled toward each other and pressed our bodies together. I didn't feel the least bit dirty about what we were doing. To the contrary, it was a worshipful experience. Somehow I knew that this was the woman I had dreamed about when I was a boy.

We spent as much time with each other as our hectic schedules would permit. Getting a date with her required competing with scores of other people and interests, yet I never minded the trouble. She had an uncanny way of making me feel as though I was her top priority. And when I was with her, all the waiting was forgotten. She had to check her schedule for everything, and it was almost always full. A few months later, I found out why. Gina was competing in the Miss Utah pageant. I was dismayed about that, for some reason, and gave her a hard time. Competing in a beauty pageant seemed so artificial, beneath her dignity. We agreed not to talk about it.

There came a week in the spring when Gina was unreachable, stuck in an auditorium somewhere, dancing and singing and otherwise competing. She called me at my apartment late Saturday morning.

"Well," she said amiably, "I know you'll be happy to hear I'm through with that pageant."

I was. But I tried to be polite. "How did you do?" I asked.

"Oh. I did okay."

"What's okay? Doesn't somebody win a crown in those things?"

At that moment, my roommate, Gary, who had overheard my conversation, walked into the kitchen with a copy of the Provo *Daily Herald.* There was Gina's picture on the front page, just below the fold. The headline read: Miss Utah Pageant Crowns Provo Beauty.

"Is that you?" I stammered. "Did you win?"

"Yeah," she said, laughing, "I won. So now that it's over, when are we going out again?"

From then on, dates with Gina usually involved meeting her at her house and driving in her brand new navy-blue Pontiac Grand Prix to some ribbon-cutting, autograph-signing, store-opening, speaking assignment, or singing engagement. I stayed in the shadows, content to watch her do her beauty queen thing. She smiled at everyone, gladly signed autographs, sang on cue, and gave her speech on the importance of self-esteem. I feigned indifference, but I secretly enjoyed studying her poise and grace—and that smile.

Three months later, I sat alone in her parents' family room watching her on television as she glided down the ramp at the Miss America pageant in Atlantic City. "There's your winner!" I yelled to the judges. She did win an award for her performance in the talent competition, which paid several thousand dollars in scholarship money, and I licked my lips when I saw her in that bathing suit. I thought about how sweet her mouth tasted, how supple her breasts felt in my hands, how soft and smooth her body felt when it pressed against mine. I thought about how beautiful our children might be. I thought all those things, without feeling the least bit dirty.

Packer had convinced me that if I was to become a TV news professional, I'd have to spend every free moment on it. So, I became a rug rat in the newsroom, grabbing every chance I could get to take a camera and go cover a story for the nightly student newscast. I put together four times the number of reports Packer required for his class. I was sure to get the highest grade in Packer's class, but I was flunking out of all the others.

I heard about a job opening at KTVX-TV, the ABC television affiliate in Salt Lake City. They wanted a part-time reporter and stringer to work mainly on weekends and holidays. I dubbed about ten of my best pieces onto a videocassette and grabbed the phone. Ron Harrig answered my call. He was the quiet and thoughtful executive producer at KTVX.

"Mr. Harrig," I said, trying not to pant in his ear, "my name is Jon Du Pre. I've been working at KBYU-TV for about the past year, and I want you to see some of my tape. When can I bring it to you?" He told me to come over right away. I hung up the phone and hooted at the top of my lungs. "I've got a job interview!" I shouted. I phoned Gina and told her.

I sat in the KTVX lobby for almost an hour waiting for Harrig. When he finally appeared, I started to tell him about myself. He cut me off. "Let's go back and view your tape." He wasn't interested in small talk. He didn't care about my table manners or how I dressed. He didn't ask about my grades, whether I was involved in student government or glee club or anything else, or what my personal best was in the long jump. He wanted to see my tape.

I followed him into one of the edit suites, careful not to say anything silly (like how the room, with all its editing and special effects equipment, looked like the inside of a space shuttle). I stood off to his right shoulder as he studied my tape.

After five minutes, well into my third report, he spoke: "Hmm. I would have put that higher."

I was embarrassed but thought I'd better say something. "You would have put what higher?"

He paused the tape and shuttled back to the beginning of the third report. "In this piece you buried your lead."

"Where?"

"Watch." He replayed the tape. About 30 seconds into the piece, I heard my videotaped self recite a line that obviously belonged at the beginning; it was clearly the most important element of the story.

"Right there," I said.

"Yup. Right there." Now it was so obvious. There was the lead line, 30 seconds into my report, presented as if it were a minor detail. I'd broken one of the cardinal rules of news writing: *Lead with a lead.* Don't make readers or viewers sift through less important information to get to the punch line. They need the main point at the top.

"Why did you bury that line?" Harrig asked.

"Probably because the police sergeant made the other thing sound more important," I said, shaking my head.

"Did he let you make the arrest?" he asked with a slight smile, the only time I'd seen him smile through his shiny black beard.

"No," I said, confused.

"Then why did you let him write your copy?"

He pointed out several other serious flaws in another piece. "What would you do differently next time?" he asked.

"Leave this tape in my file cabinet at home," I said.

Another small smile. "To the contrary," he said. "I'm glad I get to see the bad with the good. You've done some things well."

I was sitting at my desk in the newsroom two days later, answering phones and monitoring police scanners, when the call came. "Jon, this is John Edwards. I'm the news director at KTVX." My pulse quickened. "Ron Harrig says you're a talented young reporter and a quick study. Is that true?"

"I think Mr. Harrig is a fine judge of talent," I shot back, too excited.

"Oh, and you're a smartass, too," he said. "I like that. Listen, Jon, I'll cut right to the chase. I'd like to offer you the part-time reporter job. What would you say to that?"

"I'd say I'll take it!"

"Why don't you drop by Monday morning, about nine. You can sit in on the morning story meeting, and we'll give you an orientation after that."

My career had begun, not in a ceramics manufacturing plant or a paint factory or a grocery store or a gas station. I was going to work in an honest-to-God television newsroom. I couldn't move. Hell, I could hardly breathe. And yet, my thoughts were as clear as tap water. This was my moment, my stepping-out point. This was the thing I'd been working for. My first clear thought: *Gina needs to know.*

I found her in a classroom and stood outside the window until she looked up at me. I mouthed the words "I got the job!" and raised my fists above my head. She leaped from her seat and scampered out to congratulate me with an embrace. I knew I had done this as much for her as for myself. In her arms, I quietly rejoiced that, at long last, there was someone I could share my accomplishments with.

I immediately dropped out of school, not a difficult transition for someone who was flunking most of his classes, and devoted all my energies to my new job. The gig was part-time, but I worked every day of the week. Gina and I politely argued a few times over whose fault it was that we seldom saw each other, but we agreed that it was a nice problem to have.

I found myself getting more serious about things. I went to my boss three times asking for what I thought was a well-deserved promotion to the status of full-time employee. I figured that anybody who wanted to get married ought to have health benefits. When my boss said there just wasn't room in the budget for a new full-time position, I sent out my résumé tape. The news director at a station in Green Bay, Wisconsin, phoned and said, "You'll get here and look around and think this place is a dump, but I can promise you that you'll work hard and learn what you need to know to become a top-flight reporter." I admired his frankness, appreciated his interest in me, and accepted the job offer, sight unseen.

A few days before packing my bags for Green Bay, Gina and I went out on a date. I had to strain to seem pleasant and undistracted as I rehearsed the speech I'd been composing in my mind. We went to a movie, *Rocky IV.* As usual, she slept through most of it. I didn't mind. As long as she was asleep, she wouldn't notice my apprehension. And besides, I was always happy to find something to tease her about.

"How do you sleep through a *Rocky* movie?" I kept saying all the way back to her parents' house.

"I'm sorry!" she protested. "I'm just worn out." And she was. Those pageant people knew they had an extraordinarily popular queen on their hands, and they were booking her for everything they could. "You find a good horse, you ride the hell out of it," her father kept saying.

We pulled into the driveway, and she started to get out. I touched her arm to stop her. "Can I ask you a few questions?" I said. It was going to be clumsy, but I had to force the issue. Gina deserved to be warned. I'd be on the road to Green Bay in a couple of days.

"Sure," she said, looking curious.

"Gina, I just want to ask you to think about something for a minute, that's all. The question is, what if I turned out to be somebody different from who you think I am?"

She paused. "What are you getting at?" she said as she squinted suspiciously. Now I had her full attention.

"Well, I mean, you haven't met my father. And the thing is, he's not like yours. He's hardly like anybody's." I stumbled through the thumbnail sketch version of my family's sad tale—my parents' miserable marriage and our family's dissolution, my older brother's aborted attempt at being a husband and a father. And then I opened up and said what for me was nearly unspeakable.

"Gina, what if it's a genetic predisposition? What if I'm born to fail at marriage? What if I'm one of those men who can't finish anything he starts?"

The last conceivable thing I wanted to do was to talk Gina out of marrying me. But I couldn't let her go on any further thinking she'd met the man of her dreams. She'd only seen what I'd let her see. It was relatively easy to keep the carefully constructed clone of my formerly insecure self from unraveling in Provo's protected environment where there was nothing to challenge me. Being around Gina had been enjoyable, but now I was contemplating a lifetime with a woman who had expectations of herself and perhaps of me that were far higher than anything I could hope to achieve. While she was preparing to be Miss America, I was trying not to miss too many meals. What if she expected a relationship with me to turn out like the marriage her parents had? The thought terrified me. I knew I couldn't live up to her expectations. I told her as much about myself as I could think of to tell—everything I thought she might need to know, no matter how unpleasant. Then, when she'd heard enough, she pressed her hand over my mouth and interrupted me.

"I'm only going to marry once," she said, looking me straight in the eyes. "The man I marry is mine for the rest of my life, so I prefer to concentrate on what's good about him." I was speechless. All I could do was stare back into her blues. "You worry too much," she said. And with that, the conversation was over.

It was the first day of April, the day before I'd be leaving for Green Bay. This, maybe, was my last date with Gina. The Pinto was pushing its way up Provo Canyon, toward Park City. I turned down the radio. She told me years later that she knew it was coming.

"What would you say," I began, "if I asked you to take me as your husband, for the rest of your life, like you said before?"

She'd been watching the road ahead. I saw her face blossom into radiance. She turned to me. "I don't cook," she said with a twinkle, "and I don't do laundry."

"And I don't care," I said.

"Then, sure," she said. "Good idea."

I screamed and tried to hug her and almost ran off the winding canyon road.

We got to Grub Steak, our favorite restaurant, and sat at our favorite table and giggled at each other all evening. I felt drunk.

❧❧❧

CHAPTER TWELVE
The Toothless Traveler

Packing my gear into the Pinto for the trip to Green Bay, I realized I was continuing the slow, erratic, clockwise circling of America that I'd begun 12 years before, when my family had left South Carolina. This was the northern leg.

I'd hardly made it out of Utah, driving the Pinto, which Gina had named "Old Spot" for the Bondo spots on the doors and fenders, when I drove smack into the worst springtime blizzard in five years. The snow, driven by 40-mile-an-hour winds, slammed horizontally into the front of my car, rushing under my hood and clogging Spot's carburetor. Her engine sputtered and choked, and she slowed to a crawl. "Oh, no, Spot, don't fail me now!" I shouted, panicked at the thought of stalling here, 40 miles from the next town. I gripped the wheel tight and pressed the pedal all the way to the floor. Twenty miles an hour was all she'd do. For two hours I pushed Spot through the storm, and at last we made it to a gas station. Only then did I allow myself a full exhale. "Way to go, Spot," I sighed, "you hunk of junk."

Five days after I had begun my trek, I crept into Green Bay through heavy fog. A bowling convention had taken up almost every hotel room in the city. Bowling is like religion in the northern Midwest, right up there with pounding down brewskies. Except for Green Bay Packers home games, the convention was the biggest event of the year in this frozen mill town. Finally, around midnight, I found a vacancy at the fifth hotel I tried.

"What does it look like?" Gina asked me eagerly when I phoned her. In four months, when we married, Green Bay would become her first home away from Provo.

"I don't know," I told her. "I can't see a thing through the fog." Something in my voice may have hinted that she should prepare for the worst.

The sunrise woke me up the next morning, and I walked outside to look around. A few blocks in any direction and you ran into one of the major paper manufacturing plants that had driven this region's economy for three generations. They made facial tissue, toilet tissue, and cardboard boxes. Then there were the meat-packing plants, where tough nine-fingered line workers, for whom the football team was named, cut the beef and wrapped it for market.

I knew no one when I arrived at WBAY-TV, the CBS affiliate station. I was introduced to few people and was standing around talking to them when I heard a husky voice say, "Hey, kid!" I looked up. Chuck Ramsay, the station's anchorman, who still dominated the ratings as he wound down to retirement, was nodding at me and beckoning. "Hey, kid, come over here."

I walked over to where he was standing. He put his hand on my shoulder and fixed his bright, brown, energetic eyes on mine. "I'm only going to tell you this once," he said earnestly, "and if you're smart, you'll remember it." He raised an admonitory finger. "You gotta watch what you say around here. The TV biz is incestuous as hell. You never know who's sleeping with who."

"What did I say?" I wondered aloud, a little defensively.

"Nothing," Chuck said. "Nothing, yet. But you will, unless you remember what I've just told you. And if you don't, you'll make enemies. I've seen other people come in here and make trouble for themselves, just because they didn't know how to watch their tongue. I don't want to see that happen to you because I can tell you're a decent kid."

His unsolicited bestowal seemed a bit strange, but I appreciated the fact that someone had noticed the new guy. I worked hard over the spring and summer, trying hard to learn everything I could, dreaming all the while of the seventh of August, the day I would marry Gina.

The wedding was in the colossal, six-spired Mormon Temple in Salt Lake City, which the pioneers had built, three-ton granite block by three-ton granite block, a century before. We were ushered upstairs to the Sealing Room, where we'd be joined together as husband and wife for eternity. Neal Maxwell, one of the church's apostles, began by offering each of us a bit of advice. I don't remember what he said to Gina, but I'll never forget what he said to me.

"Jon," he said, "you're a young man with a quick wit but also a sharp tongue." I was astounded. I'd never met the man before, yet he had me down cold. He'd either had a divine revelation or he'd made a few phone calls. "There will be times," he continued, "when you will conjure up the cleverest, funniest things to say about Gina, and in all good humor you will want to say them. My counsel to you is this: Don't." This was the second person who had now warned me to watch my mouth.

I've often wondered whether my father had had an advisor who tried to steer him in the right direction. Having met Senator Thurmond years later, I was impressed that he'd seemed like the sort of man who would have taken his bright, outspoken young staffer under his wing. Did Bobby Du Pre appreciate the attention, or resent attempts to correct his behavior? Always vigilant to avoid my father's mistakes, I took the wise men's words to heart.

Marq was my best man. I noted with sadness that he was no longer wearing a wedding ring. "Happy for you, Bro," he said, looking me square in the eyes. This time, I could tell that he meant it. Daryl was there, too, sitting beside Marq. It was the first time in 12 years that my mother had all her boys together in one place. The sight of us was probably what made her cry throughout the entire ceremony. Afterward, Gina's father, who was misting up a little himself, wrapped his big steelworker's arm around me and muttered, "I always wanted a son." I wanted to tell him, "I've always wanted a father," but it was too emotional to say without losing my own composure.

My side of the marriage was responsible for six or seven of the guests at the reception, among them, the Jensens—as always, cheering on the Du Pre boys. The other guests were friends and relatives of Gina's. Five hundred invitations had gone out; 1,400 guests had appeared. We had fun watching their eyes widen as Daryl greeted them in the reception line, dressed in a snappy rented tuxedo, his punk-rocker hairdo bleached white.

That night, Mr. and Mrs. Jon Mason Du Pre stayed at the Silver King Hotel in Park City. The bridal suite, room 502, has a glass ceiling. Literally as well as figuratively, I saw stars that night. The next day we flew to Mexico for a honeymoon. We returned to Provo, packed Gina's things into a U-Haul, and set out for Green Bay.

No sooner had Gina arrived in town than she landed a great job at the ABC affiliate station, our chief competitor. Her first night on the air, I was standing with four or five of my co-workers, watching the ABC newscast on one of the monitors in the newsroom. When the camera on Gina came alive, I got goosebumps up and down my arms. But I quickly realized I'd have to get used to being married to someone who attracted a lot of attention, especially from men.

Behind me I heard a voice yell out, "Check out the bimbo on channel five!" It was Lanny, a producer who had come on board a week earlier. "Look at all that hair! I wonder if she's a natural blonde?" I looked around at Lanny, thinking he must be joking. He wasn't. "You gotta believe there's nothing under it but air!" I felt heat rise in my face. "I heard she's from Utah," he went on. "Yeah, man, they grow big-boobed bubbleheads in Utah!"

His banter was stopped by a blow to the ribs from Tim Blotz's right elbow. Tim was a fellow reporter and a friend of mine. "That's Mrs. Du Pre, asshole," he said quietly, glaring down at little Lanny. Lanny seemed to shrink even smaller as he realized what he'd just done. He slunk out of the newsroom and didn't show his face the rest of the evening.

"Hey, kid!" I looked over to the corner where Chuck Ramsay was sitting at his desk, observing the scene. "What did I tell ya?"

❧❧❧

Gina and I competed with each other for stories, critiqued each other's performances, and cheered each other's successes. We loved the idea that we were being paid for doing what we'd done for nothing in college. I didn't make much and neither did she, but we put our paychecks together and felt wealthy. When my old Pinto snapped a steering cable, losing its ability to turn left, we decided to trade it in. Once we'd mapped out a route from the apartment to the car dealership using only right turns, I drove Spot downtown and said good-bye, noting with sadness and glee that I was parting with one of the last emblems of my sorry old life. My melancholy lasted as long as it took to pick up the keys to a gleaming, new blue-and-silver Chevy S-10 Blazer. Ol' Spot didn't get much more of a farewell ceremony than any other member of my childhood family. I was moving too fast to look back.

The marriage, as it turned out, was the relationship I'd dreamed of, with occasional exceptions. One evening I was sitting next to Gina on the floor of our little apartment, eating dinner on our garage-sale coffee table. Gina was unusually quiet.

"How was your day?" she asked.

"Fine," I replied. "How about yours?"

She was silent a moment, then said a bit irritably, "Fine, but you wouldn't have noticed." I sensed that something was coming.

"What was I supposed to notice?" I asked.

Then she opened up. "You just let me stand there at that press conference today, all by myself," she cried, "pretending you didn't even know me!"

"Hey, wait a minute," I protested. "I was working. I was trying to concentrate on what was going on. I was trying to take notes."

"You were rude," she interrupted.

"I was busy!" I shouted, forgetting that I'd been chewing a mouthful of green beans. Propelled by the shout, vegetable fragments flew halfway across the living room, all over the beige carpet. Stunned, we both looked at the mess strewn across the floor.

Gina began to laugh, and I did, too. "Now *that*," she said, "was rude."

At work, we were both learning our craft, paying our dues. But I decided I'd paid enough one night in January of 1988 as I stood on the shore of the Green Bay, watching for the glimmer of searchlights two miles out. The bay had frozen over, but not so solid that it could hold the weight of the pickup truck an ice fisherman had driven out onto it. The truck had broken through. By the time they pulled the fisherman out, his body was frozen solid and the lobe of my right ear and the little toe of my right foot had suffered frostbite. The pain ended in two days, by which time I had slipped into the WBAY studios at midnight to assemble a stack of updated résumé tapes.

Gina and I had sifted through about a dozen rejection letters when the call came. "Jon?" a man said. "John Edwards." It was my old boss from Salt Lake City. "Sit down, Jon. I have a proposition for you. I think you might be ready to take an anchor job. How about coming back as an anchor/reporter and anchoring my weekend newscast?" With nearly four years of experience under my belt, I was a more mature newsman than the giddy college kid who had accepted his first offer without a thought.

I told Edwards I'd think about it a few days and call him back the following week. I hung up the phone, jumped in the air, and screamed, "Gina! We're going back to Salt Lake City!"

We rented a stylish, two-bedroom condominium on Salt Lake's upper east side, the perfect temporary digs for a pair of young professionals looking for their first house. Not surprisingly, Gina landed a job anchoring the noon show at the CBS affiliate. We lived in Sandy, a quiet suburb of Salt Lake City. Our two-story, four-bedroom house was perched on a bluff overlooking a plush, green valley, and beyond, a breathtaking view of the Wasatch Front. My life was looking about as close to perfect as I could have imagined. I was rapidly forgetting that it was all painstakingly manufactured. As far as I was concerned, there was no one else in the world but Gina and me.

It was all so different from the direction my older brother's fortunes were taking. His divorce from Karen in 1983 had dropped the floor out from under him, and he was free-falling. He had moved out of his in-laws' house in San Diego, leaving behind two small boys—Anthony, almost three; and Ryan, just a toddler. He had taken up residence two blocks away, at Grandma and Grandpa Peek's house, so he could be close to the kids, but it didn't take long before he found himself cut off from them. Karen, embittered, virtually banned him from seeing them, making sure they were unavailable almost every time he worked up the nerve to ask for a visit.

Blaming himself for the breakup, Marq had allowed the divorce decree to strip him of nearly all his paternal rights. Sporadically employed, he had fallen behind on his child support payments. His failure to send money all but eliminated him from his kids' lives. Over the next five years, Marq faded into despair.

With her parents caring for the children, Karen went back to college and earned the degree she had postponed for marriage. When she graduated, she went to work as a high school teacher, moved out of her parents' house, and began seeing men. Before long, she remarried—a guidance counselor she had met at work. Marq claimed to be pleased that his boys had a father figure in the home again. It was a lie. He was crushed that his boys now looked up to another man.

Marq could no longer stand to stare his failures in the face. When an acquaintance suggested that he move to Florida in search of a good-paying job, he packed a few things in a bag and threw it in the guy's trunk. He moved into an old house in West Palm Beach and shared the rent with three other guys just like him—between jobs, between relationships, and between decisions on where they would go and what they would do. For about a year, Marq worked in the luggage hangar at the West Palm Beach airport, tossing suitcases.

Only Grandma Marie knew that Marq had gone to Florida. No one knew any details of his time there.

Karen and her new husband petitioned the court to allow an adoption of Marq's two boys. That was where my downtrodden brother found enough courage to draw the line. The legal maneuver had terrified him. When he heard about it, he got on the phone and begged a San Diego magistrate not to authorize the adoption. "They're all I have in life," he told him. "What if someone took away everything that was important to you in life?" He held on to his sons by a very fine thread.

Beyond the adoption threat, something else happened to Marq while he was in Florida—something terrible, Grandma gathered after talking with him. Whatever it was, it changed him. Atop the tragedies of his divorce and his loss of his children, it was too much to endure. It broke his will and stole his self-respect. He has never spoken of it.

His Florida excursion was the culmination of half a decade during which he sank to the depths of his own personal hell. By the time Gina and I found him, he was a shadow of the person I'd known.

I was talking to Grandma Marie on the phone one day soon after Gina and I moved to Sandy. "So, what's Marq doing with himself?" she asked.

"How would I know?" I said.

"Well, you guys are practically neighbors."

"How's that? Last I heard he lived in Florida."

"Not anymore," she said. "He called me a month ago and told me he had moved to Provo."

"Provo, Utah?"

"Provo, Utah," she said. "I thought he would have called you."

I couldn't believe that Marq had moved to within 30 miles of my home and not called to let me know. He'd been the first person I'd contacted when I went to Provo in 1981. Clearly, we had grown apart, but his not calling felt like a deliberate swipe at me—his way of telling me that he wanted nothing to do with me. It was, essentially, the same thing I had done to him and the rest of the family. And maybe Marq might have wanted to get a job and an apartment, to have something to show for himself before I came marching back into his life. Maybe he was trying to salvage enough pride so that his younger brother wouldn't find him completely hapless. I didn't think of any of those things; I was deeply insulted by his quiet return to Utah.

"Get in the car," Gina said, when she heard the news. Without asking for any explanation, she drove us south to Provo to look for my brother.

We had nothing to go on but an address, and Grandma hadn't been sure she'd written it down correctly. She hadn't. The street number she gave us didn't exist. But we found the street, a line of old houses that had been converted to rental space, and cruised up and down 700 South for about an hour, knocking on doors where the numbers looked like they might match.

I was getting back in the car when I spotted him, standing in the front yard two doors down. From his basement room, he'd seen us pass by five or six times and decided to come out of hiding. I ran from the car and wrapped him in a hug.

"I'll ask quick, before Gina gets here," I said, my mouth against his ear. "What the hell are you doing?"

"Aw, boy. Don't get on me, man. I was going to call. I just figured you guys had your own thing going, and I didn't want to horn in."

"Forget it," I said. Gina walked up and gave him a smile and a hug.

We convinced Marq that we weren't going to leave without him and all his belongings, and so he piled into Gina's Grand Prix and came home with us. Marq took his pick of the three empty bedrooms and moved in. For him, moving in meant unzipping his bags and laying a blanket on the carpeted floor. We apologized for not having an extra bed, but he didn't seem to mind.

"This is the most comfort I've had in five years," he said.

Our boarder had little to say about what had brought him to Utah or what his plans might be. Before long, he got used to the comfort and began slumping around the house, brooding. He seemed to resent my attempts to make conversation, as though I were putting him down when I asked what he wanted to do or how I might help. I tried asking in different ways, careful not to imply anything that might offend him. I soon stopped asking and gave up trying to help him find a job or get back into school. Gina and I went on about our daily business as if Marq weren't there, thinking that maybe an air of normalcy in the house might help our guest relax a little.

He found work at an art supply wholesaler in Salt Lake. We congratulated him, but he scoffed, feeling patronized.

"It's nothin' to cheer about," he said with a sneer.

And it wasn't. Marq spent half as many hours making bus connections to and from the city as he spent on the job. Each evening, he would come home seeming dejected and more depressed. He withdrew into near silence, sitting at the kitchen table for hours at a time, staring at the classified ads and drawing red circles around dozens of entries. If he made any phone calls, he did it when no one was around to hear.

His welcome wore out one evening, just after dinner. Gina had prepared a delicious meal. Marq hadn't said anything, but we could tell he enjoyed his dinner because he'd gone back for seconds. I was finishing my meal, always the slowest eater. Gina, carefully loading the dishwasher, said, "Marq, you want to rinse your dish so I can put it in the dishwasher?"

Marq looked as if someone had just spit in his face. "No," he said, raising the tone at the end of it as if to say, "I can't believe you'd ask." He picked up the newspaper and pretended to be engrossed.

My eyes darted to Gina. She was already peering at me, her lips tightening and her jaw muscles flexing. I rose from my seat. "I'll get it," I said, trying to sound casual.

Gina stared at me, her eyes blazing. She expected me to do something about this outrageous affront. I winked at her and nodded, assuring her that I would take care of it.

I was angry, too. My wife, five months pregnant, had plenty to deal with, working her shift at the TV station and doing her housework. She didn't need to be insulted by a sullen guest. She didn't know Marq's way. And after the years that had passed between us, neither did I any longer.

I stopped by his room on my way to bed that night. "Pack 'em up," I said calmly. "We'll get you into your own place tomorrow."

"Fine," he said, as if he'd expected to hear it for a long time and was glad I'd finally said it.

We found a clean, airy little furnished one-bedroom on Salt Lake's west side. A few hours of shopping, and we'd put together all the essentials he would need to get started—toiletries, bedding, kitchen utensils, food, even a small palm tree. The plant was my idea.

"Hey, man, keep this plant green," I said, "and maybe it'll keep your spirits up."

He nodded. "We'll see."

We promised to stay in touch. And this time, we did. I called every few days, and Marq even called me every so often. He didn't tell me much about how things were going, but I didn't need specifics so I didn't press. I was determined that this wouldn't turn out like Provo again, the two of us drifting apart.

❧❧❧

A bright, happy new baby named Kasey—ten toes and ten fingers and a big appetite—came into our home and made us a family. I felt that things couldn't have been more perfect. That is, until the phone call.

The Saturday afternoon couldn't have been more serene when the phone rang. Those were the days when I answered the phone whenever I heard it ring.

"Jonny!" the man on the other end of the line said. My head began to throb, starting at the base of the back of my skull and crawling over the top and into my eye sockets. I instantly recognized the voice.

"It's your ol' dad, partner! You're not going to believe this . . . I'm at the Salt Lake City bus depot!"

I waited, or was frozen in fear, more like it. It was another wreck, and my mind picked up speed and started whirring. My first thought was that maybe he'd say he was just kidding, he was in Florida or somewhere. But he didn't say he was kidding. He said, "I want to see this grandson of mine I've heard so much about."

My mind scrambled for a way out of the giant spring-loaded rat trap that had just snapped down on my back. I could think of nothing. "Oh, hey, great," I said weakly. I told him I'd be right down to get him. We talked for a few more minutes, but I couldn't hear a word he said through the ringing in my ears. I hung up the phone, trembling at the thought of what was about to happen. I just couldn't fit Gina and my father into the same picture, didn't *want* them in the same picture, didn't want my father breaking into my little boy's world and defiling it.

I phoned Marq. "Dad just called me," I said. "He's at the bus station downtown."

"You're kidding!" he exclaimed.

"I'll pick you up in 30 minutes."

I told Gina about the call and told her to expect us. She said not to worry, she'd go along with whatever happened. I jumped in my truck and sped over to Marq's apartment building. He was waiting at the curb, thrilled that Dad was in town. We headed for the depot. There I was, quaking at the prospect of what was about to happen, dreading this reunion of the dysfunctional Du Pre family, and there was Marq beside me on the front seat full of excitement.

"All right, now," he was saying. "I'll get Dad into my apartment, and he can stay with me, and I'll take him to this temp agency where we can get him a part-time job, and once he has that steady paycheck coming in, he can get his self-esteem back. I won't let him drink, I'll keep him off the drugs, we'll get him cleaned up. I think I can get him rehabilitated. I think I can save him."

I sat there thinking, *Oh, Marq, please don't set yourself up like this for another failure.* I thought for a minute of reminding Marq of the last time he'd tried to help Dad, lending him money, and of the disappointment he'd suffered when he'd realized Dad had once again just used him. But I didn't say anything.

We arrived at the bus station. He'd said he'd be standing outside, but we didn't see him. I circled the block and came back around. No sign of him. I circled the block one more time. As I came back around, Marq shouted, "There he is!"

And there he was. He had been there the whole time, and we hadn't recognized him because he wasn't the man we remembered. I hadn't told him when he called that I'd be driving a silver-blue Chevy Blazer, and he hadn't told me that he was 70 pounds lighter and hunched over, a curve in his spine, and toothless, with no hair. We'd been looking for our tall, handsome father. I stared at him, hoping to find a remnant of the man I knew.

I was stunned by how bad he looked. He looked as if he'd been hungry forever. He was gaunt. His skin was dark, the blackened bronze of someone who'd been baked by the sun all day long for years. He was wearing baggy brown slacks and a cheap yellow shirt and a brownish plaid jacket with a big collar—clothes that advertised their provenance, the bin at the Salvation Army. He had a small, scuffed leather suitcase, and as he approached, it struck me that everything he owned in this world was probably in that bag.

Marq jumped out of my truck and ran over to Dad and embraced him, almost knocking him down. I walked over. From five feet away, I smelled the stale body odor coming from his clothes; they looked as if they hadn't been washed in years. Since he didn't have teeth and didn't use a toothbrush anymore, his breath was bad.

His body seemed fragile, and as I hugged him, it quivered, the way really old men shake when they try to get up and walk. Yet he was not really old; he was only 63. I felt that if I squeezed him too hard, I might break his back. But he was not fragile; he was tough and stringy. Our cheeks met. His skin was coarse and hard. As he smiled, he opened his mouth—just stubs of a few teeth that had rotted away. He still had his old dental plate, but now it was dark from age. It no longer fit, and hung from his gums at an odd angle. Seeing it brought back two memories.

I thought back to the times when Marq and I and our little brother, Daryl, were kids back in Mauldin, and Dad would play monster with us. He'd muss up his hair and let it flop over half his face, and he'd tilt the plate out of his mouth, alarmingly, and he'd stalk us through the house, growling, "Come here, little boy! Come here!" The three of us, squealing in fear and delight, would scurry off and hide under beds.

The other memory was of a seemingly insignificant incident that happened when I was five years old. My father was brushing his teeth, and I was standing on the toilet seat, next to the sink, watching him. He removed his lower plate for cleaning. As he unscrewed the cap from the toothpaste tube, he bobbled it. It fell to the sink and raced around inside it, spinning ever closer to the drain. Dad jerked forward to catch it, but his hands were occupied by his tooth brush and his denture. Just as the cap reached the hole, there was my little hand, cupped, covering the drain. I snatched the cap and handed it to Dad.

He looked startled. "Great catch!" he exclaimed. "How did you know where to catch that cap? Are you that smart?"

"Yes," I said, "I am."

Dad grinned. "Yes, you are, Jonny! Way to go!" My father, in the early days, never missed a chance to praise his boys. He had a knack for recognizing that a little thing could be a big deal to a child. That's what attracted us to him, and why we missed him so badly after he'd abandoned us.

When Dad smiled now in the bus station, all these years later, it smoothed out the long, deep crevices on his face he'd gotten from perpetually scowling. The skin inside the wrinkles was white, making it obvious that he seldom smiled, and that he hadn't had a pleasant moment in a long time.

We stood on the corner talking. "How you boys doing? Look at you, you're such a strong boy, and you, look how big you are!"

And we said, fumbling for words as though we were teenagers again, "Hey, Dad, how are you doing?"

"Look at me, boys. I've lost 70 pounds. I do a lot of aerobics now." I looked to see if he was joking. He wasn't. Clearly he was homeless, a man who scrounged his meals from dumpsters, yet here he was, trying to persuade us he'd lost all that weight on a health regimen—on a Jenny Craig diet, maybe, or working out at the gym.

"Let's have something to eat," he said. "I'm starving."

We took him to the Denny's a block away and sat in a booth as far from the crowd as we could get. As we waited for the waitress, I wanted to ask him so many things, half-fascinated by his life, and half-terrified by it. Where do you live? Where do you sleep? Where do you get food? How do you protect yourself from the weather, from the other people on the street? Where do you go when you have an emergency? Where do you go to the bathroom? Where do you find clothes? And shoes—what happens if someone steals your shoes? I was full of questions but afraid to ask them because he'd already made it clear with his bad joke about weight loss that he didn't want to talk about reality. Marq and I didn't want to talk about anything that he didn't want to talk about, so after a few minutes, we just let him have the conversation.

"I think things are looking up for me, boys," he said. "I think before long I'll get back my license to practice law in South Carolina. Yeah, I talked to a few people lately who just might have enough pull to get me another hearing before the bar association. You know those crooked bastards robbed me of my license years ago."

He dropped back into reminiscences of events decades earlier, gripes Marq and I had heard him vent a thousand times when we were boys, about who was a crook and who was honest and how he was the only one who was willing to fight for the rights of the oppressed. And so on. Here we were in 1990 in a Salt Lake City restaurant, I hadn't seen him in almost 16 years, and we were listening to him rehash his old stories.

We got our menus, and the waitress brought him a cup of coffee and asked for our orders. Marq and I began ordering up a huge steak-and-eggs breakfast for Dad, but he interrupted. "No, no, I'm sorry, boys, I can't eat that food." We sat back surprised. "Don't have the teeth for it anymore," he whispered. Marq quickly put in a new order, for two portions of scrambled eggs and mushy hash browns, and white toast and more coffee. He ordered a small breakfast for himself, and I ordered an orange juice.

When the food came, Marq and I sat and watched him eat. He didn't cradle his fork in his fingers anymore; he gripped it in his fist so that he could shovel food directly from his plate to his mouth. He used two fingers from his other hand to help him with the shoveling. He kept talking all the while, and food would fall out of his mouth and splatter onto the plate. He'd just scoop it right back up and push it back into his mouth. He ate like a dog, bent defensively over his plate, his eyes darting around the room to make sure no one was going to steal his food. It was at that moment, watching him eat, that it came through to me full strength: *This man is homeless.*

We sat for a couple of hours in that Denny's. Only the food interrupted his chatter. Marq and I didn't expect to learn anything from what he was saying; his stories had no shape to them. We didn't care. We were just glad he was getting some food. It occurred to me then that this might be why he'd shown up. He was hungry, really hungry, not just between-meals hungry, but desperately hungry to the core of his being, suffering from malnutrition to the point where he couldn't think straight, could hardly stand up—the kind of hungry that makes the stomach turn on itself and begin to gnaw. That guess proved right. Hunger was the reason he'd come to Salt Lake. He'd been kicked out of the shelter in Tucson, and he needed to eat real food. "Hell, I thought I'd starve to death," he said, "waiting for those bastards to forget what I looked like and let me sneak back in!"

He finished all the food that we could push at him, then he sat back and said, "Oooh, I'm stuffed." Then he started talking about something else.

I interrupted him and said, "Come on, Dad, let's get to my house. You've got to meet my wife, and you've got a grandson to see." I found myself wishing I could clean him up and get him a change of clothes, but there was no way of suggesting that. I wished I could slip off and phone Gina and warn her, but he was canny and sensitive, and I was afraid he'd see through me. I was afraid of offending him.

"All right," he said, "let's go."

Marq and I paid the tab, and we left. As I drove home, I watched my father in the rear-view mirror and thought, *He's here. He's here with us. He's just had a good meal, and he's about to meet his grandson.* I wondered how Gina was going to react. She'd heard all my horror stories.

I took the scenic route home, past the golf course, up to the bluff and onto Nicklaus Road so that he could get a good view. The neighborhood looked more impressive from that side, and I wanted Dad to be impressed. I wanted him to be proud of me, the way he was proud of me when I'd snagged that toothpaste cap. When we were kids, before his decline, he'd had a way of making us feel good about ourselves, and it was the fuel that stoked our fires, that made us want to excel. For the first time in years, I was feeling the need for his approval. I was a kid again, wanting to do well so my father would be proud of me.

We pulled into the driveway and got out of the truck. I escorted him up the path, opened the door, and immediately called out, "Gina, we've got a weary traveler from far away who's come to see you." I was trying to say, "My old man's here and he looks like hell, so don't be shocked when you see him."

Gina came down the stairs. She didn't hesitate. She walked right over to our smelly old visitor, arms extended, and wrapped him in a hug. My eyes immediately filled with tears. My father was overwhelmed. I'd never seen anyone so moved by an expression of affection as he was in that moment. At once, I knew that Gina's embrace was the kindest, most loving thing that had touched my father's life in many, many years. He fumbled as he tried to hug her back, clutching her sleeve, trying to hold on to a sublime feeling of tenderness so unfamiliar to him.

She kissed him on the cheek and said, "Robert, to say I've heard a lot about you would be an understatement. It's like I've known you for years. How are you? Welcome to our home."

Robert, I thought. *That was a perfect touch.* The whole thing was perfect. It couldn't have been any better if we'd rehearsed it. She didn't flinch at the sight or the smell of him. She just embraced him and welcomed him into our home. It left a lump in my throat.

My father was dumbfounded, completely taken off guard. He was immediately changed. His expression softened, and he abandoned the self-ascribed role of the chatterbox, the topic of conversation, the star of the show. He was speechless, overcome with an emotion that was foreign to him, something he hadn't felt for so long that he hardly knew how to react to it. He was connected again, for the moment, after all those years of estrangement from the human race.

We moved into the living room. I took his leather bag and put it over in the corner. We walked to the big windows and looked out onto the view. "Kasey's taking his nap," Gina said, "so in the meantime, we'll show you the house."

We took him through the living room to the dining room and the kitchen, and we showed him where the downstairs bathroom was. He followed along politely—it occurred to me he'd follow Gina anywhere—but I could tell he wasn't interested in interior decoration or the view or the cathedral ceiling. He was grateful to be there, happy to be with us. Gina took him upstairs and showed him the bedrooms and let him peek in Kasey's room and glimpse his sleeping, pink-cheeked grandson.

She brought us over to the dining area and said, "I've just put together a little lunch for you guys." She, of course, didn't know that we'd already eaten and that her guest had already stuffed himself. Marq and I puffed our cheeks as if to say, *Oh boy, Dad can't eat another bite, what are we going to do now?* But he sat right down at the head of the table, took a hamburger, and started slapping on mustard and mayonnaise, ketchup and pickles, lettuce and onions. He picked it up and crammed it in his mouth and took the biggest bite he could. He couldn't chew; he gummed and pulled at it.

"Gee, that's delicious," he mumbled. "I haven't had a hamburger like this in years." After the first hamburger, he had a second, and chips to go with it. He ate watermelon, strawberries, and grapes. We were at the table an hour, and he ate the whole time. Where was he putting it? He was eating as if he knew it might be a long time before he got another meal like this one so he might as well go all out. I also sensed he was thinking, *Gina fixed this meal, and I'm going to eat it.*

Finally he sat back and patted his stomach and said, "Whooo. I couldn't eat another bite," just as he'd said in the restaurant a couple of hours earlier.

Kasey was awake by this time, and Gina brought him down and said, "Here's your grandpa, here's your grandpa," and one-year-old Kasey said, "Papa, Papa." Three generations of the Du Pre family together—it was something I'd come to think I'd never see. The two of them, Dad and Kasey, got down on the floor and crawled around for a while. Marq and I helped Gina clean up.

That afternoon I saw the spirit flow back into my father's body. When I'd met him at the bus depot that morning, he was a dead man whose heart hadn't stopped beating. He was just there, sagging. Now, on the floor of the living room, with his grandson chortling and pulling on his shirt, trying to climb up and stand, he returned to being.

Never for a minute, however, did I dream that he could be put back together again. He'd gone too far; it had been too long. What we were seeing was only temporary. Marq realized that, too, and his brave, hopeful notion about rehabilitating our father ebbed away. He let it go, but I knew he was mournful. Marq had always taken everything harder than I had, always more affected by the things that happened to our family. He'd been introduced to disappointment early: Mother beat him; his wife divorced him. The two women who meant most to his life had rejected him. From then on, he'd refused to date women at all. It was a shame to see such a loving, trusting person shut himself off.

At the end of the day, we went out to the backyard to watch the light of the setting sun bathe the mountains above us, the Wasatch Front, a granite wall that rose 11,000 feet above sea level. The lower the sun dropped, the richer the colors it cast on the rock face. It was an enormous and breathtaking sight, one I never got tired of.

The evening air was crisp and dry and burned our nostrils. We were standing there witnessing the spectacle when we heard a call from the street. "Hello, Du Pres, can we come back and watch the sunset with you?"

It was Chuck and Michelle Cutler and their two kids. They'd been walking along Nicklaus Road, watching the view between the houses. Chuck had been an All-America wide receiver for Brigham Young while I was there, a kind of hero on campus. Now he was a financial planner and a stockbroker. I'd always admired him. He was an unassuming fellow, not at all impressed with himself. We were pals and played some city league basketball together. I waved and called, "Hey, come on back." I didn't know what to do about my unsightly visitor.

When the Cutlers had appeared, Dad had drifted over toward the patio, into the shadow of the deck. Gina and Marq and I talked with the Cutlers as we watched the sunset, a pleasant conversation until Michelle looked beyond me and stiffened. I knew what she was looking at. I knew that at the other end of her stare was my ugly, painful past, a dark figure in tattered clothing leaning up against the post of my deck. Her expression made it look as if she'd seen flies buzzing around him. "Who's *that*?" she asked. We all turned and looked.

I knew Dad had just lit a joint—you can smell pot 50 yards away. There he was, looking back at us, puffing. He smiled a wide toothless grin and said, "Hi, kids," in his gravelly old voice, and waved the hand that held the joint. Then he took another drag. He was testing me.

Michelle and Chuck gulped and Chuck said, "Is he smoking what I think he is . . ."

I cut in and said, "Yeah, smoking pot. That's my father. He came into town this morning. Marq and I picked him up at the bus depot. He rolled in from Tucson where he's been hanging out. He gets around a lot; he doesn't really have one particular place he calls home. He travels. He's sort of a vagabond, a free spirit, he moves around." But I never said, "My father is homeless."

Chuck nervously said, "Oh, yeah, sort of a hippie type, huh? One of those flower children."

I said, "Well, he's in retirement now, and he's just traveling, looking around, doing some sightseeing. So he dropped by to visit this morning." That was all I said. It was more than they wanted to hear. The conversation died. We stood around sort of scuffing the grass for a minute, everybody trying to think of something to say. It was one of those defining moments that lifts you ten feet in the air and gives you a spectator's view of the event. There it was, in my backyard: My past had met my present. And it was clear that the two sides of my life were total strangers.

"How about a tour of our house?" Gina said brightly. "You guys haven't seen it yet." And all of us immediately said, "Oh, yeah, yeah, yeah, let's go see the house." We went inside and climbed the stairs to the second floor, and we showed them the teddy bears stenciled on the baby room wall and the curtains that Gina had hung in the guest room and the drapes in the master bedroom and the Jacuzzi tub in the master bath. We were all young families in that neighborhood, all the houses were new, and it was a matter of ritual to go and see how the other people lived.

We were half an hour into the grand tour, starting back down the stairs to the main floor, when I looked over the rail. There was Dad, sitting on the couch in the family room, fidgeting, patting his pocket, looking for a cigarette that he knew he couldn't smoke in my house anyway, looking around, tapping his toe. He didn't want to be alone, and who could have blamed him? This visit, after all, was a big deal to him. So he took measures.

"Welcome," he said in his best Robin Leach voice, beaming up at us as we descended, "to another edition of *Lifestyles of the Rich and Famous.* Today our fabulous megastar from television, Jon Du Pre, escorts his lovely and talented neighbors through his palatial estate . . ." He went on and on with it, loud. It was vintage Dad. Always the center of attention—or else.

The Cutlers acted as if they didn't hear him. I thought at first, *God, shut up!* But it was so funny I had to laugh. He was an excellent mimic, and he was trying to tell us something: "Hey, enough with your neighbors. *I'm* here." We showed the Cutlers to the door and got back to Dad.

We sat around on the couch talking, and at last he asked us a question about ourselves. "You a member of that country club we drove past? You belong?" He was trying to assess my financial worth, I figured.

"Oh, no," I said. "I could never afford to play there. The membership fee is $10,000. Out of my league."

Then Marq chimed in. "Jon is one heck of a golfer. You should see him hit a golf ball. He's amazing. And he only picked up the sport about four years ago."

I couldn't remember the last time Marq had said anything complimentary about me to my face. And I didn't openly compliment him. That was just the relationship we had. So it startled and moved me when he said something like that right in front of me.

I popped up off the couch and went into the garage and pulled a few clubs out of my bag and grabbed a few balls and went back in the family room and said, "Let's go outside and bump the ball around." We all got up and went out to the yard. There was still a little daylight left, and I turned on the floodlights. Gina came out onto the deck to watch, with Kasey in her arms.

We took the pitching wedges and fooled with them a while. Then I said, "I'll tell you what. Let's go from this side of the yard to the pin, and the pin is that little maple tree in the far corner of the yard." It was maybe 30 yards away.

"Okay," Dad said, "let's go." Marq suggested I shoot first. I lined up my shot and hit it about 15 feet from the maple.

"Nice shot, boy," Dad said. "You know what you're doing."

It was like being back in the yard in Anderson with Dad pitching us the ball. We were together again, we were involved in a pleasant activity, and we weren't talking about bad things. We weren't talking about anything in particular, just enjoying one another's company.

Marq hit a shot about 15 feet away, too, and I said, "Nice shot, Marq," and Dad said, "Marq always had athletic ability." I could see Marq glow. Our touring pro got over his ball and lined up his shot and placed one ten feet from the maple. We cheered.

"Great shot, Dad!"

"Where did that come from?"

Up on the deck, Gina clapped. "Oh, don't you worry, boys," my father said, beaming. "I played a little golf in my day."

We retrieved our balls and went back to our imaginary tee box and hit another round of shots, and then another. As we played, we chatted about how to grip the club and how to swing, how to put just the right touch on the ball so as not to send it flying into the neighbor's yard. The shots were getting closer and closer to the tree.

My father stepped up for his fifth shot and got himself set, concentrating. He was trying hard now to hit a good shot each time his turn came up. We could see his confidence growing with each round.

I said, "So, Dad, where'd you learn how to play golf?"

He said, "Well, you know, I was a lifeguard at a country club between semesters when I was in college." I'd seen pictures of him lifeguarding—swimsuit, sunglasses, muscles, tan. He'd been a good-looking young man, athletic. "I used to sneak out and play some golf with one of the pros."

"When was the last time you played?" Marq asked him.

"Oh, hell, I don't remember. It's been a long time. You think I still have the touch? You think I've still got it?"

It was a question that could be taken several ways. "Absolutely," I said. "You've definitely still got it." He chuckled at that.

I said, "When was the last time you had this much fun?"

Until then, he'd kept his head down, lining up his ball. Now he stopped and looked up. "Longer than I care to remember, Jonny, longer than I care to remember." He hit his shot.

We played for another half hour. Dad won the championship round. His shot passed ours and rolled into the one-foot-wide planter hole that surrounded the base of the tree. It was a hole-in-one. In his best sports announcer imitation, he cried, "The crowd roars! Nicklaus has won the Masters!" It was a reprise of his old habit of announcing in a broadcaster's voice whenever he took part in sports. I used to say, "Dad, stop talking and play." This time it made me happy.

I was ready to ask him to stay the night, but Marq insisted that Dad come and stay with him. Dad said, "Great, great, you bet." We had two spare rooms, and I knew Marq didn't have even one spare; he was living in a one-room apartment. I sensed Marq didn't want Dad imposing on Gina and me.

Gina gave her newfound father-in-law a warm good-bye, and I drove him and my brother back to Marq's apartment. We sat around until nearly three in the morning talking, not saying anything heavy, just shooting the breeze, discussing the golf a lot and our championship tourney.

Dad stayed with Marq another day-and-a-half and never drank a drop that whole time. After church on Sunday, I came downtown and met the two of them, and we went for a walk and then came back to the apartment and talked some more.

The next morning, Marq called me and said, "Dad wants to go back to Tucson. He's dying to get on the bus. Can you help me with his ticket?" By the time I got to the apartment, my father had stuffed what he had back into his old leather suitcase and was sitting by the door. Marq was arguing with him, urging him to stay. But Dad kept saying things like, "I've got to go. Things to do, people to see." No specifics. So we gave in and took him down and put him on a bus.

Marq and I hugged him and kissed him good-bye and stood at the bottom step as he boarded. He mounted the steps, then turned to us. "Boys," he said, "I think I'm getting too old for this shit." He turned back and shuffled into the dark interior of the bus. I stood there motionless. An image of my father's death flashed into my mind. The image looked like a body curled up in an alley. For the first time, it occurred to me that my father could die out there, alone and homeless.

After that, for five years, hardly a day went by that I didn't fear getting a call from a stranger asking me to come somewhere to identify a body—the body of a homeless derelict who just got too old to live that way anymore.

❦ ❦ ❦

CHAPTER THIRTEEN
Casualties of War

S omehow, after fleeing California, I came to believe that if I were to fabricate a new life for myself, I had to leave my old life behind, turning
my back on my mother and brothers. It was like rushing out of a burning house without your family photos—a terrible loss, but survival seemed the
only consideration. For ten years, I nearly forgot three people I loved. As it
turned out, those were difficult years for all of them.

My mother had continued to seek happiness with her second husband, Bill.
She soon realized that it was impossible. He was selfish and negative and mean,
and no matter how hard she tried to keep from upsetting him, she couldn't.
One day he was changing the oil in his big green Ford LTD when a drop splashed
onto his shirtsleeve.

"Goddamnit!" he howled. "This is one of my good shirts!" He considered
every shirt in his wardrobe, most of which came from K-Mart, to be one of
his good shirts. "Marquise!" he yelled. "Get out here!"

My mother came out of the house.

"Can you get this oil out of my shirtsleeve?" he demanded.

"I don't know," she said. "I can run it through the wash and see what
happens."

"I don't want to 'see what happens'! I want the goddamn oil out of my
shirtsleeve. This is one of my best shirts!"

"I'll try," she said. "But why did you wear one of your best shirts to change
the oil?"

He looked at her scornfully, then did that hateful thing: "'Why did you bla
bla tick tick bla bla?'" he said, grotesquely twisting his face and sticking out
his tongue, mocking my mother the way children mock each other on the play-

ground. It was his ultimate put-down. Although it made him look petty and nasty, it did the job; it hurt my mother's feelings.

Not surprisingly, Bill was a loner. He didn't have any real friends, and when Mom tried to introduce him to a few of her new friends in Encinitas, he refused to cooperate. So, they had no social life at all. The fancy dancer with whom my mother had fallen in love never once took her dancing in the 11 years they were married.

Bill, who had a rule for everything, had an especially rigid one about money: Only *he* would handle it. When Mom asked him for cash to buy groceries, he made her beg for it and never gave her the amount she needed. The routine made her feel guilty and helpless for asking, even in cases of emergency, such as running out of toilet tissue, an occasion Bill turned against the rest of us.

I was sitting on the toilet one day when he opened the bathroom door and walked in. "Before you spin the roll again and waste all my toilet paper, I'm going to show you how to wipe your goddamn rear end the way they taught us in the Army." He tore off a short length of paper, four squares, and folded it into a triangular shape.

"Here. You hold your wipe like this," he said, placing the tissue on his extended forefinger and middle finger and holding it by one corner with his thumb.

"Oh, yeah, sure," I said with a raise of the eyebrows and a nod of the head, as if making a mental note.

"Well, go ahead!" he ordered, holding the tissue triangle out for me to study.

"I'm hanging a turd right now. Maybe you could give me a minute." And my bathroom drill sergeant left with a snort.

Bill also passed his wisdom on to Marq and Daryl. That night as we lay in bed, Marq commented on what he had learned. "If that fat fucker thinks I'm gonna wipe my butt with a shred of toilet paper, then he can just put his lips down there and pucker up." Daryl and I giggled ourselves to sleep that night.

Mom soon realized that quitting her job at the fabric store had been a mistake. It wasn't long before she was back on the pavement looking for anything that would bring in a few extra dollars a week. I was in college by this time, and Marq was preparing for his mission to Canada. Mom used Marq's mission as an excuse to go back to work, knowing Bill would disapprove of her leaving the house, and her chores. She told Bill she had to help support her son on his mission. She knew Bill was obsessed with the subject of women and money. He'd lost money in his four divorces, and he was taking it out on his fifth wife.

❧❧❧

Soon after Mom and Bill were married, Bill had stopped going to church. She began to see that his professions of faith during their courtship had all been part of the courtship act. His quick turn away from religion forced her to concede what she had begun to dread: He didn't want a wife, he wanted a maid and a cook.

She pled with Bill to see a marriage counselor with her. "Not that again!" he replied. He'd been down that route before.

"I think that what most disappointed me about being married to Bill," my mother said years later, "was that I was just as lonely after I married him as I had been when I was single. After what I'd gone through with my first marriage, to have this happen was demoralizing. I lost all confidence in my own judgment."

One day, in her mailbox, she found a note from an elderly neighbor with a message that confirmed her fears and forced her to admit the obvious.

Marquise,

I fear you'll think I'm a terrible snoop for writing this. But I wanted to offer a little well-intentioned encouragement.

I have seen how you hold up in the face of the abuse you're taking, and I wanted to say that I admire your strength and the way you maintain your dignity and grace in spite of it all.

Sincerely,

Louise

"Until that note," she said later, "I didn't realize I was being abused. I guess it taught me a lesson. You can be around mean people for so long you eventually get used to it and you forget that there are good men out there who treat their wives with common decency." It was the only explanation she could offer for why she stayed with Bill for as long as she did.

❦ ❦ ❦

When Marq and I escaped Bill, Daryl was left behind. His chance came at last, in the summer of 1979, in the form of a call from a desperate and lonely old man. Dad had been flushed out of the Santa Monica apartment, he said, and he was on his way to the place where he always went when his luck turned bad, South Carolina. He planned to stay until his luck ran out there, too. He wanted Daryl, his sweetheart boy, to come with him. Daryl was so frantic to get out, and so eager to be with his father, that he didn't even leave a farewell note. He got all the way to New Mexico before calling Mom to say he was headed east with Dad.

They landed in a town called Rock Hill. Dad knew a lawyer there, a born-again Christian, who he thought might throw a little work his way. He soaked his friend for all the Christian charity he could get. The two formed what Dad called a "partnership." The arrangement was actually that Dad hung around his lawyer friend's office sniffing for bones that might be tossed his way. It was the same sort of grunt work he'd hated doing in San Diego—clerking and investigating and writing briefs. Daryl noticed he didn't seem to mind doing it as long as he could make it look as if he was in charge of the operation.

Daryl and his travel companion moved into a mobile home.

"Somebody's clothes were still in the closet," Daryl told me later. "And they stunk. And there was spoiled food in the refrigerator, and a jar of grape jelly in the cupboard, half full of cockroaches. I could never figure out how roaches could get inside a closed jar of jelly. But they died happy!"

Daryl never unpacked his duffel bag during the two months he lived in that mobile home. "I never even put it on the floor."

In the middle of one night, there was a tremendous pounding on the door, and a tough, back-country voice demanded to see Dad. The two of them lay still until the man went away. Then they tossed their gear in Dad's car and sped off, never looking back.

My father and brother drove to Greenville, 40 miles to the south, and the next day Dad and Daryl went to see Miss Tilly. Dad thought he could persuade her to let them move in with her, but he couldn't. She wanted nothing to do with him. With no money and no victims within reach, Dad dragged Daryl to a flophouse of a hotel on Main Street, next door to the Daniel Building in downtown Greenville. The two would live there for the next couple of months.

It was a happy time for Daryl. He got the doorman to give him a part-time job, sweeping the lobby and the sidewalk in front of the hotel and watching the desk when he took a break. He was paid three dollars an hour. It was enough to get him into the nearby movie house, where he sometimes would sit, by himself, and watch movies all day long. The movies broke his boredom and loneliness and took him to faraway places and great adventures. He used this fantasy world to protect himself from the consequences of his father's neglect. That had always been the amazing thing about Daryl—his ability to subsist on so little money—and so little love.

Daryl had no idea where his father went when he left each morning, but he knew that the old man wasn't working, because there was barely any money to buy food. Daryl scraped enough together from his doorman's assistant job to buy a couple of cheeseburgers each afternoon at the nearby McDonald's.

Daryl was free, just as he had dreamed of being, but he was also completely unattended, and he knew that wasn't good. In September, it occurred to him that he ought to be going to school, but he didn't know where to go. One morning he left the hotel and wandered around until he came upon a high school, Wade Hampton High, four miles away. It was a scary place. The students were mostly black and angry, and the teachers were mostly white and rough. He checked out of Wade Hampton High four weeks after he walked in. Nobody knew he'd been there.

During that school year, his junior year, he enrolled himself in 12 different schools, from South Carolina to Southern California, for Dad and Daryl were on the road again.

They wound up in Long Beach, California, sharing an apartment with one of Dad's old girlfriends. Daryl got a job at an Alpha Beta grocery store, as a bag boy. It was an especially bad neighborhood—a bag boy who was a friend of his had been shot in the chest—so when Daryl's shift was over, he ran the whole five miles home. One night he slipped on a wet spot in the pavement and fell, breaking an ankle. He made it back to the apartment and told Dad.

The next morning, Dad told him to get up. "We're going to San Diego," he announced. They didn't go to a hospital, but to Mom and Bill's house. Daryl, in the living room, could hear the talk in the kitchen as Dad laid out the situation. "I just can't take care of him anymore," he said. Daryl listened as his father and his stepfather told each other why they couldn't have him around.

"I felt like a dog with fleas," he told me years later.

Since Daryl wasn't going to be able to work his shift at the Alpha Beta, he was no longer of any use to his father. Bill said he couldn't afford to feed him. Mom hardly spoke at all. Daryl didn't like the idea of moving back under Bill's roof, but it was better than the alternative. He resolved that he would never again have anything to do with Dad. He'd enjoyed the adventure of traveling to points unknown, but he hadn't liked the way his father had used him.

That day, my enormously generous and trusting younger brother reached his breaking point. He stopped hearing the debate in the kitchen over who would be burdened with Daryl, as he detached himself from everyone. From that point on, he would take care of himself. His long-held goal was now more enticing than ever. He wanted to be a hippie. As soon as his ankle mended, Daryl slipped out of Bill's house. He wandered from place to place and from job to job. He lived with friends, mostly, nomads like himself, who would jam as many people as they could into an apartment or house until they were all thrown out for trashing the property or disturbing the neighbors. He became heavily involved in drugs, mainly pot and cocaine. But his friends constantly sought higher highs, and one night somebody came home with a plastic vile of crystal metham- phetamine. Daryl, eager to please, sucked a tiny particle of it up his nose. The way it made his nerves feel, like someone had plugged him into a light socket, scared the hell out of him and he swore it off after one experiment. In due course, he went off the cocaine and concentrated on marijuana—smoking pot, he came to believe, was a religious sacrament.

Having no place to live never fazed Daryl. He created a place of his own, in a ravine on the north side of Mira Mesa, just north of San Diego, beyond the sprawling housing developments. On a ledge, he built a little shack out of wooden pallets. "It had a great view and plenty of privacy."

He got work at a Mira Mesa catering company, stocking shelves in the ware- house and trucks in the lot. It was perfect for the style of life he had chosen. He could quit whenever he liked, and whenever he needed money, he could come back to find work.

❧❧❧

Mom had reached the end of her rope with Bill. No longer could she allow herself to be his slave. Realizing that his power over her was financial, she set out to make money of her own. Daryl, who called her from time to time, had told her about Fiesta Catering, and she asked if he'd recommend her for a job driving a catering truck. He warned her about the roughness of some of the people, the harshness of their language, and the terribly early start time, 3:00 A.M., but when he told her how much money she could make, she jumped at the chance.

The former drum majorette, UCLA coed, and former wife of a prosper- ous attorney, was now driving a roach coach and living on loose change. Her first assignment was behind the wheel of what they called a "cold truck." It carried cold drinks and snacks. She proved to be dependable and valuable to the company. Anyone who didn't steal at least $50 a day from the till was con- sidered a reliable, valuable employee. Soon, the bosses at Fiesta, with a little urging from Daryl, put Mom behind the wheel of a brand new "hot truck" with a full kitchen in the back. Daryl went to work on the back of Mom's truck, learning how to cook on a moving grill.

The two got good at running their rolling restaurant. They staked out a lucra- tive route, hitting aerospace and computer companies in the area. Those work- ers, they determined, had more money in their pockets and weren't as likely to steal from the truck when the driver's back was turned. Soon the team was bringing back about a thousand dollars a day. After paying for food and supplies and handing over the company's cut, they had about four hundred dollars to share. More than that, they were establishing a bond of trust and friendship. They had never been especially close; now they found that they got along famously.

Having proven her independence to herself, my mother was ready for the next step. She went to Bill one afternoon. He was sitting in the permanent trough that his enormous buttocks had pressed into the couch. "Bill," she began, "I have something to say to you."

The tone of her voice, and the fact that she'd dared to address him while he was watching *Hee Haw,* his favorite TV program, brought him to attention.

"This marriage is a farce," she continued. "It's clear you don't love me, and I refuse to live with a man who doesn't love me. It's time to end it, right away."

It was as if a weight had been lifted from her shoulders. Bill's mouth hung open. He offered no resistance. Their divorce was quick.

The twice-divorced woman's feeling of relief and freedom was tempered by fear. She was terrified of being alone. She worried that a woman in her 50s might never find a man who would love her and take care of her. That is, until she met Sam.

Sam was a programmer for Rohr Technologies, a large computer hardware and software company in San Diego. Mom met him in the Rohr parking lot while selling snacks and sandwiches to hungry employees on their lunch break. Sam ordered two franks with sauerkraut and flirted a little, and Mom picked right up on his signals. He started coming out to the truck twice a day.

One day at noon, as a secretary was buying lunch, she asked Mom if she was married. "Who wants to know?" she replied. "Is it Sam?" The secretary wouldn't say; she'd been sworn to secrecy.

Mom shut off her engine and locked up her truck and walked right into Rohr headquarters and upstairs to the second floor. She found Sam at his desk and put him on the spot. "Are you interested in asking me out on a date?" she said.

"Uh, yes," said Sam. "I suppose I am."

The two dated for about six months before they became engaged, and two weeks later, they were married.

Had Mom finally found her knight in shining armor? God knew she deserved one. But Grandma Marie didn't think Sam would measure up. Neither did Marq. Neither did Daryl.

I met Sam during a visit to San Diego in 1989. Gina and I had sought relief from an unusually cold Utah winter. She'd insisted we go to San Diego and stay at a hotel her parents had always liked when she was a child. "We can visit your family," she had suggested, as if that proposition would make me want to make the trip. I'd told her plenty about my family by then, but I had never said that I wasn't that excited about seeing my mother. We'd fallen out of touch after I'd left the house in Mira Mesa. I didn't call or write, letting the distance alienate us. I began to notice and resent that she never called or wrote either. I started thinking of her as selfish and shallow. How could she let these years pass without checking on me? On the other hand, I wasn't phoning to check on her, either. Whatever the case, we'd become strangers.

I was ashamed to admit that to my wife. So there was nothing to do but go. I swallowed hard and got in the car.

Gina and I picked up Grandma and met Mom and Sam at Fish House West, a snug little restaurant on the beach in Cardiff. The introductions were pleasant enough, but Sam seemed ill at ease.

As in all my meetings with Sam, I couldn't pinpoint what it was about him I didn't like. He was a soft man—quite overweight—but that wasn't why I didn't like him. He simply looked like the kind of guy who never got up off his chair. He was pale, and always clammy with sweat. He might not have perspired so much if he had taken off the sweater he wore year-round. He always seemed to have a complaint about a sore neck or a sore back or a sore something. And when Sam had a sore something, it wiped him out. He'd miss weeks of work.

The rest of us chattered over dinner, but Sam had nothing to say. And then, halfway through the meal, he came to life.

"So, you guys are in TV news, huh?" he began, somewhat aggressively. "You know, I've always wanted to ask, what makes you media types think you have the right to invade people's privacy just for the sake of getting your story?"

It was a question I'd heard a hundred times before—a reasonable question—but this time it rankled me. It was totally inappropriate for the setting, a challenge to his new relatives at a time when we all wanted to make a good first impression. Sam went on to outline his reasons for disliking and distrusting the news media. He claimed the media had been responsible for destroying Gary Hart's presidential campaign, for the public's eroding trust in law and order, and for the decline of patriotism in America. *Fair enough,* I thought. The gentleman is entitled to his opinions. But why, I wondered, would he have decided to air his gripes during a family gathering at which he was supposed to be the honored guest?

I sat there, trying not to let myself be drawn into an argument over something as irrelevant to the occasion as the Fifth Estate's privileges and abuses. It was embarrassing to watch my mother and grandmother wince each time Sam lifted his finger as if to quiet his audience while he finished chewing and prepared to launch into another of his meandering soliloquies. He managed to ruin dinner for everyone but himself.

"Charm school dropout?" I said to Grandma on the way home. That opened the floodgates.

"I disliked the man from the minute I laid eyes on him!" she exclaimed. She went on to explain her intense aversion for her new son-in-law as only my grandmother could, using words such as *arrogant* and *lazy* and *phony*. My opinion exactly.

I knew I hadn't succeeded in hiding my thoughts at dinner from my mother. My face was a replica of hers, and she could read my expressions, no matter how hard I tried to conceal them. I hadn't liked Sam, and she'd surely known it. It had hurt her feelings. My poor reaction to Sam pushed my mother and me still farther apart.

Through my grandmother, the only thread that still connected Mom and me, I heard all about my mother's resentment of her family's unwillingness to embrace her newest husband. Rather than listen to us criticize him, she chose not to speak to us. Rather than try to be careful of what we said to her about him, we avoided speaking to her. I seldom spoke with her anyway. But now, my lack of enthusiasm for Mom's last-chance husband created tension that widened the gap between us. Cool relationships turn cold.

Mom lived with her new husband in the front two rooms of his mother's dilapidated little house in Chula Vista. Known by the natives as "Chulajuana," this East County neighborhood was low-income, a depressing place for the new-lywed bride. Their quarters were cramped, the atmosphere hostile. Sam's mother was a tiny, mean woman who wore the same hand-knitted orange cap on her head every day. She seldom spoke, and when she did, it was to order Sam to fetch her something, or to say a few unflattering words about her new daugh-ter-in-law.

Sam kept my mother in that house by telling her that since they could live there rent-free, he'd be able to pay his debts; then they could buy a place of their own. My mother believed him with all her heart. She handed over every penny of the money she had claimed in her divorce from Bill, about $38,000. It was by far the most money she had ever seen at one time. A portion of it went toward paying some of Sam's old debts—tens of thousand of dollars in unpaid credit card bills. The rest of the money parked itself on the dirt drive-way in front of the old house in the form of a brand-new, fully loaded Cadillac Sedan de Ville with seven coats of gleaming black paint and gold trim, power leather seats, and surround-sound stereo.

"All the bells and whistles, honey!" he boasted, happy as a drunken sailor on shore leave. He and Mom drove the car for about six months, until the finance company told them to give it back.

My mother never had a chance to be too concerned over Sam's crippling, self-inflicted money problems. She found something far more threatening to worry about.

Her work on the catering truck began to sap her strength. This was more than the general tired feeling about which she had complained for years, which she had blamed on a thyroid condition and which Grandma had said was laziness. This was heavy fatigue. It was terribly depressing to do nothing but work and sleep. She thought that perhaps it was the monotony and the depression that might be affecting her health.

In the spring of 1989, my mother visited a doctor for a severe blistering rash she'd developed. He took one look and ordered immediate breast exams, a mammogram, skin-sample extractions, and biopsies. The test results came back two days later.

"Mycosis fungoides," the doctor told her as he sat behind his desk looking down at his chart. It was an extremely rare form of cancer. And it was terminal. The dispassionate doctor told her that the case was advanced. He predicted that she might have eight years to live before the cancer moved into her internal organs and began disabling them. My mother began a series of painful radiation treatments that would go on for years.

The horrifying revelation forced her into immediate retirement. Her job had been hard and unglamorous, but she'd made a decent wage, bought her own independence, and had begun a wonderfully cooperative new relationship with her youngest son. Her last day at Fiesta was also Daryl's. He didn't see the point in staying on without his partner.

As soon as Mom got the bad news, she phoned me. I had distanced myself from her years earlier and had gone on with the selfish work of building my family and advancing my career. Now that she needed simple acts of caring— a few minutes of my time, a listening ear, a word of encouragement—I had little to give. I called every month or so, out of a guilty sense of obligation, but I sped our conversations along, avoided talk of the cancer, and tried to forget about her misery as soon as I hung up. I wouldn't admit it, not even to myself, but I was deserting her, just as surely as my father had deserted me when I was 15 years old.

Grandma Marie began asking us to bring her newest great-grandchild down for a visit. I knew that would mean I'd see my mother, and I didn't want to. But there was no way of inventing an excuse that wouldn't be suspicious to Gina, so off we went.

Mom, I knew, would be at Grandma's, waiting for us. We walked into the house, and there she was, leaning forward in her chair, trying to pull herself up by the armrests. I noticed the blue scarf tied tightly around her head. Then I saw her face. No makeup, blanched and empty. Gone was the sparkle that had always animated her beautiful brown eyes. There was little life in her expression. She forced a grin, exposing loose, yellowing teeth—not the brilliant, straight, white teeth that had always made her smile dazzling. Just trying to look pleasant seemed to tax what little energy she had.

I walked over to her and held out my hands. She put hers in mine. These were not my mother's hands. These were the hands of an old woman, a dying woman—frail and cold, veined and bony. The fingernails, once long and slender and coated with rich colors, were now brown and cracked and brittle. I was about to pull the hands up to me and help my mother stand. Instead, afraid of hurting her, I knelt.

She hadn't said anything on the phone about chemotherapy. She was ashamed of what the radiation had done to her appearance and kept trying to apologize for herself. We wouldn't let her. When she slowly and reluctantly removed the scarf from her scalp, we fought back our squeamishness and smiled.

"You have a nice round head," I joked, trying not to seem horrified by the sight of my mother with just a few strands of hair still clinging to her scalp. "Mine's all lumpy and crooked." We laughed a little.

Gina and I coaxed Mom to tell us all about her latest treatments, listening intently and humming approval when she said something hopeful such as, "This will either kill the cancer or kill me. Either way, I'll be done with it."

"You're going to come through this just fine," Gina chimed. Mom held my hands as tight as she could.

Gina and I and our baby spent the whole day with Mom and Grandma. It was the longest I'd been around my mother since 1982, when I left for Provo and my future. She apologized for being too weak to hold her grandchild for more than a few minutes. She lamented that she couldn't get down on the floor and play with him. Other than that, she never uttered a word of self-pity. I could have been crushed by her pain and sorrow; instead, being near her—touching her, hugging her, listening to her—had a miraculous cleansing effect on me.

I no longer felt afraid to care about her. I knew it wouldn't hurt me to show her I loved her. I'd changed from the way I'd felt two years earlier, when our "Welcome to the Family" party for Sam had fizzled so badly. When it was time to leave, I felt happy to give my mother a hearty hug.

The drive home from California to Utah gave me hours of quiet time in which to think about what I had just seen and felt. No longer was I ashamed of my mother. To the contrary, her courage was inspirational. I realized that I had tragically misplaced the blame for my guilt and insecurity. My mother, and for that matter, my brothers, were not responsible for our family's breakup. Rather than distance myself from them, I should have grown closer over these past few years with the only people who truly understood my disappointment. Rather than shame, they could have given me strength, if only I had recognized the truth.

Sam finally made good on his prenuptial promise. He moved Mom out of his mother's front room and into a small condominium in Mira Mesa. It was a repossessed property that a bank liquidator was desperate to sell. At last, Mom had a place of her own. She could clean it and decorate it and make it into something that looked like home.

A second round of chemotherapy treatments, along with radiation treatments and experimental drugs, sent the cancer into temporary remission, but only for a few months. Then her doctors told her she would need surgery. "I held my breast all morning long," she told me afterward. "I just wanted to remember what it felt like." When she got back home, Sam waited on her and tried to comfort her.

One week to the day after my mother's surgery, Sam came home with the news that he'd been fired. His supervisors had told him to clean out his desk and leave right away. He went into shock, sitting motionless in front of his huge computer in the dining room, hardly speaking. My mother began to worry. She asked him what the prospects were for work in his field.

"Just about zero," he said.

"That bad?" she asked incredulously.

"That bad!" he snapped back. "You just don't know anything about the computer programming industry. You don't know how hard it is to find a good, high-paying job in this field."

"I wouldn't mind if you took a low-paying job," she said gently. "Anything would help."

Sam was insulted. "I'm far too highly trained," he said, "to go back to the bottom of the ladder." In the next weeks, my mother, trying to gather her strength and recover from her surgery, watched her husband, already emotionally fragile, steadily deteriorate. He got to the point where he didn't bathe and often spoke of suicide.

She was lying in bed one day when Sam came into the room and asked her how soon she could get back to work driving the catering truck. She was horrified—not at the prospect of going back to work, but at the idea that he would ask her so soon after major surgery. It was then that she finally saw her third husband for what he really was, 260 pounds of depression.

But she had no choice. They were almost two months behind on their mortgage payment. She couldn't just lie there and let Sam lose her home. She'd waited too long for it. So she returned to Fiesta.

She bore up for several months, working her long, demanding hours and bringing home enough money to make her mortgage payments and keep the wolves away. Sam nurtured his self-pity.

One evening, after hanging up the phone, he said, "My mother needs me." His mother, he explained, had gotten into an argument with a contractor over a roof repair job. "She refused to pay him because he didn't finish. Now the guy is threatening her, and she's frightened. I think we should pack up our things and move back in with her."

That was it for my mother. "No," she declared. "I spent seven years there, and I can't go back. If you go, you'll have to go without me."

Mom drove him down to Chula Vista the next morning. She didn't get out of the car as Sam carried his bags into the old house. She phoned me that night. "I don't know how long I'll last," she cried. "I can't afford to keep up the payments on this condo, and I don't know how long I can keep working on that truck. And the worst of it is being alone. I can't stand to live this way."

I felt helpless to do anything but try to encourage her, but my words seemed hollow. Marq, however, with boundless compassion borne of his agonizing divorce and hopeless longing for his sons, was stirred by Mom's predicament. The one who had pulled me out of so many jams when we were kids was about to rally to his mother's rescue. He got in his rusted old Toyota pick-up truck and drove 750 miles to tell her that he had a plan.

"I have to do it face-to-face," he told me on the phone before he left. "I have to convince Mom that my plan will work."

He told her that his Amway distributorship was beginning to take off and that he would need some administrative help. He said she could come to Salt Lake City and share his small apartment, and the two of them could work together, much the same way in which she and Daryl had been partners.

"I can generate sales, and you can process orders and manage inventory," he plotted.

Marq didn't know whether or not his hastily sketched plan would work; he'd improvised it on the drive to San Diego. But he felt he had to do something, anything, to bring her close to him, where he could help her. His mother's disaster had somehow, suddenly, given him a new purpose that energized him.

"It was the best offer I'd had in a long time," she told me later. In fact, it was her only choice. It was also a late-in-life chance to forge a relationship with her eldest son. Her job-sharing arrangement with Daryl had been so rewarding, perhaps a similar partnership with Marq would bring them together. Maybe, she thought, the man of her dreams might be one of her long-lost sons.

✤✤✤

In 1989, when Mom heard the cancer diagnosis and her wonderful partnership with Daryl broke up, Daryl moved on to other jobs. He drove a shuttle van at the airport and parked rental cars, barely making enough to live on. He staggered along for three years as poverty, drug abuse, and loneliness beat down his self-respect and his trademark positive outlook. There came a time, in the summer of 1993, which he barely remembers, when he ceaselessly wandered San Diego on foot in a hallucinogenic haze. He became obsessed with the idea that he must see the mayor, to tell him about a program he'd devised to generate money for underprivileged kids by collecting and restoring brokendown bicycles. In anticipation of the meeting, he went to the extreme of putting on a coat and tie. Wardrobe not withstanding, he was escorted from city hall by a pair of security guards.

He continued his roaming, and soon found himself at the main gate of the Naval Training Facility on San Diego Harbor. He told the shore patrol at the gate he wanted to see the base commander. The shore patrol were polite and professional, but they didn't let him in.

In protest, and because he was hot and sweaty in his old wool suit, he stood in the driveway and began removing all his clothes. When he got down to his boxer shorts, the polite shore patrol carefully joined his wrists behind his back, locked them together with a pair of handcuffs, put him in a paddy wagon, and took him to the base stockade.

After a few hours, the commander appeared. He ordered a guard to give Daryl a blue Navy shirt and a pair of blue slacks. Then the shore patrol drove him a few miles from the base and let him out on a street corner.

After a time, he noticed two San Diego police officers observing him from a squad car parked across the street. That irritated him, and he yelled at them to leave him alone, underscoring his request by holding up the middle finger of his right hand. Instead of driving away, the officers swung their car around and crossed the street to Daryl's side, pulling up right in front of him. They got out, handcuffed him, and put him in the back seat. At the station house, he was placed in a padded room with no windows. He was there for three days.

He began to feel that the only way to get out was to threaten suicide. The guards took him to the psychiatric examination room at the hospital across the street from the jail. There, Daryl managed to convince the examiner that he was not mentally ill, but had been strung out on drugs. A day or so later, Daryl appeared before a judge who told him that the charges had been dropped, and invited him to leave the building and go his own way.

That was the beginning of a series of drug-related difficulties with the police. Eventually, he was written up on a marijuana citation and told to appear in court the following month.

Daryl the free spirit, the wanderer, the vagabond hippie, was trapped. If he appeared in court to answer the citation, he would have been thrown in jail for his previous violations. If he ignored the order, they would have found and arrested him on a "failure to appear" warrant.

Clearly, it was time to move on, so when his mother told him of her plan to go to Utah, Daryl was ready to ride.

❦❦❦

C HAPTER FOURTEEN
Demons at the Door

I 'd been working in Salt Lake for five years, and I was getting restless. I was ready for a new job, this time in a bigger city—a major market, as they say in television. Moving up in my profession—making more money, making a name for myself—seemed essential to the goal I'd set many years before: reinventing myself and rebuilding my life. One more step, a big step upward, would prove that my father's horrible fate would not be mine. Gina understood the business, and as happy as she was in Utah, where she'd been raised and where her parents lived, she had prepared herself to pull up roots when the time came.

NBC called and invited me to New York for a few days of interviews. The visit ended with the bosses telling me that they wanted to hire me as a correspondent for a new magazine show in development, and that I would soon get a contract in the mail with a job offer. The offer never came. When General Motors sued NBC over a botched *Dateline* segment, a management shake-up ensued, and all bets were off. I turned to the next best available thing. It was an anchor position in Boston. It would be an important advance, and it was the kind of job that could carry me all the way to a comfortable retirement.

Gina and I sat on the family-room couch discussing the decision facing us. On the fluffy white carpet at our feet, Kasey played with Jessie, his new-born baby sister. We now had a boy and a girl, the perfect American family. And if I took the Boston job, we'd be the perfectly wealthy American family.

"Lynn Packer will say I sold out," I argued with myself.

Gina smiled knowingly. She too had survived Lynn Packer's demanding courses in broadcast journalism, and she knew he'd want us to follow in his footsteps as investigative reporters. "You know what he'd say," she said. "'You're throwing away your note pad for a can of hair spray.'" We both laughed;

that was exactly what he'd say. "On the other hand," Gina went on, "I've always thought New England would be a lovely place to live."

"Those bright red leaves in autumn . . ."

"Those places where history was made . . ."

"Those Celtics games at the Garden . . ."

Who were we kidding? The money was great. We jumped at the offer. I set out for Boston in August of 1993, a few months ahead of Gina and the kids.

From the moment I walked into the WLVI studios in the city's South End, all eyes were on me. I could sense the station managers' nervous anticipation the first day I went on the air. They patted me on the back as I made my way to the studio and wished me a tight-lipped "Good luck!" as if I were going off to war. Their nervousness made me wonder whether they weren't second-guessing the decision to hire me. I could hardly have blamed them. They had taken a risk, hiring a virtual unknown, a veritable youngster.

After the first broadcast, which went smoothly enough, one of them took me aside. "Boston television viewers are the toughest in the country," he said. "They're leery of newcomers. You can't just flash your smile and expect them to invite you into their homes. You'll have to earn their loyalty. It could take five years." He paused. "If we're lucky."

Unnerved a little by that observation and by the constant doubtful stares, I got cautious. My performance soon became stilted and unnatural. I needed to relax, but the harder I tried, the tighter I became. My co-workers saved me. They were remarkably friendly and seemed eager to make me feel welcome and needed. With their encouragement, I managed to settle into the anchor chair.

Gina and I built a house in Hingham, a tiny coastal town founded in 1635 just up the road from Plymouth Rock and carefully preserved—something like "Main Street USA" at Disneyland, only real. The schools were academically superior to any that Gina or I had attended. Contrary to the warnings we'd heard about New Englanders, the neighbors were the friendliest we'd ever met. Our house was beautiful—a classic hip-roof colonial, with modern features built in. Browsing the little country stores where century-old antiques sold for five dollars became a hobby. Piling in the family car and driving down Route 3 to Cape Cod's long, white beaches became a weekend ritual. And those mornings when we'd climb to the upper deck of the ferry and sail to Martha's Vineyard, where we'd shop and stroll and watch the sunset and eat at the Black Dog Tavern, became our special treat.

Gina and the kids were thoroughly enjoying our adventure into prosperity, but I was worried about it. More than ever before.

❧❧❧

There is boredom in the anchorman's job—the same routine every day, reading other writers' stories. Maybe that was the problem. Or maybe it was some sort of early midlife crisis. Or perhaps I had one of those psychological ailments that pop scientists write about in trendy magazines, the kind of thing that strikes successful young people, makes them impotent, and causes them to drop out of seemingly promising careers. Or maybe it was the pattern. The strange fact was that after a year in Boston, I was getting edgy.

I kept having this feeling that something was missing, that although I had everything I wanted, it wasn't right, not because it wasn't enough, but because it was too much. All the trappings of success raised the stakes. The thought of losing it all when the world figured out I had faked my way into it was too much for me to bear. My secret fears tortured me and shattered the God-given certainty that once I'd created my own sweet family and won a measure of prosperity, I'd possess a lasting contentment. It hadn't happened.

My anxiety began to spill out onto Gina. I became notoriously good at finding things to criticize. The rebukes became almost a part of our daily routine as I found temporary pleasure in putting her down, sort of a salve to ease my own personality itch. She made my haircut appointment with the wrong barber. She bought salad in a bag instead of fresh lettuce. For that matter, she wasn't a very good cook. She brought prints home from the Fotomat, and most of the pictures were lousy. She ruined our trip to Martha's Vineyard because she booked us at the wrong bed-and-breakfast and then didn't want to ride the rented mopeds. She talked on the phone to her mother too much. She was getting lazy at sex. I'd lie in bed beside her at night and wonder when her patience would run out, and when my problems would burn up our marriage. I was confused and a little ashamed.

Then came the blizzard, the first I'd reported as a Boston anchorman, and the stock footage of the old derelict curled around a manhole cover. My father's words started ringing in my ears again: "I'm too old for this shit, boys." And so did Kasey's words: "Whatever happened to Grandpa Bob?"

I was mortified that I couldn't answer my son's simple question about my father, but it was just one of many questions I couldn't answer. I knew so little about this man who was the source of my anguish . . . what had formed him, how he became the sort of person he was. I began to think that learning about him might be the key to my salvation—that the very act of asking would help liberate me.

I started by reaching out to people who had been significant when I was growing up. My first call was to the Du Pre family matriarch, Aunt Ann, my father's eldest sister, now 70. She was possibly the tallest, broadest, loudest woman I'd ever known, and yet, when I called her at her home in Chattanooga, the sound of her voice brought back memories of tenderness. I remembered that voice booming a welcome across the yard when we arrived at my grand-father's for family reunions, "Well, look who's here! Bobby's beautiful boys!" I also remembered her breasts, her enormous breasts. Their cleavage above the neckline of her dress was the last thing I'd see before being pulled into one of her smothering hugs.

"We've tried so hard to help Bobby over the years," she said when I phoned, "but it's just never worked out. He doesn't seem to want our help because he thinks it will tie him down and he'll lose his freedom. He wants to be free to go where he pleases and do what he wants. We've put up money to get him into an apartment and to get him started in business again, to no avail."

My Uncle Frank, whom I'd remembered as a large, swollen, gruff old man who breathed his liquored breath on his nephews while telling us how spoiled we were, was friendly and candid and supportive when I told him I was try-ing to find out what had happened to my father. "I think it's an admirable thing you're doing," he said. "I wish you luck. I've bailed Bobby out so many times I can't count them anymore. I just think he prefers to live out there the way he does. Maybe he just got tired of all the rest of us."

All of the relatives who'd grown up with Bobby Du Pre seemed happy to speak with a member of the family who they had thought had been lost along with him. I realized, much to my astonishment and pleasure, that I had rela-tives all over the country, people with whom I hadn't spoken in years, who cared about me and my brothers and our parents. They had been trying to keep track of their lost kinsman as I had been trying to forget him.

Talking to them all made me realize that I had not been alone in my sor-row over the loss of my father and the breakup of our family. For all those years, they had watched it happen and had mourned with us. We had moved out of their reach and neglected phone calls and cards and letters that would have kept us in touch with caring relatives. We had denied ourselves their love and support. Reconnecting with them was as easy as saying, "Hello, this is cousin Jon." They were eager to offer encouragement and help, and very interested in what I might learn when I found my father. I realized that in my personal and private quest, I actually represented everyone who'd ever loved and lost him.

My cousin Catherine, Ann's third daughter, offered an astounding insight. She had met her husband, whose name was also Jon, while the two were in college at the University of Tennessee. They lived together for a couple of years, then married. They built successful careers and were raising two children in their home in Atlanta when Catherine learned she had breast cancer. The news unhinged her husband. While she was still in bed after the surgery, he told her he was leaving her and the children. He moved in with an old high school girl-friend, a younger woman with two breasts.

I asked Catherine why she thought he'd deserted her in her moment of great-est need.

"He was afraid," she said. "He was afraid that he wasn't man enough to deal with adversity."

"Why was he so afraid?" I asked.

"Because Jon, my Jon, had a father who'd deserted him and his brothers and sisters when he was a child. His father just up and left one day, and he never knew why. He hated his father for that. And as much as he hated him, he always feared that he would become just like him."

The similarities between his story and mine were stunning. "So who says I won't collapse the same way," I asked her, "if the pressure gets too intense for me?" I thought of how I had shunned my own mother during those years when she needed her sons' support. "What's the difference between me and your Jon?"

"Well, the difference," she said, "is fundamental. My Jon never faced his demons. And so, when the crisis came, they beat him."

"And me?" I coaxed, sensing that this cousin might have something impor-tant for me to hear.

"You? Well, the fact that you've called me with all these questions makes it perfectly clear. You're facing yours."

It had been about 30 years since I'd seen Cousin Catherine, not since the family reunions when we played in the field behind our grandfather's house. And here she was, explaining my anxiety better than I'd been able to explain it to my wife, and defining the challenge before me. I needed to know what had happened to my father because I needed to be certain it wouldn't happen to me. I wanted my wife and children to know that I would be there, always. To convince them of that, I had to be sure of it myself.

❧❧❧

The closest person to my father over the years had been Uncle Jimmy, his younger brother. I called him to reestablish our friendship and to see what he could tell me about my father. We talked many times on the phone, and each call yielded a little bit more. Eventually, from Jimmy and my other rel-atives and various people they referred me to—people who'd known Dad when he was young—I assembled a portrait of Bobby Du Pre and an account of his origins.

My father was born in a farming and textile-mill town called Walhalla, in the far western corner of South Carolina. Walhalla's main street was two blocks long and lined with brick-faced storefronts. Most people lived in the surrounding countryside tilling plots of red clay. You couldn't see beyond the edge of your field, where the rows of corn and beans ended and a wall of tall pines covered with kudzu vine began. People in Walhalla didn't have much interest in what lay beyond those trees and those mountains. They were content to live their lives and go about their business. The entire town was eerily quiet under a thick blanket of humid air that seemed to muffle even speech and thought—not the sort of place that could long contain or satisfy an ambitious upstart like my father.

Our family name was originally Du Pré, with the accent mark, pronounced *du-pray.* The Du Prés were Huguenots, French Protestant farmers who, fleeing religious persecution, landed in Charleston, South Carolina, in 1686. Their American neighbors ignored the accent and said *du-pree.* That pronunciation stuck.

Charleston in that day was already a thriving port and cultural center. But it was a city, and the Du Pres wanted to farm again. During the next two centuries, the family moved steadily west across the state, looking for good land. Some members of the family settled on a flat spot in Carolina's Piedmont region and called the place Abbeville. Others continued the westward migration until they reached the foothills of the Blue Ridge Mountains, the southernmost stretch of the Appalachians. One of those Du Pres, Julius, my grandfather's grandfather, fought as a foot soldier in the Confederate army and received a medal for his wounds. After the war, he worked in various county jobs and then became the first chairman of Clemson College's Department of Horticulture. "Du Pre had no formal horticultural training," said one memorial, "but he was a naturally gifted man and anything he touched seemed to grow."

My father's father, Mason, whose name I was given as my middle name, served as Oconee County's postmaster his whole adult life. He was also known as the most powerful and effective chairman who ever ran the Democratic Party in that district. His second son, Robert, the fourth of five children, is said to have been his favorite. Or at least my father's brothers and sisters all tell it that way: "He was the apple of Papa Mason's eye."

I knew my grandfather when I was a boy. He always had a fat cigar clenched between his teeth and a shot glass of bourbon cradled between his thumb and forefinger. Biting down on the wet end of that stogie and peering through the cloud of smoke that hung over the La-Z-Boy recliner that was his throne, he appeared sinister to us grandchildren. The red bags under his eyes, the purple vein that crept across his swollen nose, and those huge ears that drooped from the sides of his head made us shudder, and we dreaded his wet, smelly kisses.

"What are you no-good rascals up to?" he would growl. "Come to beg a nickel off poor ol' Papa Mason, did ya?"

We would cower as he coaxed us closer to his throne with the nickel in his palm. The game was to snatch the nickel and scamper away before Papa Mason could grab your hand and pull you onto his lap and kiss you.

He was a hard man, but one evening my brothers and cousins and I discovered to our amazement that Papa Mason had his tender side. We were rummaging around his attic, through the old trunks of old-fashioned clothes, hoping to find Civil War uniforms or even weapons, and we came across two cardboard boxes full of love letters he had sent to his young bride while he was off in the army in World War I. "My dear Sally," he wrote in one, "I can't wait to caress your lovely skin and to see your beautiful face and taste your rosy red lips." We giggled for hours as we took turns reading those love letters to each other.

Whatever his romantic feelings about his wife, he was of the view that women were meant to obey men. Sally's job was to keep Mason fed, his house clean, his liquor glass half-full, and her mouth shut. All these things, she did.

Grandma Sally seemed to love to cook for us. Or if she didn't, she never complained about it. We sat at her yellow-topped kitchen table and eagerly gobbled down her chicken, her ham, and her okra—all of it fried in the same black grease she'd used the week before. "That's how I cook in the southern flavor!" she would brag from her position at the stove. She served up her fried delicacies with piles of black-eyed peas, lima beans, creamed corn, grits smothered in gravy, and collard greens soppy with vinegar. We'd eat until we could hardly walk, then go outside and lie belly-up under the huge oak tree by the garage.

After Papa Mason died, Grandma grew old quickly, suffering from diabetes. She refused to be taken to a nursing home, which meant we grandchildren had to take our turns nursing her, feeding her, administering her insulin shots, bathing her, changing her clothes, and helping her use the bathroom. It was a terribly unpleasant assignment. She was senile and incontinent in her last years, but she wanted to die in her own home.

My father and his two brothers and two sisters grew up working hard on their grandfather's farm, which he called Chigger Hill. The Du Pre boys were sturdy, good-looking, and popular. The eldest brother, Frank, was "the toughest, meanest S.O.B. in four counties," as the usual description put it. Frank turned his mean streak into legend one Friday night in the fall of 1941 when the Walhalla High School football team lost to the Seneca High Bobcats. He stormed Seneca's team bus and challenged the entire team to a fight. "He bloodied about a dozen of them before they threw him off that bus," Uncle Jimmy, my father's younger brother, told me with satisfaction.

Life for my father and his brothers was good. Thirty-five cents would buy you an R.C. Cola, a can of vienna sausages, a pack of saltines, and a moon pie, with enough left for a ticket to the double feature at the Walhalla Cinema. They had 300 acres to roam, land Mason had bought with his Army mustering-out pay for two dollars an acre. Mason had fenced off 18 acres and made a small farm, where he intended to grow a crop of strong young men. As soon as a boy was old enough to carry a shovel, Mason put him to work.

"We were planting watermelon starters one afternoon," Uncle Jimmy said. At age nine, Jimmy was the runt in the family of five children, three years younger than Bobby. The west field was freshly plowed, and the boys were told to start at the top of each row, walk one pace, stoop, open the earth with a trowel, and insert a melon vine. This was early summer, but it was hot, nearly 100 degrees. Steam rose from the soil and freighted the heavy air. Frank, then 17 and already strong as a man, worked far ahead of his two younger brothers. Papa Mason mostly stayed on the porch in the shade, but came out now and then to bark directions.

"After about five hours, Bobby and I got tired of planting," Jimmy told me. "So we started a little game of tackle. He knocked me down and ran. I got up and chased him. I tackled him and ran in the other direction. This went on for a while. Country boys that age never get tired."

When Jimmy threw his ninth or tenth tackle, Bobby didn't get up. Jimmy didn't notice at first. He'd run to the other side of the field. But when he wasn't tackled back, he turned. "I looked over and saw Bobby, still lying face down where I'd tackled him. I hollered at him, 'C'mon, Bobby. Bobby, c'mon!' He didn't move. Papa Mason called over from the edge of the field, 'Bobby git up out of that dirt!' But Bobby was unconscious.

"Frank picked him up and carried him to the house, and somebody ran to get the doctor. We didn't have a telephone, and doctors still came to the house back then. He said Bobby had suffered a severe heat stroke that had stopped his heart for a few seconds and shut off the blood to his brain. He said the best treatment was to keep Bobby cool—pack him in ice. Somebody jumped in the buggy and rode to the ice plant and came back with a big cake of it. Mama and Daddy darkened the front room and set up a bed and laid Bobby out in it, putting bags of chipped ice around him. Members of the family stood vigil over him for three days and two nights. It was touch and go. We thought we were going to lose him."

On the evening of the third day, Bobby awoke, took a breath, and looked around the room. He was shivering and confused but seemed as good as new.

My aunt and my uncles felt that Papa Mason always treated my father a little differently after that. Maybe it was the thought of losing his second son that frightened Mason into favoring Bobby. No one knows. But everyone agrees that by the time he was a teenager, he was the one who got all the breaks. Mason didn't let any of his children go without the necessities, but he made sure Bobby got the advantages. My father learned to expect he would get what he wanted, and that somebody would be there to bail him out, whatever trouble he brought on himself.

Bobby displayed intelligence early—all his teachers commented on it—and his friends teased him for his habit of walking around with his nose in a book. At the same time, he developed a lively appetite for the more physical pleasures. During high school, he found he had a way with women, and apprenticed with the local girls in the back seat of his father's Oldsmobile and on the young ladies' rear porches. But it wasn't until after high school, when he joined the Navy, that he learned just how easy it was for him to talk his way into a skirt. Over the years that followed, uninterrupted by his marriage, the desire for women would turn neurotic, progressing into compulsive womanizing.

Like most American boys, Bobby had been caught up in the excitement and patriotic fervor of World War II. He begged Papa Mason to let him quit high school on his 17th birthday and sign up. Papa Mason said no; he had to graduate. By the time he did, it was 1945, and the war was almost over.

The Navy assigned him to easy duty. "It was two years of high living," my father told us once. "We could eat in the officers' mess and shop in the officers' store. We ate steaks. We stayed drunk. I trained to be a rear gunner in a fighter plane, but what I really learned from the navy was how to drink."

Uncle Jimmy remembered that his parents worried about Bobby the whole time he was in the Navy. "They actually celebrated when he got back in one piece," Jimmy said. "Heck, the worst that could have happened, he might have tripped on a beer bottle coming out of a bar."

Heavy drinking, which in the world of my father's youth was considered one of the manly arts, developed into another destructive, addictive behavior that would plague him throughout his life.

My father had played football in junior high and high school, well enough to earn a scholarship to Dayton University in Ohio, where, in his freshman year, he starred as a tailback and punter. When my brothers and I were little, Dad used to love to pull out the brittle, yellowed articles he'd clipped from the *Dayton Sentinel* and make me read them aloud. "The speedster from the south scampered around end to pay dirt," one read. His most memorable moment came when he broke through the line on fourth down and blocked a punt. "We didn't wear face guards in those days," he told me. "That punter caught me square in the jaw. Broke it in three places." There were no team doctors, no x-rays. Dad's lower left molars rotted and had to be taken out. From that point on, he had to wear a lower plate of false teeth.

Whether it was the injury or just homesickness, he never said, but at the end of his freshmen year, the speedster sped home. He tried out for the team at the University of South Carolina, but they didn't offer him a scholarship. His father had to help pay for college, which meant that for the first time in his life, Bobby had to knuckle down and study. When he did, he got good grades and, assisted by his father's influence, was accepted by the university's law school. Thanks again, perhaps, to his father's connections, an appointment as a special agent in the FBI awaited when he graduated.

After his time in the FBI and with Senator Thurmond, Dad had returned to his native region, to live in Mauldin and work as a prosecutor in Greenville. If he hadn't quite been trailing clouds of glory, he'd certainly been carrying strong credentials and glowing with professional promise. Out at Chigger Hill, Papa Mason sat back in his recliner and watched his golden boy shine. He himself had passionately wanted to be a lawyer, but times had been hard, and there hadn't been money for it. Now his son Bobby had realized his own frustrated dream.

"So at last there was an attorney in the family," Uncle Jimmy told me. "That meant an awful lot to ol' Mason, and it put a lot of pressure on Bobby. Poor guy. He was expected to achieve his own ambitions and his father's, too."

❧❧❧

The emerging portrait of my father seemed to explain some of the things about him that had troubled me so—his attitude toward women, his erratic, self-destructive career, and his drinking. It helped me see him in a new way—not just as someone who hurt people, but as someone who'd been injured himself, by his father's favoritism and by the selfish, indulgent behaviors that young Southern males were permitted. I began to think that if I found him, I could receive him in a different, more understanding spirit.

But what else would I find if I found him? I was shaped by this tormented man. His blood ran in my veins. I could see his face in my face. If I looked into this dark mirror, would I see myself?

I knew Jimmy kept track of Dad's whereabouts, as well as anyone could. "You know how he roams around," Jimmy said in his comfortable Carolina drawl. "He drops by about twice a year, but only for a few days. Then he hears the call of the wild, and off he goes. I don't know how he does it on what little money he has, but Bobby's always been real resourceful, and, as you know, Jon, he can talk a raccoon out of its skin."

What little money my father had to live on came to him from the Social Security Administration, via Jimmy. As the arrangement went, Dad would call monthly and tell Jimmy what town he was in, and Jimmy would send the welfare check to general delivery there. Anytime I wanted to find my father, I could track him through Jimmy.

From then on I called Jimmy toward the end of each month, to laugh at his bad jokes and to get updates on my father's movements. Dad had gone from South Carolina to San Diego, then doubled back and landed in Arizona.

When I called in February, Jimmy sounded worried. "I think he's in trouble, Jon," he said. That made me sit up. Jimmy, a calm, undemonstrative man, had always been one to play down trouble, not wanting to alarm anyone.

"To tell you the truth, Jon, I think he's ill. It sounds like he might have the flu or pneumonia or something. He phoned a few days ago, and he didn't talk clear, so I'm not sure what he was saying, but I think he might have been arrested and put in jail. I think he said he was in Tucson, but like I said, he didn't talk clear."

That did it. I went straight to Gina and asked the question she'd been dreading. "Will you let me go try to find my dad?"

My timing was terrible. Gina was with child, seven months into her term. She didn't need turmoil; she needed serenity. For years she'd endured my tortured self-examinations, my unanswerable questions, my temper flare-ups, and my frustration. It was all a blurry, sometimes frightening mess to her. She couldn't possibly understand such things. She'd come from a family that worked. She'd just wanted a calm, peaceful, normal, happy life with me. Not all this. We had argued about it many times. She felt this fixation of mine was disrupting our marriage and our family life. I'd shouted her down many times, insisting that it was absolutely essential for me to resolve this thing about my father.

She'd seen it coming. By the time I got around to having the conversation, she knew I was going to tell her I wanted to go and try to find my father. All the hours-long phone calls in the other room, all the note taking, all the quiet introspection—it was just the kind of behavior that had always made her jealous of my inner thoughts, where she wasn't the most important person. And I'd anticipated her protest. All the sideways glances and subtle verbal digs whenever I'd come out of the other room after another long phone call. I'd sensed her displeasure for weeks, and I'd grown steadily angrier that instead of showing interest in my research, she'd disapproved of it. When it came time for us to have the conversation, we dispensed with the formalities and went right to the ugly part of it.

Listen, Gina, I want to talk to you about my going on a trip—"

"I knew it!" she interrupted.

"I can't believe your imaginary family is more important to you than your real family here," she said in the most impetuous tone I'd ever heard from her. Her comment sparked an explosion like she'd never seen from her combustible husband.

"Imaginary?" I screamed. That's how I'd always done it. The sheer volume of my voice paralyzed her. Once she was disarmed and I was loaded with explosive rage, she didn't have a chance. I stood and ran across the living room at my pregnant wife, and she cowered as I swelled with hot, angry air and launched the worst verbal attack she had ever endured.

"My miserable life is just my imagination? Is that what you think? All those years of doubt and shame? I just imagined all that? You think I invented this torment? Just to inconvenience you? Just to interrupt your perfect little life? I told you it would turn out this way. Did you think I was just making it up? Sure! Of course you did! I wouldn't have dared tarnish your perfect little picture of your perfect little life!" I screamed.

I continued my rampage. "This is all just a big inconvenience for you because you have no idea what I'm going through. And you have no idea what I'm going through because you've never bothered to ask. And you've never bothered to ask because you're afraid of the answer. Welcome to the real world, princess, where not everyone is happy. For once, this one's not about you, you spoon-fed, spoiled-rotten bitch. This one's about me. I'm going to find out why my father fucked up my life, and piss on you for trying to make me feel guilty about it!"

"Please stop," was all she could utter.

The next day I was on a flight to Phoenix.

❧❧❧

CHAPTER FIFTEEN
Street Lawyer

I arrived in Phoenix at dusk and made a couple of phone calls to Tucson hospitals before leaving the airport. Still, no word of a Robert Du Pre. First thing next morning, I jumped in the rental car and headed south on Interstate 8 to Tucson. The desert was empty and made me think how big the world is and how small we people are and how nearly impossible it might be to find my fugitive father. *What if he didn't want to be found?* After 20 years on the road, the old guy was probably more streetwise than anyone on the face of the earth. Even the IRS had given up on finding him. What made me think *I* might? I couldn't let myself think about how overmatched I was.

Getting off the freeway, I saw my first Tucson resident, a bearded man standing on the median strip of the exit ramp holding a sign that said, "Will Work for Food." I slowed my car and studied his face; it wasn't someone I recognized. At the bottom of the ramp, there was another man with another sign— "Vietnam Vet. Need Help. God Bless You." Two more beggars sat on a bus stop bench as I drove up Broadway into Tucson's downtown district. Just ahead there was another, pushing a grocery cart filled with cardboard. Was it just my imagination, or was this place crawling with homeless people? Certainly, I was seeing this city through a filter I'd never used before. But yes, Tucson was teeming with indigents. The city's abundance of services and shelters attracted them . . . and my father, I hoped.

The need to cover a huge area and the complete lack of clues made me decide to start at the most obvious places and work my way into this unfamiliar territory. The young woman behind the counter at the Travelers' Aid office at the bus depot gave me a suspicious look when I asked for the names and addresses of all the homeless shelters and food pantries in Tucson. I knew she was wondering why a clean-shaven young man wearing jeans and a fresh button-down cotton shirt might be interested in finding a free bed and a meal. Five shelters and four pantries—I might be able to get to most of them before nightfall.

At the Salvation Army, the man in the navy-blue uniform wore a badge that read: "Mr. Sosa, Assistant Director." I asked if my father was staying there and was stunned by the answer. "I'm not at liberty to give out any information on our guests, sir," he replied.

"You're not able to respond to an inquiry from a member of a guest's immediate family?" I said, getting out my wallet. "Mr. Sosa, I'd be glad to show you identification if that would help you clear my request through your supervising officer." As I pulled out my driver's license, I managed to display my press credentials, my gold credit cards, and the $200 in cash stuffed in my wallet. "I'm sure my father would be upset to find out I traveled all the way from Boston and missed him. I'm only going to be in Tucson overnight. Are you sure your supervisor wouldn't clear this request?" I spoke in a polite tone, but Mr. Sosa got my message. I wasn't about to leave without information.

"What's your father's name?" Mr. Sosa asked reluctantly.

"Robert Du Pre," I said.

He didn't show any sign that he recognized the name. "Just a minute," he said as he stepped into his office. He came back and read from a clipboard.

"Mr. Du Pre has been banned from staying in this facility," he announced. I could practically feel my father's presence. I was standing where he had stood. I needed more information. How close was I?

"Listen," I said, "I flew all the way from Boston looking for my father. What would it cost you to tell me when my father was last here and where he might have gone? How about it? Then I'll be on my way." My offer to leave must have sounded good to Mr. Sosa.

"Robert Du Pre checked in to this facility on November 26, 1994. He took a room, but after showering and shaving and changing his clothes and eating, he left the same night without checking out."

Sosa then said something about the rules and a requirement that guests stay the night once they check in. He said Du Pre had failed to return his key and never bothered to pick up his photo ID card.

"I want the ID card!" I practically shouted. "Give me the ID card!" I could see what he looked like if I could get a look at the card.

"That's out of the question," Sosa said sternly. "Even if I had it, I couldn't give it to you. You've already gotten more than I'm allowed to say."

I turned without thanking Mr. Sosa, and left, thinking how his explanation sounded so like the man I was looking for—unwilling to abide by anyone's rules. More important, how much distance had Dad been able to put between himself and this place since November 26, four months and a week ago? The world seemed big again, and I felt small.

I went to a place called Primavera, the largest shelter in Tucson. The man at the door looked as though he was a guest who'd gotten a temporary job watching the front door. His eyebrows raised when I gave Dad's name.

"Ah, the street lawyer," he said. "Saw him last month. He came in several times. Never stays—just takes a shower, throws his shirt into the bin and grabs a clean one, shoots the breeze with some of the regulars, and leaves." I could practically feel my father's presence in this place, too. It made me uneasy, as though he were hiding around every corner watching my movements, staying two steps ahead of me. I left a note for Robert Du Pre and told the man I'd check back with him first thing in the morning. None of the other three shelters had heard of the fellow I was seeking. I looked at my watch as I left the last one. It was four P.M.

I was startled by how quickly the day had passed. *The post office!* Following my city map, I found the Cherry Bell station, the main post office, in an industrial park on the western outskirts of the city. I told the woman at the general delivery window that I was looking for my father, too hurried to explain. She gazed at me with a knowing look, sort of smiling that she was pleased someone would be going to the trouble of looking for one of the hundreds of vagabonds she saw coming through her office every week, and yet, a little confused that my clean-cut, well-dressed appearance didn't seem to connect me with one of them. She graciously suggested that I leave a postcard for him, care of general delivery "When he picks up his VA check, he'll get the postcard."

I hadn't said anything about a VA check. *Does this woman know him, too? Is everyone in this goddamn town standing watch for him?* I had to quickly clear my head. I couldn't afford to let anyone get the impression I was just another street crazy. Obviously, the postal clerk had done this drill before. I wasn't the first person to come through the Tucson post office looking for a lost loved one.

I bought a 45-cent postcard and ran to a phone booth outside. Convinced that my prey was two steps beyond my reach, I had to think three steps ahead of myself if I was going to have a chance of catching up. The note would be no good without a phone number where he could reach me. That meant I had to check in to a hotel. I phoned the closest place I could find and hurried back to drop off my postcard. "Dad," it said, "I'm in Tucson looking for you! Please call me at the Strand Hotel, 297-0700, room 513 . . . please! Love, Jon."

Sitting in the rental car, all I could do now was review. My head was still full of day-old adrenaline. Everything was still clear. I'd covered every possible base. If Dad were in Tucson, then he must be shacking up with somebody. Surely he'd go to the post office to pick up his survival rations from the VA. I'd stake out the general delivery drop box and find him there.

Now it was 5:30. As soon as I let myself relax a little, the adrenal glands shut down, and my body went limp. Suddenly, all I could think of was that I had been going nonstop for 14 hours without food or drink. As soon as I spotted a familiar "Kenny Rogers Roasters" sign, I pulled in and grabbed a box of chicken on my way to the hotel. The touch of the warm cardboard and the buttery aroma that filled the car made me conscious of how easy it was for me to get food—and that the one I sought might be starving that night. *I'm coming, Dad. By God, I'll find you.*

I flopped on the floor in room 513 and tore open the brown paper bag, letting the flavored steam waft around my face. It made me think of Grandma Sally's Sunday fried chicken feasts in the kitchen of the old homestead in Walhalla. I took a bite and dialed Uncle Jimmy in Walhalla. "Have you heard anything else from my dad?" I asked.

"Jon," he said, excitedly, "Bobby called about an hour ago. He's not in Tucson, buddy. He's in San Diego! I guess he hitched a ride down there."

The hair on my neck and arms stood on end, and I could feel my heart pump harder.

"Did you tell him I'm looking for him?" I asked.

"You bet, buddy. And I got a number where he said you could reach him. I told him you had to get in touch with him tonight."

Uncle Jimmy had made the connection. This development made me anxious. Gone was the element of surprise. If my father didn't want to see me, he had until the next day to take evasive action. Someone as crafty as he, who knew the road map like I know the hallways of my house, could disappear without a trace and I might never find him. My hope was that the phone number was good, that even if Dad wanted to avoid me, he wouldn't admit it to his brother.

My fingers trembled. It had been three years since I'd seen the guy and nearly 20 before that. Now here I was, about to reconnect with the mysterious menace from my past. Was this wise? Sitting on the floor of that hotel room in Tucson, the phone in my hand, I realized I didn't want to talk to him and I didn't want to hear his voice. I didn't know exactly how to explain to him what this trip was all about. I was afraid he would bolt and run, like a cockroach disappearing down the drain when you turn on the bathroom light. And I was angry and frustrated. I'd focused all my energy on finding him in Tucson. All my instincts had told me that he was here. I'd felt his presence all day. Now, finding out he'd skipped town made me feel foolish. And I thought of Gina, and how I'd told her to put her pregnancy on hold while I went on this ghost hunt.

I dialed the number. Ten rings—ten rings that seemed longer than normal. My grip tightened on the receiver. I was about to slam it down when I heard a click and then a voice. I asked for my father. "Um, he was here," a man said, "but he left to go see Chuck."

"Who's Chuck?" I inquired.

"Uh, Chuck's a friend of his."

"Maybe I could call him there. Do you have that number?"

"Uh, yeah, yeah, I have it. Let's see. I got it written down on my sheet. Okay, 234-7353. Excuse me, that's 7535; my eyes aren't too good. So you're his son. My name's Jerry. Nice to meet you."

"Jerry," I said, "you have no idea how grateful I am."

I called the other number. "Hello, I'm looking for Robert Du Pre. I'm—"

"Yes sir," the man interrupted. "He told me you'd be calling. You're his son, right? Well, he's just sitting around with us drinking beer. He's only had four. We're not drunk. It's just a social gathering. I'll pass the phone to your father."

Dad came on the line. "Hello, Jonny!" That old familiar Carolina drawl, raspier than I'd ever heard it.

"It's me, Dad." I heard myself talking. I sounded younger than I wanted to sound. My throat was tightening.

"Dad, I'm in Tucson looking for you. What're you doing down there? Are you all right?"

"Not too bad," he said casually. "I just came to San Diego to get briefed on a couple of cases I've been working on and to do a little surfing. I might stay here through the summer. Summers are easier on the coast."

His flippant, nonchalant answer was maddening. I had been struggling to make this phone call for years, and now the man on the other end of the line was practically mocking me with outrageous babble about casework and surfing. As I listened to him, my emotions turned on a dime. No longer was I nervous. I was angry.

"Listen, Dad," I interrupted. "I'm catching a plane down to San Diego first thing tomorrow morning." We set a meeting point and a time. He started talking about how he was going to sue somebody on behalf of his friend Chuck who'd been falsely accused and imprisoned for a crime he didn't commit.

"Well, listen, Dad," I said, "I'm coming to see you tomorrow. I'll look forward to hearing all about it then. Right now I need to book a flight." I knew that there wasn't much use talking to him now. And I realized I still hated trying to make sense of him when he was drunk.

Sitting on the floor of that dark hotel room in Tucson, I realized I was fatigued. The first day of my odyssey had sapped my mental and emotional reserve. I exhaled hard and sank lower as a feeling of utter foolishness overwhelmed me. I could practically hear the voices of the doubters echoing in my head. Uncle Jimmy, as soon as he'd hung up the phone, must have been wondering if his brother's middle son hadn't turned out as crazy as Papa Mason's. My father, as soon as he'd hung up the phone, must have been sobered, already mustering his formidable faculties to resist my approach. He had surely noted that I hadn't called from my Hingham home to say I was thinking about him and the kids and wanted to talk to him. Rather, I'd called from a place uncomfortably close by, where I'd scoured the town in search of him. He saw me coming even before I'd left Boston.

Without the element of surprise on my side, I would have no advantage when I confronted someone as cunning and resourceful as he was. Even if he let me find him, what then? Worst of all was the thought that I was about to confirm my wife's doubts about this insane undertaking. How would I even begin to apologize for shaking up our precious little family by dragging them through my tormented past? And that five-year-old boy waiting at home—how could I face him once he realized his father was a fool?

✤✤✤

It was a dramatically different San Diego than I'd ever seen before. The picture of paradise—gleaming downtown towers cloistered on the waterfront, accented by thousands of sailboats, and backdropped by the clear blue Southern California sky—all faded from my view. My focus narrowed to the width of the rear-door window of the taxicab that carried me to the appointed spot. I inspected the dingy side streets and the swarms of panhandlers I passed along the way, trying to detect someone I might recognize in the crowd. I could feel myself being drawn into their otherworld. It was a cold and suffocating feeling, like being lowered into a hole.

Under ordinary circumstances, the sinking sensation might have caused me to stop and turn back. But this was an emergency. Of all the second thoughts that streaked through my brain, bailing out was not an option. My most pronounced fear was that I would let the deadline pressure unnerve me, that I might mishandle the interview, get impatient, and ruin everything. As a control on myself, I decided to face the confrontation the only way I knew how, as a journalist would approach a story. I'd stay detached and objective. I'd "cover" the meeting the way I'd been taught to cover an event. I wouldn't get caught up in it and lose my cool. *Yeah, okay . . . just cover it . . . just like any other story.*

I spotted the familiar red-and-yellow McDonald's sign and knew I was fast approaching the intersection where India Street crossed Broadway, two blocks ahead.

"Stop right here," I barked. The driver jerked and peered at me in the rear-view mirror and protested.

"You said Broadway and India."

"Pull over!" I was starting to panic, like the back of my seat was pushing me toward the dreaded spot. I had to go the rest of the way on foot. I had to see him before he saw me.

Automobile exhaust mixed with the salty flavor of San Diego's familiar breeze. My senses were enhanced. My eyesight was sharper. My thoughts moved faster, two steps ahead of me. I patted my back pocket to feel my slender reporter's notepad, and touched my shirt pocket to check for my pens, two of them, just in case one ran out of ink. Without glancing down, I grasped the Pentax hanging around my neck and wound the film, removed the lens cap, and set the aperture. I wanted to get a good look at him, in context, and maybe get a photograph of him.

Crossing to the far side of the street, I hurried along Broadway, trying to scan every face on the opposite sidewalk. When I was across from the McDonald's, I stopped. The arteries on the sides of my neck swelled, and my ears rang louder than the traffic noise. This was it. A thought sprang into my mind: *Wasn't it a little absurd to be sneaking up on him this way?* But this was how I'd planned it. I'd rehearsed this scene in my mind countless times. I forced myself to concentrate.

I examined the area in front of the restaurant. A man wearing a trenchcoat and a white baseball cap came into focus. Everything else in my field of vision blurred when I saw him. He looked so alone on that crowded street corner, a snag in the torrent of people flowing by. From behind drooping eyelids, he was peering at every cab that rolled past, looking for me.

He carefully held a white styrofoam cup in his right hand, his morning coffee. Tucked under his left arm was a plastic grocery bag. Under the open trenchcoat he wore a light blue dress shirt, buttoned to the collar, and a red-and-gold-striped necktie. His pants were baggy gray polyester. On his feet were a pair of mailman's shoes, soft black leather uppers with rubber soles, just the thing for a guy who spent all day on his feet. He had obviously dressed to look his best, for a special occasion.

That got me. My eyes filled with tears. "Dad!" I blurted out, unable to contain it. "Right here!" I crossed the street.

He turned and looked straight at me. He had to study me before he was sure who it was. "Jonny!" His voice was raspy and dry. Coffee splashed over the rim of the styrofoam cup as he fumbled to place it on the newspaper machine that had supported his elbow. He put out his arms, and I put out mine, and we squeezed each other, with Dad's plastic bag pressed between us. "There's my boy," he murmured.

"Here I am," I murmured back. The embrace lasted only a few seconds, but I knew I'd remember it the rest of my life, along with the four other times I'd hugged my father in the past 20 years.

"Well, we got the obligatory hug out of the way," he said with a nervous laugh, backing off and trying to regain his composure. And without hesitation, he started talking, as if he'd been interrupted in the middle of a conversation with the newspaper vending machine.

"I regret not seeing you standing at the line at Brigham." The reference was to my time as a long-jumper on the track-and-field team at Brigham Young University. Marq had undoubtedly told him about it. The reference surprised me. I had no idea he'd even known I attended school at BYU, let alone that I'd competed in a sport.

"It's not wrong for us to deify you and to look up to you," he went on, "because you achieved more than anybody in the family. I achieved more in the way of professional and educational accomplishments than anybody in the Du Pre family. Well, that doesn't necessarily mean that the others have to be jealous. That means that I was fortunate. And now, you're the fortunate one."

His monologue seemed premeditated. He'd been contemplating my arrival and the reasons behind my visit. Although I didn't realize it at the time, his indefatigable chatter, meaningless at first, came from a cleverly calculated purpose—to disarm me from the start. My host would not stay on one topic for more than a few minutes before he'd jump to another observation, almost as I would imagine a patient might freely associate random thoughts to a psychiatrist. This session, however, was being directed and controlled by the patient. I was in his world now, where very little made sense, where a kind of insanity made him feel safe, but turned everything crooked and weird for me.

"When was the last time we saw each other, Jon?" he asked, as he reached into his pants pocket and pulled out his wallet. "Four, five years ago in Utah? I'll bet you didn't think that by this time I'd have a bank account! That's right, Jonny, I got me a bank account!" He opened his wallet, pulled out an ATM card, and held it up for me to see. I didn't react with any audible response, causing him to think I was unimpressed. He put it away and quickly changed the subject again, holding up a plastic bag and opening it to display what the proud smile on his face indicated must be coveted contents.

"Jonny," he said, "take a look at what's in this bag." Two sweaters, one white, one light blue. He pulled out the white one and held it up for display with the cachet of a department store sales clerk. "Good-looking, huh?" he eagerly prodded.

"Sure, Dad," I answered with hesitation. It was a white cable-knit sweater—stained dull by an unknown liquid, maybe perspiration—with a V-neck collar and an "NBC Sports" logo stitched onto the left breast.

"Got it for two dollars at the Goodwill," Dad proudly announced. "How's that for a bargain, Jonny? Two dollars for an authentic NBC Sports sweater!" I raised my eyebrows and nodded with feigned approval. *Authentic?* Sure it was authentic, like the "authentic" Atlanta Falcons football helmet Dad had given me when I was nine. It must have been evident to him that I wasn't impressed by the sweater. I just stood there and nodded at it. Dad held it up for a minute or so, until he realized I wasn't inspecting the sorry-looking garment, then he quickly stuffed the gift into the plastic bag.

It was several days before I realized what had happened in that moment. Dad had gone to the Goodwill thrift shop that morning to buy his shirt and tie. He'd noticed the sweater with the NBC Sports logo and thought it would be the perfect gift for his son, the TV announcer. He'd bought it for two dollars and put it in the plastic bag to present to me on the occasion of our reunion. I'd just ignored it, and he'd been too embarrassed to insist I take his humble offering. I wondered whether my visit might have gone more smoothly if I'd accepted the gift.

What he wanted to do that morning, he said, was to take me on a little tour of his world and introduce me to his friends, the other men and women who lived on the streets of San Diego. We began walking east along Broadway, the busiest street in the city.

"I want to comment on this young fellow here," he said, pointing at a man in his late 20s who was standing about 30 feet away, holding a bowl in his outstretched hand, silently begging for change from people as they walked in and out of a store.

"Hello, partner," Dad said brightly. "Remember me?" The man looked blank. "Robert Du Pre. I'm the retired lawyer. We've talked before. You're Steven, right?" The man slowly nodded, reluctant to talk to us.

"Steven here is from New York City, Jon. He served in the Navy. The Navy brought him out to San Diego. And then they released him, and Steven has had some bad luck. So here he is, out here on the street, panhandling. From the high seas to the bottom of the gutter, isn't that right, Steven?" The man nodded again. He seemed not to take offense at his presenter's remarks, or at the way he was being studied like an exhibit in a zoo.

"Steven, this is my son," Dad continued. "Name's Jon. He's my second son, my middle boy. He's probably your age. He's an NBC television

announcer. He's come here from Boston, Massachusetts, to visit me." I offered
my hand. Steven reluctantly shook it. He was clearly uneasy about these two
people who'd approached him, but too intimidated to turn away or ask us to
leave him alone. I was embarrassed for the man, but, like Steven, I was caught
up in my father's spell.

"Steven, do you need a sweater?" Dad asked. "I've got a couple of good
ones here that I don't really need. What about a blue one?" The young man
shook his head no. He just wanted spare change. All I had in my wallet by this
time was a $20 bill. I'd kept it in my wallet when I'd tucked my luggage and
valuables into an airport locker. The money was for an emergency, although I
couldn't have imagined what sort of emergency might be resolved with 20 bucks.

"Steven, everybody treating you all right?" the advocate asked. Steven shook
his head yes.

"Okay," Dad said. "Well, you take care, Steven, and I'll see you around."

I couldn't tell whether my tour guide genuinely cared for this man or was
just performing for me. Whatever the case, one thing was clear—my father
was still uncannily adept at making himself known to strangers and making
himself at home in any situation. This was a skill that amazed me when I was
a child, one I emulated to some advantage when I became an adult. The ability to speak freely with people of varied backgrounds and opinions had been
extremely useful in my work as a news reporter and broadcaster. I watched
my father banter with people on the street that day, thinking how pathetically
useless his skills seemed now.

We made our way along Broadway. It was crowded with well-dressed people who blankly ignored the wretched underclass with whom they shared the
sidewalk. This street would be my home for the next little while, and the homeless wanderers who lived out their lives on it would be my neighbors.

We moved on. "You do that all the time?" I asked, trying to sound like a
reporter conducting an interview. "Talk to just anybody out here?"

"Oh, yeah," he said. "I talk to everybody. That's what I'm here for. When
I have something to give, then I give of myself. I always say, everybody knows
how to complain, but nobody knows *where* to complain. And so that's where
I come in. I'm the street lawyer. I give out information, guidance, advice. And
then, when my government check comes in, I usually give away about $50 of
it the first day. That's what I'm here for, Jonny. It's my mission."

As he walked, Dad squinted and peered as if expecting to meet someone,
or avoid someone, or fight someone. I remembered the squint from the rear-
view mirror of the old Mercedes diesel. I'd studied it many times when I was
a boy, sitting in the back seat as he drove my brothers and me to school. Watching
his eyes as they darted back and forth, I always wondered why he sweated so

much, even on winter mornings when it was so cold inside the car that we could see our breath. He still looked haunted, all these years later. But by what, or whom? Who could hurt him any worse than he'd hurt himself?

I met quite an array of characters along my tour. Bo was a very tall, very black man, agitated by the apparent fact that my father owed him money. Bradley was a long-haired, leather-vested, Bible-thumping street preacher who winked when he shook my hand, as if to assure me he knew exactly who I was and why I had come to his neighborhood and that he approved. On practically every corner, we encountered someone who knew my father and had heard his story, and who had told theirs to the street lawyer. I began to realize what these disenfranchised people wanted most, other than money to buy their next meal or their next bottle or their next fix or their next trick, or a white sweater with an NBC Sports logo. What they wanted was someone to listen. The simplest yet most comforting act of charity for homeless people, it seemed, was to pay attention to them. Not in the way I'd paid attention in the past—marching into the soup kitchens of Salt Lake City, Green Bay, or Boston and shining bright lights in their faces and shooting videotape footage for the newscasts, so our audience could see for themselves that poor people got free turkey dinners on Thanksgiving and Christmas. No wonder, then, the people at the long tables crouched over their trays and looked confused between gratitude and anger. They didn't want to seem ungrateful, yet they knew the news coverage was society's way of patting itself on the back and forgetting about them once the holiday season ended.

We reached Horton Plaza, and I immediately remembered my teenaged days and nights when I prowled the city with my buddies. In those days, Horton Plaza was a dormitory for vagrants who hadn't been able to get into a flophouse. It was here, when I was 16 years old, that I'd first seen the homeless. My buddies and I called them "the gray people." That's how they looked to us—tinted gray, as if they'd been lifted from some faded old black-and-white film and pasted on the lush, green plot. They lay there in their filth—harmless, helpless, practically motionless—offensive to shoppers who steered around them on their way into the mall.

"They used to let us lie on the grass here," my father said nostalgically, lamenting the loss of what, for him, had been a place of comfort. "Then, J.W. Robinson's department store said we couldn't lie here, that we were killing business. So the city sent in construction crews and ran us off."

A colorful bed of flowers now decorated the spot where the gray people once gathered. To me, it seemed like an improvement, but to my father, it was a forbidding reminder that he wasn't welcome here, or anywhere decent people passed. I stood for a moment looking at the flowers, imagining my dad lying under a palm tree on the grassy spot that Horton Plaza used to be, shuddering at the thought that my own father was one of the gray people. And today, at least as far as the shoppers were concerned, so was I.

"They went out of business," he said with rueful satisfaction, still talking about Robinson's department store. He then embarked on a tirade against selfish, cold-hearted companies, and moved into an account of his lifelong struggle against entrenched power. I didn't listen. I was thinking instead of a time when I too was homeless, a cast-off, shut out of a warm building and left to sit on a curbstone in the dark.

"One quick question, Dad, if you don't mind," I said, interrupting his monologue. "How come Marq and Daryl and I spent so much time on that curb outside the Anderson YMCA, waiting for a ride home?" He didn't even flinch. His answer was quick and glib.

"Well, hell, son, I don't know why your mother couldn't have driven in and picked you boys up."

It had taken me 25 years to work up the nerve to raise the issue with my father, only to discover he'd hardly given it a thought. He'd never connected our pain with his behavior. I suddenly felt foolish for having asked, and angered by the response. I felt a twinge, an urge to slap the man next to me. *Keep your cool, boy. Don't screw this up.*

This little drama we were playing, this first day in San Diego, was following my father's script, and he had all the lines. "We homeless people get moved off of the curbs all the time," he said, in a segue that any news anchor would have envied. Stunned, I decided not to press the question but just let him talk. I'd observe and listen for as long as I could.

The same apparent indifference would be Dad's reaction to all my questions that day. Still, I clung to my plan, however tenuously—to remain emotionally detached and use the same calculated approach I used on every story. Throughout the first day, I watched his every move and expression, looking for signs of what he might really have been thinking, trying to keep track of the contradictions. As he gave me his civil rights lecture for the zillionth time, I asked myself why, if he was so consumed with keeping his poor clients out of jail, even the ones who couldn't pay him, he had been seemingly so unconcerned with keeping his own children from going hungry?

We came across a knot of men who had huddled at the patio of the McDonald's on India Street to smoke a joint. One of them was a burly, disheveled fellow named Mike, an armed robber from New York who had violated parole and fled. He claimed he was looking for work. What he was looking for was cheap dope and a good fight.

"Hey, Lawyer Bob!" he shouted, causing everyone in the back section of the restaurant to look over at us. "Where the hell you been, man? I thought I was going to need a lawyer last night when I cracked down on a couple of niggers who jumped me."

Mike got up and came to our table. He stood over us, breathing heavily, rocking back and forth like an ape. He bled from the mouth, and his right hand, carelessly wrapped in a dirty ace bandage, was also bleeding. His left side appeared to be shriveled, by childhood polio, perhaps, or a birth defect.

Dad appeared to be glad to see him. "How you doin', Crazy Mike? This here's my son Jon. He's visiting me from Boston. He's a TV announcer for NBC."

Mike looked down at me with a wild expression on his face. "Hey, TV guy," he said in a loud, mocking voice, spitting as he spoke, "this your old man? Ha! So what you doin' here, some kinda exposé on the life of a bum? I'll tell you what it's like. It's kill or be killed. If you can't kick some ass, then you'll get yours kicked, know what I mean? That's how I got this busted hand."

Mike proudly held up his right hand for inspection. It was swollen and twisted. He couldn't clench his fist. The crooked knuckles appeared to have been broken. "You should see one of those black motherfuckers," he said with a proud smile. "I took him out before his partner got over on me. I'll finish it next time."

Mike invited Dad to take a hit on the joint. In a flash, Dad was on his feet and in the middle of the group, eagerly watching the joint as it went from person to person, making its way around the circle toward him. Each man ceremoniously received the joint, took one drag, and passed it on. Mike took two hits when it came to him.

Shepherd, a dog belonging to Rusty, the oldest member of the group, pawed Mike's leg. Mike kicked the dog under the snout, and Shepherd yelped and streaked away. Rusty yelled at Mike, "Hey, man, don't kick my dog. He ain't hurtin' nobody!"

Mike handed the joint to the next guy in the circle and turned on Rusty. He grabbed the old man around the neck with his good arm and pulled Rusty's head down to his side, forcing the old man over backwards. "I'll kick your fuckin' dog if I want to, you old piece of shit. And I'll kick yer ass too right now if I feel like it, you got that?"

Rusty offered no resistance; he just went limp. Mike looked up at the others to make sure they were watching, then jabbed two fingers of his free hand into Rusty's eyes. The old guy whimpered in pain. He needed help. My stare shot to my father ten feet from the tussle. I expected him to intervene, to yell at Mike or at least distract him from Rusty somehow. Instead, Dad quickly turned away, pretending not to notice what was happening right in front of him. I was incensed. I rose to my feet, not very eager to get involved, but worried about the old man.

"Mike!" I shouted, louder than I'd intended. The volume startled even me. The voice that had terrified my poor wife in so many one-sided arguments, and even my children on rare occasions, brought everyone to attention.

The bully hobo looked up at me. I shook my head, just once, waggled my finger, and made a "tsk-tsk" sound. Mike's menacing grin faded and his grip loosened. Without taking his eyes off me, he helped his victim straighten himself. The fracas was over, no thanks to "Lawyer Bob," champion of the downtrodden.

"I know how you feel, Rusty," I muttered to myself. "Where's the lawyer when you need help?"

The incident was brief and would have been meaningless, except that it made me see something I hadn't seen. I'd had command of a situation in which my father appeared hapless. That made me think I might have more control of our conversation than I had realized.

My somewhat deflated host and I left the McDonald's patio and walked along Broadway toward the Senior Center at the corner of Seventh. Dad was quiet for the first time that day, chagrined, no doubt, that I'd seen him cower. I was hoping he'd attempt a witty explanation for having turned away, so I could confront him with it. He didn't mention it.

I waited on the corner as Dad entered the Senior Center, only to emerge seconds later with disappointment on his face. "What's wrong?" I asked.

"I missed the lunch tickets," he said, sighing. "They only have about a hundred tickets. They hand them all out in ten minutes."

"So you don't get lunch?"

"Not today. Not here."

"So, what are you going to do for lunch?"

"Nothing," he said. "I don't mind. They're serving fish sticks and fries today, anyway. I don't like their fish sticks and fries." My father's nonchalance was transparent. I knew he was hungry. He'd been living on short rations for a week. What really bothered me was that he'd missed lunch because he'd been smoking a joint with his buddies, and maybe because he was distracted by my presence. Still, he didn't ask if I had money, and I didn't offer.

Whatever its merits, my plan was to follow his every step and do whatever he did. I realized that might mean skipping a few meals, but I didn't care. I'd told myself that I wanted to try to understand my father's life. That premise, I later realized, was incredibly naive. How could I have understood how my father felt when he missed a meal? My hunger was a mild discomfort. His was an emptiness in the pit of the belly. And no doubt, the anxiety of not knowing where his next bit of food would come from surely sharpened the pain. He said nothing about it, just changed the subject and kept shuffling along.

"I think I might have been better off in jail in Tucson than on the street in San Diego," he said.

"What do you mean?" I asked. "If you weren't here, you'd be in jail in Tucson?"

"Probably," he said casually, as if going to jail was no big deal for him.

"What for?"

"Disturbing the peace, public drunkenness . . . ticky-tack bullshit. Some of the people who run the shelters there think they have to tattle on you whenever you have any fun or attempt to live like a normal person." It was as if he were talking about Mr. Sosa at the Salvation Army, as if he knew I'd been there because he'd been watching me all along. This time, though, the thought didn't unnerve me the way it had for the past two days. Instead of thinking that my father had some sort of omniscient power over me, I just took his rambling talk with a grain of salt.

"So, I got out of town and hitched a ride here," he continued. "I'd just finished a case that I'd ghostwritten for some people, so I took the money and took off. Usually I can just step out onto the freeway and catch a lift. But this time I didn't get a ride. I walked 30 miles in two days before I got a ride. I get these wild hairs to go somewhere, and I just start walking." He laughed.

Again he changed the subject. "That's one of my homes when I'm in San Diego." He pointed across the street to a dilapidated six-story brick building. The red neon sign over the front entrance blinked "Pickwick Hotel." At one corner of the ground floor was a yellow sign that read "Bail Bonds/Checks Cashed." Eight or ten men were gathered near the entrance, some leaning against the brick wall, panhandling the people who tried to avoid them as they passed.

The Pickwick Hotel. I just stood there for a minute, looking across at it. This was the closest thing to a home my father could claim, a flophouse on Broadway.

"Okay, $25.95, plus room tax, makes it $31 a day to stay there. I'll sleep on somebody's floor before I'll pay that kind of money for a room." My father didn't seem to mind telling me that he slept on the floor of a dirty flophouse. He said it matter-of-factly. It was a condition of life for him and had been for many years. He'd gotten completely accustomed to the idea.

"There's the old county hall of justice," he went on, guiding me along my tour. I looked across Broadway to the north, half a block up Front Street, to see the county jail, a four-story structure faced with sheet metal. Years earlier, my mother, Daryl, and I had gone there one Monday morning to pick up my older brother, who'd served a week in jail for shoplifting.

"So, Jonny," Dad said with a smile, "you want to find out about your old dad?"

"Yeah," I said. "That's why I'm here."

He motioned for me to follow him, and he set out along Front Street. For the first time all day, he seemed to move with purpose. For the first time since I'd set out on my journey two days ago, I thought I might be getting somewhere.

"When I hit San Diego in 1973," he said, "I'd never been here before in my life. Marquise and I were eating dinner at Fisherman's Wharf. I was complaining that I couldn't talk to these lawyers in this town. 'How am I going to get a job with them,' I said, 'if I can't talk to them? The silly assholes walk too fast and talk too fast.' And the guy sitting at the table next to ours leaned over and said, 'Am I included?' I said, 'Included in what, sir?' And he said, 'I'm an attorney here in San Diego. I was just wondering if you thought I too was one of the silly assholes.' His name was Condra, Crandall Condra."

I remembered having heard that name many times when we lived in Encinitas.

"We talked for a while," Dad went on, "and Condra referred me to a big law firm. They were in that building right there with the flag on it." He pointed to a gold-roofed office tower, the Federal Savings Bank building. "The partners thought I was overqualified for the position they were trying to fill. Said I'd quit in a week. I wanted to say, 'Come on, men, I'm on my ass. I have three children and no money. I can't even borrow money on a car. I need work!' They didn't know how desperate I was. I didn't tell them I'd had to close up shop in South Carolina and get out fast. But for some reason, the senior partner had me hired. And I was grateful for the menial labor."

I had never realized how desperate my father was when we first landed in San Diego. "What did you do for this firm?" I asked.

"Hell, all I did was grunt work for leech lawyers."

"Leech lawyers?"

"Personal injury lawyers. I'd go photograph victims, take statements, and make measurements. You know. It was grunt work. A monkey with a Polaroid could have done it."

A monkey with a Polaroid . . . or a TV news reporter. I couldn't help but think that Dad's description of his so-called demeaning grunt work sounded a lot like the kind of thing I did every day in my profession—take pictures, write down notes, tell people what happened.

"I got my training in the FBI and the U.S. Justice Department," he went on. "That firm was getting a real bargain. It paid me $8,000 a year."

"Eight thousand?" I asked, astounded.

"Eight thousand a year. And I was glad to get it. I'd made my own bed. I'd taken a loss on the lake house. I'd had more property I could have sold, but everything got foreclosed. Eight thousand dollars a year was enough to feed you boys."

This was a stirring realization for me—that my father had been willing to take a job he thought was beneath him, a job that paid so little, just so he could feed his children and pay the rent on our dank little two-bedroom apartment. I remembered hearing him grumble about the downturn of his fortunes. I remembered hearing my mother complain about our family's sorry predicament. I remembered thinking that my dad, the invincible attorney, seemed terribly down on his luck at the time. I had never, until now, realized that that frustrating year, my 14th year, marked what might have been the most noble, honorable, and courageous act of fatherhood Robert Du Pre had ever performed. It was in that year, I realized, that my father had done what countless American working men do routinely, what my father-in-law had done for most of his adult life—go to work to support their children. It was in that moment that I acknowledged that the hero of my childhood was at his best as a father when we all thought he was at his worst.

If only I'd realized it then . . . maybe I could have told him how grateful I was to have a father who was willing to go to a job he hated just to feed me . . . maybe he wouldn't have left. But that was ancient history. This was now. I was learning something about my father, the man. I was beginning to think that there might be hope of salvaging success out of this folly after all.

Three blocks past the jail, Dad and I came to the law library. He strode in, and I saw him change as he went through the door. The man who was a bum on the street somehow transformed into a lawyer again as he entered the building. His face lost its pinched leer; he looked confident. "Let's see," he began, eager to show me everything at once. "You want to see the first thing I ever wrote that's published?"

"Of course," I replied.

He led me through a door opening into a hallway that brought us to the elevators. He pushed three. As we got off the elevator, he stepped without hesitation into a labyrinth of bookshelves. Lawyers and their clerks stood around scratching their heads, checking their notes for the references they sought, peering at the guide numbers posted at the head of each row. Dad walked calmly through them to the fourth aisle from the end, stopped, and looked up at the row of maroon, leather-bound books just above his eye level.

He brushed his hand across the row of book bindings, then pulled a book from the shelf. He nudged it open with his right forefinger and let it spread. He licked the tip of the finger and tickled his way forward through the pages until he came to the entry he was looking for. Without saying a word, he handed me Volume Six, Number One, of the *South Carolina Law Quarterly,* published in September 1953. There it was, at the top of page 80: "Remedies for a Creditor for Setting Aside a Fraudulent Conveyance, with Recommendations for Changes." The byline was "Robert Owen Du Pre."

The author stood by as I pored over the article, even reading the footnotes. I found nothing I understood in those six pages, but was fascinated by all of it.

"They thought I was promising," he said. He no longer seemed to be bragging. "So they asked me to write an article."

"Who asked you to write this article?"

"The board of editors of the *South Carolina Law Review,*" he answered. "They wanted to see if I could write. When they reviewed my article, they decided I could. I was 24 years old at the time. This is still referenced as law in South Carolina, by the way."

I just stood and looked at it, as if it was some precious artifact from a museum. I was awed to hold in my hand a piece of something my father had done when he was a young man, younger than I.

"How about the first criminal case I ever prosecuted?" he said. "You want to see that?"

"Sure," I said quickly, starved for more confirmation about my father's lost status. Dad wove his way back to the elevator and led me to the fourth floor. He navigated this level of the library just as easily as he had the third floor. Walking ten feet behind him, I noticed some of the well-dressed library patrons looking at my father as he passed, wondering what a man in a dirty trenchcoat and a baseball cap might be doing there. "Here you are, Jonny," he said with satisfaction when he found the book. "United States versus Othello Campbell. It was a major bootlegging case. I was a cocky young federal prosecutor. My boss threw this one at me to see how I would handle the big ones."

"And?"

"And I got convictions on all counts. Read it for yourself, my boy."

I buried my nose in that book, scanning the three-page citation as though I was cramming for an exam, reading aloud the parts that quoted the young assistant prosecutor, Du Pre. His arguments looked brilliant to my willing eyes, his prose poetic. There I was, as impressionable and adoring as the little boy who used to follow him everywhere he would let me. "I've got to get a copy of this," I said excitedly. "Where's the Xerox?"

"Take your time," he said. "There's plenty more where that came from. Want to see the first case I ever took to Federal Appeals Court?"

"Show me the way."

Again and again, we hunted down volumes, up and down elevators, from floor to floor, through the maze of shelves. My father was thoroughly enjoying himself. It was obvious that he cherished the chance to show me who he'd been and what he'd done.

About an hour into the exercise, he said, "Do you want to see the transcript of my disbarment?" I was taken by surprise. Not only did I not know that such a record existed, I'd never have thought my father would want to show it to me. As far as I knew, it was the single worst event, barring nothing—not even his divorce or the deaths of his parents—of my father's entire life. It was the end of him as far as any of us who knew him were concerned. After that horrendous defeat, he'd remained among us only a few months, then disappeared. Now here I was, standing with him two decades later, about to see it for myself.

"Why would they record your disbarment in a law book, forever?" I asked, troubled that my father's humiliation had been posted for the world to see.

My father stopped walking when I asked the question. He turned and looked me right in the eye, something he'd hardly done all day. "To make sure my life doesn't amount to shit for as long as I live," he said. "It's a warning . . . that Bob Du Pre is no good. Anybody who wants to look up my name can come over here and find out how I screwed up . . . and why I will never be a lawyer again."

I was impressed by his rare candor, and the finality of his decree. I had never heard him concede anything about his disbarment. He'd always spoken of it as the result of a craven conspiracy: The good ol' boys who hated him for turning their corrupt system of justice on its head got even with him by trumping up charges against him with the bar association.

"I had a bad habit of not taking care of my banking," he said. "That got me into a lot of trouble. You read this report, and you'll see that my disbarment was mostly about bad banking. Ninety percent of it was that."

Dad led me back down to the third floor and into the far northeast corner of the vast room. He walked a little slower than he had when he was leading me to the books that recounted his accomplishments. Back we went, to the corner of the floor. He examined the shelves. *"South Carolina Reporter,"* he said, weariness and dejection in his voice. "This is it." He tugged the book from the shelf and opened to the index. "Page 92," he read. He thumbed through the pages. An entry caught his eye. "Here's a guy who pleaded *nolo contendere* to embezzlement, criminal conspiracy, obstruction of justice, bribing witnesses . . . he got the same punishment I got." He shook his head and flipped more pages.

"Here's mine. 'Matter of Robert Owen Du Pre.'" He handed the book to me. "Read it aloud."

I looked at the pages. There was the title, near the bottom of the left page. As I read, continuing at the top of the right-hand page, I saw that the citation was about someone else's case. "This isn't about you," I said, confused.

Dad took the book and looked at it. "Mitchell," he said. "Who the hell . . .?" He fell silent for a moment, then gasped and said, "Oh my God." Then I saw what he had seen. The pages containing the record of my father's disbarment had been torn from the book.

"Who would have torn these pages out?" I asked.

"I have no earthly idea," he said, looking truly baffled, as surprised as I was to find the pages missing.

"You think you just got drunk one day," I gently suggested, "and that maybe you were thinking about your disbarment, and you got mad and came in here and tore out the pages?"

Dad stood motionless, rubbing his chin and staring past me, trying to remember. "I bet that's what happened," he finally said. His eyebrows lifted as if he'd just solved a mystery. Then he snapped his fingers. "That's all right," he said, perking up. "I know where to find the record in the *Federal Reporter.* Come on."

We returned to the fourth floor. Dad hurried along the side aisle, then took us between two shelves stacked to the ceiling. He stopped at the section that housed the *Southeastern Reporter,* scanned the numbers on the bindings, and pulled Volume 241 of the second series. He consulted the index and anxiously flipped to page 896.

"I'll be damned," he said, half-confused and half-angry. I took the book. It, too, had been defaced. The pages containing the report on the disbarment of Robert Owen Du Pre had been ripped from the binding.

"Same thing, maybe?" I asked.

"I'm sure it was," he said. It was easy to imagine—my father stomping into the library and yanking the books and tearing out the pages as if trying to expunge the disbarment itself.

"Well," I said softly, "I can always look it up in another law library when I get home. For now, at least, why don't you just tell me what you remember of that day."

"I can't remember a meeting I didn't attend," he said.

"What?"

"I said I wasn't there."

"Where were you?"

"In a bar about two blocks down the street."

The discoveries of the missing pages deflated Dad's enthusiasm for prowling through the law library. "Let's get out of here," he said and headed for the elevator. I stopped at the service desk, made copies of all the citations we'd found, and followed him out the door, back onto the streets of San Diego.

Months later, I talked to Charlie Porter, an assistant DA in Greenville and "the best friend I have in the world," according to Dad. "All Bob would have had to do," he said, "was to go in and write a check for $2,000, and the matter would have been resolved." The $2,000 was reimbursement to two clients who had complained about his failure to provide legal services.

One more tragic contradiction, maybe the final one: My father hadn't even defended that which was most precious to him—his ability to be a lawyer.

"Before too long, we're gonna have to start thinking about where we're going to sleep tonight," Dad said as we walked back to the corner of Front and Broadway. "You got any ideas?"

I knew that he wanted me to say that I would put us up in the Holiday Inn or someplace like that. I didn't want to disappoint him. I didn't want him to fly into a rage and accuse me of holding out on him. I knew that part of the reason he was happy to see me was that he thought I might prop him up and keep him from falling out onto the street. And of course I would, but not tonight. I was hungry, and I thought about how great it would be to have a nice meal and relax in a hot bath, but I took a chance and told Dad what I'd planned to do.

"I have a proposition," I said. "Tell me if you don't like it." He nodded. "I want to go where you'd go and do what you'd do if I wasn't here. I mean, wherever it is you usually sleep, I want to follow along. Will that work?"

He didn't seem to mind at all, or if he did, he didn't show it. "Well," he said, "in the winter months, I just usually hustle for space."

He took me back to the Pickwick Hotel. The lobby smelled of ammonia, and there were stains on the worn carpet. "Every time I get in good with one of the desk managers here, they bring in another one. This guy, I don't know so well. We'll just have to see if he plays by the rules." He went up to the desk. "Room 310, please, sir."

The man handed him the house phone. Dad put it to his ear.

"Hey there, Jerry," he said after the click. "Bob here. I'm in the lobby. I got my boy with me. I want you to meet him, and I need to drop my bag in the corner. How 'bout we come on up, buddy?"

Dad handed the phone back to the desk manager and started to walk toward the elevator.

"I'll need to see one form of picture ID before you go up, please, sirs," the man said.

Dad bristled. I recognized that look in his eye. He had always detested being required to conform to any rule, and he still hated it. That was another apparent contradiction. My father made his living, for many years, as a prosecutor, enforcing laws, yet he hated abiding by them. "I got all the ID in the world, sir. The boy's ID is with NBC, and I'm a lawyer with . . . are you gonna hold us up here, just because you want to see some goddamn ID? All I need to do is drop this bag in my friend's room." His feigned patience was strained to its breaking point.

"I have a driver's license," I interrupted, before Dad managed to piss off the desk man and get us kicked out of the hotel. I quickly pulled my license and a business card from my wallet and, with a smile, handed them to the desk clerk.

"Please sign the register," he said.

"Gladly," I replied.

Dad squirmed as I signed. The security guard watched us closely as we walked to the elevator.

"I'm not gonna sign their fucking book," he whispered to me. "What the smart-assed new guy doesn't know is I'm a blacklisted refugee. They threw me out of here a few years ago. Told me never to come back. But it's not like a shithole like this can keep a manager. The bosses have changed about five times. The new ones don't know all they have to do is look up my name on the blacklist and I'm outta here. I can bullshit my way in whenever I want. And when I get in a pinch, the night security guard covers for me. I've done some legal work for him."

I was getting a full picture of my father's life. From sunrise to sunset, it was one long con game for survival. First thing in the morning, he had to wheedle money from other homeless people to get a cup of coffee. Around midday, he had to play the lunch lottery at the senior center, hoping he got there before the tickets ran out. He had to sweet-talk his way past a security guard to be able to sleep indoors at night. I wondered how he managed to hold up under the stress of knowing that his luck could run out at any time and he'd be destitute.

I couldn't imagine why Dad, or anyone, would choose to live this way. I knew perfectly well that my father could come in from the street anytime he wished and be a part of society again. I wondered what it was about my world that was so repulsive to him.

"Dad," I said as the battered elevator clanked slowly toward the third floor, "that brings up a question I've had for a long time. Why do rules bother you so much?"

"The rule in this place," he said, "is that you give them your identification and they hold it while you're in this building. I don't give anyone my identification."

"Why wouldn't you want to show ID if it would help you get into a shelter?"

"Because they might lose it," he shot back. "And then what do I do if I can't get another one? Hell, man, it's not like I have a spotless record and I can just walk right into the VA and get another ID."

The elevator reached the third floor, and Dad pushed the door open. "Is that who gives you your ID?" I asked.

He pulled his wallet from his back pocket and produced his Veterans Administration identification card. "The beauty of this little card," he said, whispering as if government agents were hiding in the hallway listening, "is that it ain't got no address on it. So when the cops try to make me tell them where I live, I just say, 'Fuck you, pig. I live nowhere. I'm an American who lives in America.'"

This was the kind of talk that made me want to slap him. I'd listened to it for years. It had always brought trouble for him and all the rest of us. He'd been tireless at erasing his identity and making himself untraceable. I didn't know what he'd done or who he thought might be after him, but I'd always wanted to ask. Didn't he realize that when he ran from society, he'd left his children behind? Didn't he understand that if the police or the IRS or the VA couldn't catch up with him, it would be as hard as hell for his sons to find him? Didn't he care?

The hall was wide, with a high ceiling. It was dark, lit only by a single bare bulb at its far end, but I could see the cracks in the wall and the mold along the baseboards. There was a strong smell of old urine, kind of like ammonia mixed with a little stale beer. The scent burned inside my nostrils. We reached room 310. Dad knocked on the door, careful not to tap it too hard or too many times.

"This is Jerry's room," he told me under his breath. "He's a laid-off steelworker from Michigan. He's been staying here, off and on, for a few years. I usually crash on his floor when I don't have a place, late in the month, when I'm waiting for my check to come in. Jerry is the frugal type; he won't waste a dime, so he usually has a room."

The door slowly opened just a few inches. "That you, Bob?"

"It's me, Jer," Dad said. "How ya doin', partner?" The door swung open. "I've got my son with me today, Jer. Name's Jon. Look at him. Is he as big and handsome a kid as you've ever seen, or what?"

"Pleased to meet you, Jerry," I said pleasantly, helping Dad butter him up so he'd let us sleep on his floor. I entered the room and was greeted by the occupant's outstretched hand, undoubtedly the largest I had ever seen. Altogether, Jerry was an enormous man, about 6'5" and 250 pounds—and homely, with big ears and a swollen nose. Each of his eyes seemed to wander off in a different direction, making him seem confused. The corners of his mouth turned up, giving him the eerie appearance of smiling all the time. His thumb touched his middle finger as he squeezed my hand in his powerful grip and greeted me with his meek and friendly grin.

The room was painted a shade of mustard, and the carpet, once orange, had been darkened by decades of filth; at its edges, it curled away from the walls. There was a rickety, pressboard dresser with a shadeless brass lamp. Through an open door, I could see into the bathroom; the mirror above the sink had been broken diagonally, and half was missing. There was no cover on the toilet tank. Yet, when I looked closer, I saw that despite the apparent squalor, the room wasn't dirty; it was clear that Jerry had cleaned it as well as a person could clean a room that was so badly in need of renovation.

Dad walked over to the corner and put his plastic bag onto a small pile of other bundles. "That stuff all yours?" I asked casually.

"That's my stuff," Dad said, seemingly unaware that I might be distressed to see that everything he owned in the entire world could be piled in a corner. He bent down and unwrapped a camouflage-printed Army-issue sleeping bag to reveal a small, blue duffel bag in which all his clothes and toiletries were packed. Inside the bag there was a yellow blanket, a white T-shirt, a gray sweatshirt, and a pair of blue swimming trunks with thin, white stripes down the sides. He started changing clothes. "I need to get out of my business attire," he said lightly. I stood and watched. When he took off his trousers, I saw that his legs were still muscled and athletic, the legs of a halfback, the Speedster from the South.

"Is that your bed?" I asked, pointing to the sleeping bag.

"That's my bed," he said, "when Jerry is kind enough to let me crash on his floor."

"You betcha," chimed Jerry.

Dad put on his shorts and sweatshirt. We sat and visited with Jerry. He was pleased to have company, and he did most of the talking. Like my father, he was preoccupied with the idea that the world had dealt him a terrible hand of cards. His lament centered on the shutdown of the steel mill in Flint, Michigan, where he'd worked for 20 years before being laid off. "Them goddamn Brazilians and them goddamn Japanese make that cheap steel and undercut our prices. Pardon my language, gentlemen. But anyway, U.S. steel companies just can't compete with that goddamn cheap steel."

Dad mostly sat and nodded in agreement, doing his best to ingratiate himself with Jerry. The big, slow man kept talking, all the while getting himself more and more worked up.

"As soon as I save up enough money, I'm gonna get on a bus and head to northern California," Jerry said. "That's where I need to be. There's not so many of them goddamn Mexicans up there to bother me. Please pardon my language. I just need to get away from them. These goddamn Mexicans have ruined San Diego. This used to be a good place for people like me and Bob. Right, Bob? Pardon my language, but these goddamn Mexicans have just taken the place over. You can't find work here, because the illegals will work for cheaper. You can't find good weed here, because they hoard all of it. And they bring their diseases from south of the border and poison all the good pussy out there, so you can't even get laid around here anymore! Pardon my foul mouth, gentlemen."

Jerry was getting agitated. I watched him closely, measuring the distance between me and the door, just in case he reached into his dresser drawer and pulled out a knife or a gun. He seemed like a perfectly kind and gentle racist bigot, but I reminded myself that I didn't know him and that I'd promised Gina to come home in one piece.

"I tell you, Bob, today I was just out there walking around, and I saw so many of them, I just decided to come back to my room and sit down, before I grabbed one of them by the neck and killed him. You know I'd do it, don't you, Bob?"

"He'd do it," Dad said to me, vouching for Jerry. "And why not? See, Jon, the truth is, the fucking Mexicans have abused the hell out of their privilege here, and they've worn out their welcome in this country."

My father, the ex-civil rights advocate, was trying to curry favor with Jerry, softening him up before asking him to let us sleep on his floor. What he was accomplishing, though, was to inflame Jerry, who had been sitting by himself for hours in this tiny room, fuming about a brush with a Mexican man on the street that morning.

"Not just that!" Jerry exclaimed, waving his arms. "We just got through giving them, what, $48 billion! Which everybody knows they ain't never gonna pay back."

"They're the world's biggest leeches," Dad said.

"You're goddamn right, Bob!" Jerry shouted. "Now these fucking Mexicans are taking all our money!"

"We're living like dogs," my father went on, "and the fucking Mexicans are taking over our border towns."

Jerry stood. "I'd kill one if I had one here right now!" he yelled, pounding his huge fist into the palm of his other hand. "I want to take my money back, *out of their little asses!*"

Jerry's outburst frightened me and startled my father. He realized he'd incited the hulking man and that we might be better off looking for lodging somewhere else. Dad surveyed the room, looking for what he might need to take as he made his way out. I was rising to my feet, trying to signal Dad that I wanted to go. Just then, there was a knock at the door. Jerry and my father looked at each other as if to ask who might be calling on them. Jerry opened the door an inch. "Is Bob inside?" a woman's voice inquired.

"Just a minute," Jerry said as he shut the door.

"It's that goddamn skinny nigger woman from down the hall," Jerry said. "Do you want to talk to her?"

"Sure, I'll see her," my father responded as he hastened up out of his chair.

A thin black woman greeted Dad when he opened the door and peered into the darkened hallway. "Hello, Bob," she said as she put her arms around his neck and let her hands hang limp. She groaned faintly as she pressed her torso against his belly, a lusty reminder of the last time they'd been together.

"Hey, baby," he said, pulling away, hesitant about returning her embrace. He didn't want me to see, nor Jerry, I was sure.

"This is my son Jon," he said. "He came here to visit me from Boston." The woman stepped back and briefly examined me, then looked away. "Jon, this is . . ." He stopped. "Uh, this is one of my friends here. She lives in 327." He was embarrassed that he couldn't remember the woman's name.

"Amy," she said, scolding him with her look.

"How do you do, Amy?" I smiled and extended my hand. "It's a pleasure to meet you."

A beautiful, hungry little boy clung to Amy's leg as she stood in the dark hallway. He peered up at my father and me with big, innocent eyes. His young black skin shone in the light coming from Jim's door. His eyes reminded me of those two sets of eyes that floated in the dark on the other side of Miss Tilly's living room years earlier.

"And what's your name?" I asked him in a playful voice, dropping to one knee. He hid his face behind his mother's leg. I stroked the boy's pointed, nearly bald head and said, "My name is Jon. Pleased to meet you, little man." I picked him up and propped him on my hip. "You're a big boy," I said, trying to coax a smile out of him. I felt compassion for this lost little boy, and I missed my own children. He decided he'd seen enough of me, and, reaching for Amy, whimpered, "Mama." I handed him back to his mother. She took him and put him on the floor, and he clutched her leg again.

Amy leaned into my father and whispered something in his ear. He turned and looked at me. It was apparent that the two of them wanted some privacy. "Excuse us for just a second, could you Jon?" Dad said, as he stepped three or four paces down the hall with Amy.

This was familiar. Good ol' Dad had tried to get rid of me many times before, when I was a kid, so he could talk dirty to some woman. The memory was like a recognizable old smell. The stench of it was that no decent woman would be attracted to some fat old man saying dirty things. Even when I was a boy, I knew Pop was paying for his sex. And I knew he was paying for it now, on credit. It made me feel dirty, and I just wanted it done with. The last thing I wanted to do now was reminisce about those shameful visits to Miss Tilly's house.

My father disappeared with Amy, leaving me alone with the volatile Jerry. I seemed to remember newspaper accounts of gentle giants like Jerry suddenly snapping, when provoked, and suspected that with his big, leathery, steelworker hands, he could snap my neck. For a while, Jerry and I tried to chat. I could see his disappointment when he realized I didn't bring my father's zeal to discussions of Jerry's favorite topics. The conversation dwindled, and then we just sat looking at each other.

I was relieved to hear a knock on the door 20 minutes later. Our roommate was full of explanations. "She just showed up here at the hotel about a month ago," he began, without my asking. "Her boyfriend threw her out. Now she's waiting for her first SSI check, and she's scared it's not going to come."

"Why did she come to you?"

"Well, you know, they all come to me when they're in trouble. I ain't got nothing now, but she knows I'll find a way to get her through this jam. Isn't that right, Jerry? That's what Lawyer Bob does. He helps the needy."

"That's right, Lawyer Bob, especially if it's a needy nigger woman!" Jerry guffawed and looked at me. "Your dad has a taste for dark meat." He laughed again and Dad laughed, too, nervously.

I gave my father a significant look, and he picked it up. "Listen, Jerry," he said, "Jon and I had planned on going up and checking in on ol' Chuck. Can I use your phone and give him a buzz?"

"Go right ahead, Bob," Jerry said. "You know you're always welcome to use my phone anytime you want."

Dad went in and dialed Chuck's number. "Hey, Chuck! It's Bob. I've got my boy here, and I told him he needs to meet you. How 'bout we come on up and pay you a visit tonight?" He was trying to sound as pleasant as possible, the way he'd talked when he called me back in Utah.

We said good-bye to Jerry, picked up my driver's license at the front desk, and left the hotel, Dad still in his blue shorts. Once on the sidewalk, we headed for Chuck's apartment on the north end of San Diego's downtown, about 20 blocks away. My hunch was that Chuck's apartment was a better place to bed down than Jerry's room, and that my father was going to try to talk us into an overnight stay. We climbed the hill up Seventh Street to the Maribelle Apartments. We climbed the narrow stairway to the second floor and knocked.

"Come in, unless you're the fuzz!" Chuck shouted from inside.

Chuck sat on a recliner, barely visible through the smoke of his marijuana. Dad greeted him. "How ya doin', Chuck ol' boy! Jon, this is the smartest man you'll ever meet," Dad said to me, careful to make sure Chuck heard him. He was laying on the bullshit with a housepainter's brush.

"I've heard a lot about you, Jon," Chuck said. "And don't believe that shit your old man says. Your old man is the smartest son-of-a-bitch on the face of this earth, and don't you forget it."

Chuck was high, and he would get a lot higher before our visit ended, telling me his life's story in the process. Our host was a convicted kidnapper, out on parole. He had a story six miles long about how the system had framed him, falsely imprisoned him, corrupted his appeal process, and ruined his life. As Dad and Chuck told it, Lawyer Bob had been working on his case for about three years, whenever he popped into town. Chuck, by all appearances, was content to sit in his tattered old La-Z-Boy recliner drinking beer and smoking pot and living off what little his wife, a Salvadoran immigrant, brought home from her two jobs.

Chuck was an affable host. He poured a glass of iced tea and offered it to me. I thanked him, and hoping not to be noticed, placed the glass on the floor and let the ants in it drown. Dad went into the kitchen. It was busy with roaches, especially around a piece of chicken on a paper plate on the table. The chicken looked as if it had been left out several days, but that didn't bother the hungry visitor. He picked it up and daintily ate every scrap of flesh from the dried bone. The sight nauseated me, and made me feel greedy for keeping my $20 bill in my wallet. My guilty conscience abated, though, when I saw how much beer my father and Chuck would drink that night, and how much pot they would smoke. The inane and relentless chatter was maddening.

Just before midnight, Chuck's wife came through the front door. Her entrance put an immediate stop to the festivities. They'd been drinking her beer and smoking her weed, and they'd known they were going to catch hell when she found out. The woman was exhausted, and the sight of the two drunks in her living room enraged her. She greeted me politely, then tore into them in

Spanish. My fluency in Italian allowed me to understand a few phrases. I picked up on ". . . lazy, good-for-nothing bastards."

"Let's go," I said. And we exited quietly. We'd wasted four hours at the ex-con's pot party. My head ached from breathing in all that smoke, and my stomach felt as though it was looking for a smaller internal organ to eat. Worst of all, it was almost midnight, and we didn't have a place to sleep. Neither of us said anything as we walked back down the Seventh Street hill, until we passed a cluster of street people wrapped in blankets and cardboard, sleeping on the steel grids over the sidewalk exhaust vents outside the San Diego Gas and Electric building. I slowed and stared, but Dad hardly looked at them. The scene was a little too familiar and seemed to make him uncomfortable.

"Are we going to sleep on the street tonight, Dad?" I asked.

"Oh, no," he responded. "I can get us in the Pickwick." I could tell he was worried he might not be able to pull it off.

If he was angry with me for not whipping out my American Express gold card and checking us into a room somewhere, he still didn't show it. I was grateful for that. I didn't want trouble with my father. I was still hoping, at the end of that first day, that he would open up to me and give me the answers that were 20 years overdue.

"Act like you have a room here," he said as we entered the Pickwick lobby. I didn't know what that meant. I just followed him. The night shift was running the hotel. The desk manager observed us but didn't seem to mind that we were walking past his post without stopping to check in. The night security guard looked at us from his position in the middle of the lobby, but dropped his gaze back to his newspaper.

We stood at room 310 for about ten minutes as Dad carefully knocked on Jerry's door. Finally, the sleeping giant awoke and opened the door a crack. "Sorry to bother you, Jerry," Dad whispered. "It's me, Bob, and Jon. Just wanted to know if we could crash on your floor."

"Sure, Bob," Jerry said in a hoarse voice. "You know you're always welcome here. And you too, Jon. Come on in." He winced as he switched on the lamp on the nightstand by his bed. He was wearing only his boxer shorts.

"I apologize, Jon, for the poor accommodations here," Jerry said. "You're probably accustomed to nicer surroundings. But this is home for now."

Jerry's friendliness and kindness contradicted his paranoia and his murderous hatred for Mexicans. I was willing to ignore his rantings of earlier that day, grateful that he'd let us in and that we wouldn't have to sleep on an exhaust vent on the sidewalk.

"Let me get you a sheet to lay on, Jon," he said. He stumbled to the closet to get the sheet. I could see inside the closet. There were several garments neatly folded on the shelf, and three clean and pressed shirts hanging from the rod at carefully spaced intervals. Then I saw a white poster-board sign leaning against the closet wall. "Will Work For Food." I quickly swung my head, not wanting Jerry to notice I'd seen his sign.

I wondered how many times, on street corners, at intersections, at mall entrances, and outside restaurants, banks, and churches, I'd passed people who'd been holding signs with that same familiar proposition. Hundreds of times, hundreds of people. Now, one of them had opened his door and welcomed me in and given me shelter and a sheet to cover myself. Here I was, lying on the floor next to his bed.

"I feel terrible this lousy bed ain't big enough to share with you, Jon," Jerry said.

"No problem, Big Jerry," I said. "I'll be fine down here. Thanks for the sheet."

Our host put out the light. Dad lay on his sleeping bag in the corner and pulled the yellow blanket over him. "Hey, if your neck starts to hurt," Jerry said, "you just roll up that sheet and use it as a pillow."

"Thanks," I said. "That's good advice."

"Hey, I know what it's like," Jerry said. "Sleeping on concrete's a bitch."

This might have been as close to homelessness as I would ever get. It was certainly closer than I'd ever cared to be. *This is how they survive,* I thought. They lower their standards. Bedding that would have once been intolerable was now comfortable—almost.

Ten minutes after the light went out, both my roommates were snoring. I was exhausted and painfully hungry, but I couldn't sleep. I kept going over the day, its revelations and frustrations. My worst fear was happening. My father had dragged me down into his rut. Very little made sense. I had completely lost control of the moment five minutes after our reunion and had done nothing to get a grip since then. I couldn't stay. What would I tell Gina when I came home with no answers? The tension made my head pound until I couldn't see straight anymore. By two in the morning, the air was cool, and I tugged part of Dad's yellow blanket over me. By five, fatigue knocked me out.

❧❧❧

CHAPTER SIXTEEN
Day of Reckoning

D ad woke me at six o'clock sharp, just as the sun rose. "Rise and shine, Jonny boy," he said gently, as if I'd been a lazy child lingering under the covers. "Up and at 'em." He nudged me with his foot. "We've got a big day ahead of us."

My father was perfectly pleasant. He showed no signs of a hangover. The fact that he'd slept only a few hours on a concrete floor, or that he'd eaten only a few bites of spoiled chicken during the previous 36 hours, didn't seem to bother him. He acted as if it had all been normal.

Big Jerry was already gone when I got to my feet. Pain shot from my right shoulder down the length of my arm, and my right hip and ankle and foot were numb, all this from sleeping on my right side on the hard surface. The hunger pangs of the previous day had become cramps. These complaints had soured my disposition a little, but what completely fouled my mood was knowing that I was halfway through my long-awaited visit with my father and I hadn't yet confronted him with the questions I'd come to ask. My return flight would leave San Diego at six that evening. I didn't have to take it, but I felt I should. On the other hand, I realized that this might be my last chance to be with my father, my last chance to get answers, and that he could die at any time and leave part of me forever wounded. I decided to press the issue and see if I could force the direction of the conversation.

I began as soon as we hit the street. "You scared the hell out of me last time we were together," I said. He didn't respond. I tried again. "Do you remember the last thing you told Marq and me when we put you on that Greyhound bus in Salt Lake City?"

"No. What did I say?"

"You said, 'I think I'll settle down and get a place. I'm getting too old for this shit.' Man, it scared me. I mean, all I could think of that night was the image of you curled up dead, in an alley somewhere. And I'll tell you something else. That thought has stayed with me ever since. I can't shake it. I deal with it all the time. It bothers me that my own father would end up that way, and it bothers me that I can't seem to do anything to prevent it."

My voice quivered as I felt the relief of confiding a fear to my father. It was hard to talk about, but it felt good once I'd said it. I was opening myself to him and didn't know how he might react. I studied his face. Nothing. He just kept walking and looking up the street, scanning back and forth, searching.

His mouth opened and he licked his lower lip. "You worry too much, son," he said. A brush-off.

I gathered myself and tried again. "That's a lot easier said than done, Dad. I go to bed most nights wondering if I'm going to get a call from some police station somewhere, asking me to come identify a body. Is that any way to live?"

"No. That's no way to live," he said, looking away from me. "You're wasting your time worrying about it."

"Well, tell me something that would put my mind at ease," I said. "Where do you think you'll end up?"

"Patrick!" Dad shouted at a wrinkled, crooked man who was leaning against a lamppost. We stopped.

The man grasped my hand. "Patrick Levy, Private First Class." He tightened his grip and held on with both hands.

"Where did you serve?" I asked.

"Vietnam. Seven years. M.P. Finance Officer. I was a trusted soldier. But I don't kill no gooks . . . just kill to live . . . and heal." He breathed hard as he talked. I relaxed my handshake and tried to retract my hand. He maintained his grip, straining to hold on to me.

"Nice to meet you," I said.

"Yes, sir!" he said.

"Can you let go of my hand?"

"No, sir!" he shouted. "I like you too much. You're a good man, a helluva good man."

Dad stood by and watched. He wasn't going to interrupt; the old fool was blocking for him. The man just stood there, gripping my hand and gaping at me.

I grasped the man by the wrist and squeezed. "Anyone who served his country is a friend of mine," I said, smiling, hoping my squeeze wasn't hurting him. I squeezed a little harder and said, "You can let me go now, Private Levy."

"Yessir!" he shouted, releasing my hand and saluting me, trying to bring his feeble body to attention.

"Are you ready?" I asked Dad.

"Let's go," he said.

Neither of us said anything as we went along. Dad's little diversion had worked, at least temporarily, so he promptly began to hail other friends—anyone he could grab. He was burning up time. After the fourth encounter, I decided to resume. "Now really, Dad, where do you think you'll end up?"

"Probably I'll end up in a seat in Congress when the new political party is set up," he said without hesitating. He launched into a monologue of nonsense about how the political realignment of the late 1950s pitted conservatives against liberals, much along the lines of the British Parliament. He babbled about how the power base in America was constructed on a religious belief, totally contrary to the philosophy of our founding fathers and the rule of law. Unable to ignore my question, he was trying to smother it. He was fighting me off with an old, familiar weapon of his: verbal sparring. As long as he kept talking, I couldn't ask questions. When I tried to force the questions, he talked with even less coherence. I spent another precious hour trying to bring him to earth, but he was shrewd and slippery. I let him go on a while, hoping he'd talk himself out. When he began to slow, toward noon, I chose my moment and hacked my way in, determined to command his attention.

"Who's supposed to be impressed by your speeches, Dad? Hey, I don't mean to seem uninterested in your views on politics and economics, but I've heard all these speeches before. I'm hoping for a chance to just sit down with you and talk through a few things. Can we get down to something a little more personal? Just you and me? A little father-to-son chat?"

Silence.

"Dad, I've got to level with you. I've come a long way to be with you. We don't have much time together. Can't you give me something that I can use?"

"I'll tell you what you can use," he snapped. "You could use a shot of tequila and an attitude adjustment. That's what you could use. You should have somebody help you with your anxieties. They're getting the better of you." He was hearing me again.

"All I'm asking, Dad, is for some straight answers to some direct questions. I've been with you for more than a day now, and you're still talking in circles. I want to talk about you and me. Won't you do that?"

"Naw. Naw. Naw. You're going to have to change your attitude first, and then you'll get answers."

"Okay. What do I have to do?"

"Relax," he said. "Do one thing at a time. Don't try to do more than one thing at a time."

"Wasn't I relaxed enough for you yesterday?"

"Yeah, you were fine yesterday. Yesterday, you were all right, because you minded your manners and let me do the talking. The difference today is that you haven't had anything to eat and you're ornery."

"You're probably right," I said. "I probably am ornery, and it may be because I haven't eaten or slept. But it's also because I realize I have to leave this place tonight and go back home. I only have a few more hours, and I'm not getting any answers."

"Well, you'd better think of some different questions," he said with a sneer.

"Fine," I said. "Let me try another question."

"Shoot," he said and started walking faster.

"How often do you think of your children?"

"Every day."

"How often do you think of me?"

"Not as often as I think of Daryl."

"Why is that?"

"Because he needs me to think about him more."

"What do you think when you think of Daryl?"

"Helplessness."

Dad still saw Daryl as the fat, soft boy he'd been when we lived in Anderson. He had no idea that Daryl had grown into a determined and self-sustaining young man, despite the hardships his father had heaped upon him. But I didn't correct Dad. He was answering my questions, and I didn't want to argue.

"And what about Marq?" I asked. "What do you think of when you think of him?"

"Danger. Volatility and danger."

"What's dangerous about Marq?"

"Hell, you never know what's going to set him off. The boy's always been that way. Tried to kill me once, back in 1980."

"Tried to kill you?"

"Tried to assassinate my ass!" He told me about the time he'd passed through Encinitas and looked up Marq at his grandparents' house. Marq was working two or three odd jobs and trying to save as much money as he could so he could marry Karen and go to college. Marq had brought Dad along for a day of landscaping. The two of them would split the pay.

As they drove from one job to the next, they began to argue, as they often did. They'd found some copper tubing at their last clearing job, and Dad had wanted to toss it into the back of the pickup, on the theory that it would be worth something at the salvage yard. Marq said it was worthless.

"You fucking moron," Dad snapped back. "You wouldn't know a business opportunity if it hit you between the eyes."

Marq exploded. "Don't you call me that! Don't you ever call me that! I'll kill you before I let you talk to me that way!"

"We were going about 50 down La Jolla Village Drive, that long slope to the beach," Dad told me. "Marq jerked the wheel and headed us toward the concrete embankment. I swear to you, Jonny, he would have killed us both if I hadn't grabbed the wheel. He *wanted* to kill us!" The fear in Dad's eyes made me think the story was probably true. I changed the subject.

"What do you think when you think of me?"

"You've got it all together."

"Do you resent that?"

"No, not at all. It means that I don't have to worry about you. I don't have to worry about anybody jumping you and taking your stuff or conning you." He was moving fast now, shooting glances in all directions but mine. He was getting twitchy, and it was showing, and I felt that for the first time since I'd arrived—for the first time since I'd known him—I was beginning to get control of the conversation.

"Does the fact that you can't con me bother you at all?" I asked, hoping that my loaded questions would stir him up enough to bring out his feelings.

"No," he said. "The fact that you think you're too smart to listen to anything I say is a testament to the fact that you have no idea who your father really is."

"That's what I'm here for! Why do you think I came all this way to find you? I came here to find out who you really are. How am I supposed to do that if you won't talk to me? Why can't you tell me who you are?"

"What's that anger from?"

"I'm not angry, I'm just getting a little frustrated. I've been with you for 36 hours, and I still can't get a straight answer from you."

"Well, you might not get a straight answer," he said. "You might go through your entire life and never get all the answers you want. You can't have everything you want. Maybe that's your answer."

"You accuse me of not having any idea who my father is, yet you refuse to talk to me," I shot back. "You refuse to acknowledge what we both know I'm here to do. You refuse to give me the answers you know I need. How can you justify that?"

"What you don't realize," he said, "because you're too self-centered and narrow-minded, is that I'm changing. I'm trying to get away from all the questions. I'm getting away from the establishment."

I paused. That one knocked me back a bit. "Does that include me?" I asked. A light seemed to turn on in my mind as I heard myself ask the question.

"Do you think the Veterans Administration sends me a check for $333 a month because they like me? I'm sick," he said.

We walked an entire block, saying nothing. I didn't know how to respond, but I knew I couldn't let him shock me with his talk of sickness and make me lose my focus. I had to keep pressing.

"You said you conned your way into that check. You've bragged about it on many occasions. I remember your bragging about it when you lived with me in Santa Monica. Now what's the real story, Dad? Are you sick, or are you just a con man?" He veered into Seventh Street and tried to walk away from me.

"That's the sickness I've got," he called back over his shoulder. "I con my way into everything. I've done it all my life."

"How do you explain bullshitting as a sickness?" I asked as I jogged to catch up with him.

"I don't explain it," he said, stopping abruptly and turning around to face me. "I don't have to explain it to you or any other judgmental motherfuckers in this world. It's like I said in first-year law when the professor woke me up and asked me to tell the class what the most precious of our constitutional rights was. It's the right to be left alone."

"So you just want to be left alone?"

"Now you're starting to figure it out, hotshot newsman." He set off again. He was beginning to wheeze a little.

"Is that why you're here?" I asked. "You just want to be left alone?" He didn't answer. "Well?" I insisted.

He kept walking, refusing to look at me and now refusing to speak. We reached Broadway, and he stopped, looking in both directions, searching for a way to escape me. He walked west along Broadway, into the busiest two-block section of the city. I guessed he was trying to lure me into the crowd, where he hoped I would back off.

"So what is it, Dad?" I continued. "Is it that you want to be left alone? Is that why you're homeless?"

"I don't causate," he said. "I won't attach causes to every event in my life or every decision I make."

"I just want to know why you're homeless, Dad."

He stopped, not to address my question but to catch his breath. "Hell, Jon, I don't know," he said with resignation.

"Because you want to be left alone?"

"Yeah, I guess so, mostly. I'm just here to get away from all you people. You're wasting your time here. You won't find the secret of life by pestering me."

"Pestering you! I'm pestering you?" I was losing control of my temper and losing what little control of the interview I'd wrested from my hostile witness. He was trying to deflect my questions by insulting me, and it was working. I was having trouble remembering what I'd planned to ask. My shouting drew looks from people on the street, and those looks were distracting me. I tried to regain a little composure.

"You know why I'm doing this, don't you," I said. "I'm doing this because I need to know what happened to you. It's important for me to find out."

"Well, it's a classic Fourth Amendment question here. And I'll give you a little lesson, son. When the public's need to know encounters an individual's right to privacy, then the individual's right to privacy wins out every time." He stopped. We were on the corner of Broadway and India, right where we'd found each other the day before. He looked me square in the eye and pointed his finger under my nose.

"Take my advice, Jon," he said. "You just get out of my face right now, before I sue you for invasion of privacy. I have the right to be left alone. I have the right to get sick. I have the right to take ten years off, if I want to." He was trying to get stern with me, hoping that perhaps he could back me down. Instead, it infuriated me.

"How much time off do you need?" I shot back, even louder this time. "How much space?" Louder. "How long can a person be sick?" Louder. "What made you sick, old man? Were you just sick of being a father? Sick of being needed?" Louder. "You make me sick!" Louder. "You people who think you can quit on the people who love them just because you think you're sick. Being a chickenshit is not a disease, Dad. I'll tell you who's sick. I'm sick! I'm sick of your excuses! Quitters like you make me want to puke!" Louder, until my voice cracked, and I was hissing. He tried to turn away but he couldn't. His face was an inch from mine. He looked me right in the eyes. His expression was one of confusion and fear. His head began to jerk back and forth, then front and back, like he was having some sort of seizure. Was this some kind of stunt?

Only then did I realize I was gripping the lapels of his old trenchcoat, nearly strangling him with it as I lifted him off the ground and shook him.

"Quitter!" I heard myself shriek, but it sounded like someone else, off in the distance, beyond the ringing in my ears.

I heard, "You're no lawyer!"

Then, "Your clients didn't love you!"

Then, "We loved you! Marq and Daryl loved you!"

Then, " . . . fucking quitter!"

The last one came out like vomit, like the dry heaves, when you think your eyes are going to pop out of their sockets. His eyes rolled back in their sockets. My father was muttering, "God, help me . . . oh, God, deliver me from evil."

I felt something like a clamp on my right shoulder that squeezed so hard it made my arm tingle down to my wrist. It startled me, enough to make me aware of myself. I was still standing on the sidewalk in front of the McDonald's at Broadway and India. Dad was sitting at my feet, slumped forward, whimpering like a child. The people who rushed by us seemed oblivious to the plight of the homeless man sitting on the sidewalk. And he and I were oblivious to them. Now, they were the gray people, now that I had completely immersed myself in my father's otherworld. Their faces were unidentifiable, all blurred into one opaque picture of people. All except Big Jerry, the laid-off steelworker, standing about five feet from me, glaring at me with a look of amazement on his large, distorted face, as though he'd just seen a ghost; amazement and anger, like he wanted to kill me; anger and fear, like he was afraid someone was about to arrest him and throw him in jail. Jerry stepped back and disappeared into the crowd. I stood there, looking into the throng, trying to find Jerry, hoping I could catch a glimpse of him so I could thank him for saving my father's life.

I stooped and grasped the crumpled man at my feet and pulled him up, only half noticing he was sitting on Jerry's cardboard "Will Work for Food" sign. I threw one of his limp arms over my shoulder and sort of dragged my father to the alley behind the McDonald's and sat him on the bench where I'd sat the night before and watched him and his friends smoke a joint.

Neither of us spoke. Neither had a voice. Two hours passed. Then three. And then the silence broke.

"Grief," he said.

I turned and looked at him. His face was pale and limp, but his eyes were completely clear, as though he were reading something from a sign across the street.

"Grief, for the rest of my days," he continued a few minutes later. "That's my punishment."

A long pause again. I stared at his profile, and he stared across the street. "I'm being punished for what I did to my family," he said in a perfectly level tone. "I had to leave because I was no longer worthy to lead. I've been grieving ever since, Jon. Not a day goes by that I don't grieve the loss of everything that was important to me."

I knew he meant his family more than his law practice.

"It wasn't that I walked away. It was that I was banished. I didn't deserve it any longer. You couldn't have understood. You were just a child. I had to leave before I did any more damage. I didn't look back because I couldn't bear to see what I couldn't have anymore."

He went on. "You're trying to figure out how I screwed up my life because you hope you'll learn how to prevent the same thing from happening to you and yours." This was the wise man I'd known as a child.

"I didn't set out to cause trouble. Really. I would have been an English teacher, like Jimmy, if only someone had told me that practicing law was going to destroy my life. I was never the type of person who wanted a fight. It's just that I was good at it. I only wanted what everyone else wants—my family around me, to watch the ball game on TV, float around in the boat on Sunday afternoon. But Papa Mason said I was the gifted one. I had to be a lawyer. I had to run for office. Continue the Kennedy legacy. Right the wrongs of racial injustice. I had to end the war."

My father's childhood ambition had been the same as mine—just to be quiet and go unnoticed.

Then his head dropped. The muscles in his shoulders constricted, and his neck stiffened. The old man on the concrete bench let out a wail like I'd never heard a human make. And he sobbed, so hard it caused him to quake on his seat. This lasted 20, 30, 40 minutes . . . longer than that. Then it subsided to a whimper. Then silence again. Another 20, 30, 40 minutes. Then he spoke again, this time, looking at me.

"It's not the past you came looking for, is it, Jonny?" he said with a weak but knowing smile. "Young man, what you're interested in is the future."

He stood and spread his arms. "Look at me. What a wretched sight I must be, dragging myself around the country, living like an animal. What happened to me? The grief of my guilt took hold, Jonny. And it won't let me go. I live in the past. I live here because I have to, because this is where I belong. My grief will never end." He sat back down and looked straight ahead again.

"Do you want to live here with me? Do you want to spend the rest of your life trying to unscrew your screwed-up childhood? What could you ever accomplish, in the end, but to revisit your father's sins on the heads of your children? I'm history, Jonny. And you, my beautiful son, are the future."

His words were pure intelligence. They answered every question, even those I didn't know how to ask. The answer was that I'd had it all wrong.

I was wrong to deify this man. Wrong to give him power over me, power he never wanted or deserved. And without that power, he could no longer be the object of my scorn or the cause of my insecurity. In that moment, perfect justice prevailed. I let go of my anger. I was liberated.

The man who took my father's place on the concrete bench was a defeated and helpless old homeless man. He couldn't hurt me even if he wanted to. Indeed, he feared me for what I had just demonstrated I could do to harm him.

And then I thought of Gina and the children. Suddenly, I wanted to be with them, like I was underwater and needed to get to the surface. I wanted my family to see me this way, all grown up and perfectly content to be a man. I didn't belong here, in the past, anymore. I belonged at home, in Boston, 2,500 miles from here, with my family, my future.

"God almighty!" I gasped. I looked at my watch. It was 5:30 in the afternoon, and the sun was dipping into the harbor.

"Follow me, Dad." We walked along Broadway to the Wells Fargo Bank building. I stepped up to the automatic teller machine and slid my Visa card into the slot.

"What are you doing?"

"Just getting a little cash," I said. I watched his reflection in the plexiglass cover of the machine. He folded his arms and looked around quickly, as though he expected the police to rush to the scene and stop a bank robbery. Fifteen $20 bills appeared from the slot at the bottom of the machine. I took them, folded them twice, and said to my father, "This ought to get you a month at the Pickwick. And an extra pair of shoes. You should have an extra pair."

His eyes opened wide. "Jonny! Son! I . . ."

"I've got to get to the airport," I said. "You understand, I've gotta get back. Gina's pregnant and I promised . . ."

"Go, boy. Get the hell out of here."

We crossed to the north side of the street and stood at the curb together, looking for a vacant taxi, neither of us saying anything. A Checker finally approached. I whistled and waved it over.

"I'll be damned," my father said. "Where the hell did you learn to whistle like that? I always wanted to whistle like that. There was a guy on my ship in the Navy who could whistle like that. He tried to teach me how, but I could never get it. What do you do, just tuck your tongue in behind your front teeth or what?"

I hugged him hard and felt his arms wrap around my back and neck. He squeezed me just as hard, the way he had hugged me when I was a boy. I kissed him on the cheek. His tears wet my face. I kissed him again and squeezed him harder.

"I'm sorry I shook you," I said.

"Jon, I have to thank you," he said, grasping my forearm and squeezing.

"For shaking you?"

"Hell yes, boy. You shook the truth right out of me. You didn't let go until you got your answer." I thought how Packer's training paid off in a way I'd never expected and that maybe this was why I'd stayed in his class.

"Son, I did something worthwhile today. It feels damn good." I nodded and got in and rolled down the window.

"One more favor, Jonny, if you don't mind."

"Name it," I said.

"Could you tell Marq and Daryl your ol' dad is sorry for the pain . . . so sorry for the pain, Jonny." And he started to cry again, but this time it was for joy.

"They don't need to come looking for me, son. I'm too old for this shit!" He laughed, almost as though he remembered that those were the words from years earlier that had beckoned me to come find him.

"Airport," I said to the driver. "East terminal. Southwest Airlines."

The cab pulled out and headed down Broadway, then swung onto Grape Street. I stared at the red numbers flashing on the meter. My mind was thousands of miles away, back at the house in Hingham with Gina and Kasey and Jessie and our unborn baby. I imagined opening the front door and coming through and hearing the shrieks of happy children, and dropping to my knees and letting them run to me and pull me to the floor and tickle me and bathe my face with wet kisses. I needed to see Gina's face and tell her how sorry I was for the way I'd left and that I knew why I'd been so abusive and how sure I was it would never happen again if she'd just forgive me. As the cab headed along the bay toward Lindbergh Field, I realized I hadn't looked back.

It was 2:30 the next morning as I walked up the ramp to my arrival gate at Logan International. Boston felt like home again, especially when I saw her waiting at the top. Two sleeping babies in tow and one more doing flips in her belly, Gina had come to meet me, unable to wait for me to take the long cab ride to Hingham. She wore no makeup on her face, leaving uncovered the natural, virginal beauty that had drawn me to her in the first place. The idea gave me the feeling of starting over with this woman. She was gorgeous, despite her exhaustion from being worried. And her expression told me she was desperately hoping for good news.

Neither of us said a word as we held each other and rocked back and forth, unborn Jonny swaying in the middle of our love. And then, "Well?" She looked earnestly into my face. And my tears began to flow, tears of relief . . . and repentance.

"It's done," I said, thrilled at the sound of the words. "All is forgiven. I just hope you can do the same for me."

We've spoken no more of it since. Whether Gina has ever understood why I had to go or what happened to me when I went, I don't know. What matters is that now I understand what she knew all along: It's not about me. It stopped being about me when Kasey was born. It's all about the children.

❧❧❧

C HAPTER SEVENTEEN ❧
Kasey's Answer

J onny joined our family on May 1, 1995. Friends and relatives said he was the happiest-looking baby they'd ever seen. I guess I didn't blame him a bit. Ours was a happy home now—no longer was there an irritable, preoccupied father skulking around the house. Jonny's mother was especially appreciative of his pleasant disposition when we moved six months later, to Phoenix, Arizona. When station managers told staff that the station had been sold to a new owner, I decided it was a good excuse to move my family back to the west, where Gina could be close to her parents and—it feels strange to say this—I could be close to mine.

I took a job as reporter and anchor for the NBC affiliate in Phoenix. In a way, I made an honest man of my father, who was still fond of telling everyone he met that his son was "an announcer for NBC."

Yes, Dad was still roaming the country, but he spent more time in Tucson than any other place. He knew where to find me, and he also knew that he was welcome in our home. About six months after I'd arrived in Phoenix, he decided to take me up on my standing invitation.

I was on the golf course, sneaking in a quick round before work. Standing at the ninth tee, I looked out and saw Gina hurrying toward me from the clubhouse. "They called you from work," she panted. "They said your father showed up this morning, and he's asking for you." Gina didn't seem at all nervous about the fact that her smelly old father-in-law was nearby, just anxious that I get to the station and meet him.

I dressed and dashed downtown early. There he was, sitting at my desk, wearing a smudged and faded "Georgia Bulldogs" baseball cap (no doubt from a Salvation Army clothing bin) on his head and a tired, tattered duffel bag on the floor beside him. He was leaning back in my chair, sipping coffee and reading the newspaper.

"Hey, stranger!" I called as I approached.

"Jonny boy!" he exclaimed, exposing dark, coffee-stained gums and those yellowed false teeth. We hugged each other right there in the middle of the newsroom. I didn't mind that everyone knew that this dusty hitchhiker was my new friend.

We spent the rest of the morning and the afternoon together, talking not about race relations or government oppression or social injustice, but about how nice it was to sit down and relax and enjoy one another's company. He came home with me that night to have dinner with my family, but mostly to reacquaint himself with one grandchild and meet two others.

Gina was as gracious a hostess as the day she'd first met him five years earlier. The children, for the first time seeing the man behind the name they'd heard all their lives, studied him carefully as he walked through the front door and sat on the living room couch. Jonny sat on his lap and patted his big belly and giggled. Jessie, his only granddaughter as far as I know, stood on the couch next to him and held his face between her tiny hands, gently touching the deep wrinkles in his darkened, leathery skin. Kasey, whose innocent inquiry had spurred my painful yet marvelous quest, stood at our visitor's feet and studied the old man's withered, drooping face.

"Kasey," I announced, "this is Grandpa Bob." My five-year-old son gazed at his grandfather's face.

"I know you," he said with a sneaky smile.

It was early the next morning, just as suddenly as he'd appeared, that our guest quietly informed me he had to go.

"I need to get back to Tucson, Jon. Today's my day to pick up my food stamps for the month. If I don't sign in at the shelter, I'll lose them. Then I'll have to do all that goddam paperwork all over again to get back on the rolls. You know I hate that goddam paperwork."

I told him he needn't worry about food stamps, that his credit was good at our house anytime and for as long as he needed it. He wouldn't hear of it.

"I'm not going to interrupt your wonderful home life, my boy. Your family doesn't need some ol' vagabond getting in the way around here." His tone made it clear he didn't want my pity nor my handouts, at least not when he had an allotment of food stamps in his pocket. "Don't get me wrong, it's nice to visit your home, but I'm not comfortable here. I'm only happy when I'm on the move."

His bag was already sitting by the front door. As before, I knew I wasn't going to talk him into staying. And honestly, I didn't want him to move in. I'd never aspired to be his rescuer, as Marq had. Dad and I were content know-ing that we were close enough that he could call whenever he wanted to visit or needed a hand.

He kissed his grandkids, and I took him downtown to the Greyhound depot, where I bought him a ticket and handed him a little spending money for the road. He hugged me hard, just the way I'd hugged him when I left San Diego. I knew what it meant: He'd liked it and wanted it to be our little tradition.

"Thanks for the good time, Jonny boy," he said. "I hope you don't mind my intruding on your wonderful family this way."

"You know you're always welcome, Dad."

"It's nice to know. It'll be a comfort when I get weary out there." That made me well up inside. I didn't want to show that much emotion, and I knew he didn't want to see it, so I turned and climbed back in my Jeep.

As I pulled out of the parking lot, I turned and looked before I sped away. It wasn't a sad sight. Not at all. The old street lawyer was already bending some stranger's ear, no doubt bothering the poor man with marvelously overblown stories about his boys, and hopefully his newfound grandchildren.

❦❦❦

CHAPTER EIGHTEEN
Amazing Grace

I don't know whether it was coincidence or some instinctive emotional timing mechanism, like whatever it is that causes a bird's migration, that brought my mother together with my brothers at the same time I was setting out on my quest to find my lost father. Whatever the case, it was nothing short of a miracle as far as I'm concerned.

Mom had arrived in Salt Lake City at the end of a hot, dry day in August of 1994. She found no job waiting for her. There was no booming Amway distributorship. Marq hadn't sold much soap, or anything else, for a long time. There were no orders for her to process, no inventory items for her to organize. Despite what wasn't there, my mother found what she hadn't known she was looking for. In the tiny living room of Marq's apartment above a furniture store on Salt Lake's southeast side, my mother found two of her sons, in the same place at the same time, for the first time since they were children. Marq's beautifully thoughtful and generous plan had worked perfectly.

Daryl, fleeing legal entanglements back in San Diego, had come north with Mom. When he found that there was no job waiting for her and that he would have to help support her, he rose to the occasion like Aslan of Narnia. Calling again upon his uncanny resourcefulness, he found work within 48 hours, as a maintenance man at a Holiday Inn and as an apprentice painter with a building contractor. Daryl's paychecks, along with what Marq brought home from his warehouse job, were enough to keep the threesome afloat while Mom recovered from her mastectomy.

As she gained strength, she took on all the domestic duties, turning Marq's apartment into a home, and turning mealtimes into special occasions. Daryl saved enough money to buy a used pickup truck, and with Marq's help, got it running. Mom found a job she loved, creating floral arrangements for an interior design company. Her job enabled her and Daryl to move into an apartment of their own.

These three acted as a family again. They shared their efforts and their gains. Whatever the need, one of the three seemed to have just the right answer at the right time. When Marq's car broke down, Daryl's truck rolled to the rescue. When Daryl's truck broke down and Mom was too tired to catch buses, Marq cranked life back into his old car. When Marq was hungry and a little lonesome, he was welcomed as a special dinner guest. He always brought an offering from his Amway inventory, and Mom and Daryl never wanted for household soap products.

My mother's cancer continued its slow spread under her skin. She learned to manage the pain and ignore the discomfort. "Working with the flowers . . . that's my best therapy," she often said. That, and the constant companionship of her two beloved sons, kept her going.

I called every month or so and talked to Mom and Daryl and sometimes Marq. We celebrated Christmas of 1995 together, in Mom's apartment in Salt Lake, for the first time in 21 years. Daryl delighted my children with a train set he built, piece by piece. He is still full of fun and still has that brilliantly childlike imagination.

"Someday I'll meet Miss Right," he says often and good-naturedly and with complete conviction. I believe him. There's a woman out there with the keen insight and boundless sense of humor it would require to appreciate Daryl's genius.

Marq continued in his quiet suffering, but he no longer had to do it alone. At last, he had the love and support of his brothers and his mother, and he knew it. And I knew likewise. Not once has any of them uttered a word that would suggest they harbor ill will for all the years I detached myself from them, unfairly blaming them for my torment.

This amazing trio makes its way through each day with forgiveness, tolerance, cooperation, and good humor—kind of like the way I always thought real families did it.

❧ ❧ ❧

Am I cured? Maybe. My eyes were opened to a tremendously encouraging insight one day in the spring of 1995, shortly after my San Diego odyssey.

It happened on a plane. Ordinarily, I'm not one to strike up a conversation with a stranger on a plane, usually more content to just sit back, be quiet, and observe. But the woman next to me seemed extraordinarily pleasant and inviting. She was a handsome, vital woman in her 70s—blue eyes, pink cheeks, and upswept white hair. I thought she might even be someone I should know, someone famous. Rather than wait until we were well into the flight, when it would be more awkward to introduce myself, I spoke up and asked her about herself.

She told me she was a retired Harvard psychologist. Before I knew it, I found myself telling her my story, right through to my time with my father in San Diego.

She listened intently to the whole thing, and when I finished, she asked me several questions, ones that made me think hard so that I could answer adequately. I think she was examining me, as she would a patient. Then she said, "I've worked with many people with troubles like yours. You sound as if you've been enduring the syndrome that used to be called 'shell shock' or 'battle fatigue.' Now it's called Post-Traumatic Stress Disorder [PTSD]."

She described PTSD as a mental condition suffered by people who had gone through an overwhelmingly awful experience—combat, rape, and sexual abuse are well-known examples. The victim, she said, repeatedly relives the traumatic occurrence. When exposed to some image that symbolizes the traumatic event, the victim goes through intense distress. "In your case," she said, "the image was the homeless man you saw on the video monitor. To you, he symbolized your father and his escape into a world as impossibly remote from you as he could manage."

Shame, she said, which is almost always a large factor, seemed to be significant in my case. The traumatic loss of my father was accentuated by the shame I felt over his behavior with women, his drinking, and eventually his life on the streets. I was ashamed that my parents neglected us, let us go hungry, and let us wear worn clothes. I was ashamed that although we once had lived in a big, beautiful house, we had come to live in a shabby building on a shabby street behind the high school. All that, she suggested, might have intensified the trauma of abandonment.

Guilt was another factor. She'd treated many Vietnam vets, she said, and had witnessed the extreme guilt a lot of them felt because they'd survived a fire-fight while buddies to the left and right had been blown apart. "In your case," she said, "you felt guilty because you survived family troubles that had badly injured your brothers."

PTSD sufferers are often irritable and have outbursts of anger, which their "bed partners," as she put it, take the brunt of. *My own beloved bed partner,* I thought, *could testify to that.* They can also feel detached or become estranged from others. I'd distanced myself not only from my partner, but from my mother and brothers as well. I'd worked hard for years to keep them out of my new life. And with my cruel words, I'd tried to estrange myself from Gina.

"When children or adolescents suffer deep shame and consequent guilt, as you did, they tend to deal with it in childish ways. They're old enough to know guilt because they know they could have made other choices in dealing with their problems. And since failure surrounds them, they think they were the ones who made bad choices—and then they grow even guiltier. In other words, you took on the guilt that rightly belonged to your father. You got stuck in thinking that way, and as you grew, you kept repeating those childish errors."

There are many ways, she said, to relieve the symptoms of PTSD. If I'd gone for professional counseling, a therapist would have put me through a series of treatments, some of which, she said, I undertook on my own. In one of them, the sufferer is urged to confront the horrible experience. Vietnam vets, for example, may be shown a film like *Platoon*, which brings back the horror and then, while they're churned up, they're encouraged to relive their own traumatic event. "When you went to find your father and stood toe-to-toe with him on the sidewalks of San Diego," she said, "you were confronting your trauma head-on."

Patients, Dr. Murray went on, are also urged to break through the suffocating confines of their distress and reach out for additional information that will enlarge their perspective. They might talk with others who have experienced similar events or read something on the subject. "That's what you were doing instinctively," she said, "when you started phoning your relatives and various other people to learn about your father. You were reaching out for fresh, perspective-giving information. You were opening the windows." I thought how my wise and compassionate cousin Catherine, who had learned hard lessons of survival through her mastectomy and her heartless husband's subsequent abandonment, had been right all along.

Dr. Murray and I talked the entire trip away. I was spellbound. After it was over, I was immensely grateful. Thanks to this spur-of-the-moment but powerfully accurate explanation of my condition from a person with renowned expertise, I no longer had to think of myself as a chaotic mess. I wasn't just randomly "screwed up." Because of common and well-understood causes, I'd developed a recognized mental disorder. It had a name. This knowledge, together with the realization that I had almost instinctively found a cure for my troubled heart without any professional guidance, was enormously reassuring.

In the time it had taken to fly from Boston to Phoenix, I'd acquired an explanation for three things that before had seemed inexplicable.

One was how I could have been so cold to my mother and brothers and so harsh to the woman I loved.

Another was how, before I'd left on my trip to San Diego, I could have believed I'd actually accomplish anything by finding and confronting my father.

Some people thought it preposterous and futile, but the psychologist had shown me why it had been the right thing to do, perhaps the *only* thing to do.

The third was how I could dare to believe that my two brief days with my father had "fixed" me. The doctor showed me why it actually could have worked.

Toward the end of the plane ride, as we began our descent into Phoenix, Dr. Murray smiled and said, "I hope you don't think I'm trying to put you in therapy. I just want to say there's one technique doctors find very helpful for people who've suffered as you have."

I asked her what it was.

"Tell your story," she said.

And so I have.

❧❧❧

❧ ABOUT THE AUTHOR ❧

Jon Du Pre now lives in Ventura County, California, with his wife, Gina, and their three children, Kasey, Jessie, and Jonny. Jon makes his living as a correspondent for the Fox News Network. When he's not covering earthquakes, riots, plane crashes, or presidential elections, Jon spends his time volunteering as a scout leader, Little League coach, cheerleader at dance recitals and school award ceremonies, and playing with his children in the backyard.

Jon can be reached via e-mail at: **jdupe@gateway.net.**

❧❧❧

✤✤✤

We hope you enjoyed this Hay House book.
If you would like to receive a free catalog featuring additional
Hay House books and products, or if you would like information about the
Hay Foundation, please contact:

Hay House, Inc.
P.O. Box 5100
Carlsbad, CA 92018-5100

(760) 431-7695 or **(800) 654-5126**
(760) 431-6948 (fax) or **(800) 650-5115 (fax)**

Please visit the Hay House Website at: **hayhouse.com**

✤✤✤